GENDER EQUALITY AND PRAYER IN JEWISH LAW

By Ethan Tucker and Micha'el Rosenberg

HADAR PRESS
New York

Hadar Press is supported in part by the Levine Library
in memory of Rabbi Jonathan D. Levine, *z"l*, a lover of Jewish books.

Gender Equality and Prayer in Jewish Law
Copyright © 2017, 2025 by Ethan Tucker and Micha'el Rosenberg
SECOND EDITION

ISBN 978–1–946611–08–6
This book is licensed under a Creative Commons Attribution-NonCommercial-ShareAlike 4.0 International License.

Library of Congress Control Number 2025930237
Interior design by Rachel Jackson | binahdesign.com

HADAR PRESS
The Hadar Institute
210 West 93rd Street
New York, New York 10025

This Hadar Press edition of Gender Equality and Jewish Prayer is supported by members of The Lehrhaus Book Club, led by Rabbi Ethan Tucker, in his honor and with gratitude for his many years of guiding our learning journey.

CONTENTS

PREFACE TO THE SECOND EDITION

In the years since the initial publication of *Gender Equality and Prayer in Jewish Law,* we have been gratified to see a deeper substantive engagement with the halakhic issues we discussed. Many communities that in the past would have taken gender difference in synagogue practice for granted now take seriously the possibility that greater inclusion is possible within a halakhic discourse. Others who understood gender equality in prayer to be an essential change required for the modern world that stands outside the realm of *halakhah* can now see that these ways of thinking are firmly grounded in premodern and early modern sources; indeed, "there is nothing new under the sun" (Kohelet 1:9).

The publication of this updated second edition brings us an opportunity to clarify our purposes in writing this book. From the beginning, we have had two goals for it. On the one hand, we believe the arguments we put forward here will help those who are exploring greater gender inclusivity in Jewish prayer for the first time. For some who enter this conversation with a prior presumption of gendered rules for prayer, the most convincing and reassuring path for exploring gender-egalitarian practice is one that does not require large reworking of broad conceptual frameworks (like the redefinition of who falls under the category of *nashim*), but rather one that sticks to the close reading of premodern texts and their implications for halakhic practice. Such readers will find that this kind of argument composes the bulk of this book—reading sources in relatively narrow ways to highlight pathways of halakhic practice that can expand the role of women in traditional prayer settings with an incrementalist methodology. These arguments are not dependent on any broader claims about the "fundamental nature" of gender in the past, present, or future. To put it more bluntly: Most of the pages in this book contain a careful and methodologically conservative argument for gender-egalitarian prayer that is not dependent on any paradigm shift in thinking about gender.

At the same time, we also have always intended this book as well for those who are already deeply enmeshed in halakhic egalitarian practice. These readers are not necessarily in search of a conservative interpretive approach to justify their preexisting practice. To the contrary, for some of these readers the technical arguments for gender-egalitarianism seem too small to speak to why we care so much about the topic. These concerns are reflected in our discussion in Appendix A of a paradigm shift with regard to the meaning of the word *nashim*. Precisely because we live in a world where classical descriptions of *nashim* do not align with our reality, these halakhic questions arise with particular insistence. We understand that this more radical approach will speak better to many of our readers' reality. Beyond this, however, we believe that the incrementalist arguments also demonstrate that our contemporary concerns and practices are, despite this, deeply continuous with the halakhic past.

Even for readers less interested in the questions of gender that animate this book, we believe that this book offers an honest and reverent methodology of how generally to approach halakhic sources and their relevance in today's world. In many halakhic circles, two modes predominate. One mode says that *halakhah* is a fundamentally stagnant discourse, and that "**the** *halakhah*" has already been determined based on the conclusions of the majority (though often framed as "consensus") of decisors in the past. The second mode looks to past rulings as a menu of options to be chosen from; where the "consensus" is at odds with our contemporary outlook, one may turn to a minority view (as long as it is found in a "canonical" past voice). Where no such minority view exists, however, we are stuck with a *halakhah* that we understand as fundamentally unethical.

In this book, we view all of the voices of halakhic conversation as binding, even if their specific conclusions may be culturally conditioned. That is to say, using Part Two of this book as an example: Both Rabbeinu Tam and the Levush impart important truths that are binding on us to take into account as we decide how to live our lives and manage our communities. Therefore, rather than rule "like" Rabbeinu Tam because it would appear that a majority of later decisors followed him, or "like" the Levush because he offers a stricter view, we believe halakhic rulings must take into account the concerns of both opinions. This does not necessarily mean a ruling that follows their literal conclusion, however; rather, sound halakhic conclusions are accountable to the concerns embedded in each. We offer this approach as a way forward in many thorny halakhic issues in today's world.

The framing, conceptual language of this book is mainly focused on "gender," even as most of the sources we are working with speak in the simpler, binary terminology of men (*zekharim*) and women (*nashim*). (One important exception is the Oraḥ la-Tzaddik, a source in Part Two, which engages someone of a nonbinary gender.) We follow the vocabulary of the sources as we discuss them directly, leading to the text-based analysis in the book's body to be about "women" and their status with regard to aspects of prayer. We will also use phrases like "gender-blind" or "gender-equal" or "non-gendered" interchangeably; this reflects our adaptation of ancient terminology to modern categories. Most significantly, however, many of the sources we analyze highlight questions of social status—not gender *per se*—as the substantive basis for inclusion or exclusion from various ritual roles and obligations. Sources that begin by talking about women's inclusion or exclusion lay the groundwork for speaking more broadly about equal social status, paving the way for equality in various ritual roles and obligations irrespective of gender. We hope our framing of gender in this book is not only clarifying as a point of halakhic analysis of sources that refer to men and women, but also makes the arguments in this book versatile as society continues to grapple with shifting gender roles and definitions.

We are grateful for the help of many in producing this second edition. Our colleagues in Israel, R. Nadav Berger and R. Jason Rogoff, were instrumental in the 2023 publication of *Gender Equality and Prayer* in Hebrew.[1] As part of that translation project, many improvements were made, including the new appendix; Jason and Nadav ensured that this is also now reflected in the new English edition. Hadar's Content Manager, Dr. Jeremy Tabick, prepared the manuscript of this current edition for

---

1 Tucker and Rosenberg, *Hen Hem Yodu: Shivyon u-Tefillah ba-Halakhah,* trans. Kroizer; Berger, ed., (Yediot Aḥaronot Books, 2023).

publication, reading it in its entirety and providing invaluable feedback on both substance and style, as well as preparing the new indices. As Senior Director of Content at Hadar, R. Effy Unterman oversaw the development of this second edition from start to finish with impeccable professionalism and care. Editorial Director Elisheva Urbas has worked tirelessly in both the editing and production of this book. Rachel Jackson is responsible for the beautiful graphic design, allowing our ideas to reach readers unencumbered by visual distractions. Michelle Kwitkin carefully copyedited, both catching errors and improving our clarity throughout. Finally, thank you to the Price Book Group for providing generous support for the publication of this second edition.

The state of the Jewish world in 2025 is so different from that of 2017 when the first edition was published, and all the more so from the early 2000s when we were engaged in the bulk of our researching and thinking about this topic. Those years have also made even clearer, if this were possible, how essential it is to create authentic spaces of deep Jewish practice and learning where people of all genders can participate as equals, bringing their full selves to the service of God. We pray that this second edition plays a role in further building, growing, and strengthening these spaces, bringing us closer to a world that fully reflects the will of the One Who spoke the world into being.

Ethan Tucker and Micha'el Rosenberg
AUGUST 2025 | MENAHEM AV 5785

ACKNOWLEDGMENTS

THIS BOOK WAS more than a decade in the making. We began teaching the material at the heart of this book in various settings that were grappling with a way to integrate gender-egalitarian practice around prayer with a robust commitment to the discourse and practice of Jewish law (*halakhah*). The earliest presentations took place during the founding stages of Kehilat Hadar and the DC Minyan, both prayer spaces and communities that have embodied the values of this book for years. It quickly became clear that what began as sessions in independent *minyanim* and university settings needed to become an accessible resource for many more people than we could reach in person.

As is the case with all such projects, our voices and insights here channel the wisdom of our ancestors, our teachers, our colleagues, and our students. We begin with thanks to our parents, who have, each in their own ways, supported our journeys in *talmud Torah* and who remain a source of inspiration to us as models of committed Jewish life. Ethan would like to thank his father and teacher, R. Gordon Tucker, for teaching him Torah from his earliest years: Abba, thank you for giving me this gift of access to, and love of, Jewish texts.

Our teachers are many and we proudly stand on their shoulders. We both benefited from an extraordinary undergraduate Jewish experience that was centered around Harvard Hillel. The dynamic vision of that institution, which allowed for a deep and meaningful interchange of ideas among the kinds of Jews who too rarely learn from each other, was essential to who we have become and the kinds of teachers we strive to be.

Dr. Bernie Steinberg, now of blessed memory, directed an extraordinary Jewish community, and a rich variety of undergraduate *minyanim* enabled us to imagine a world in which Jews practicing differently could nonetheless share core values and speak a shared language. In particular, the Orthodox and Student Conservative *minyanim* were, for us, models of commitment and respect that continue to inspire us until today.

We are also both proud to be alumni of the Wexner Graduate Fellowship. The Wexner Foundation's investment in both of us, including support for complex training that combined rabbinic ordination in Israel with doctoral studies in the United States, made the scholarship at the heart of this book possible. We are also deeply indebted to the Wexner Foundation for connecting us with colleagues from across the spectrum of Jewish belief and practice. Our experiences with them helped inspire us to believe that it is possible to construct shared and respectful discourse around even the most contentious issues.

Many teachers over the years have encouraged, prodded, and challenged us, both generally and in particular with regard to the texts and arguments in this book. Some of them will agree with our conclusions and others will not, but we hope that they will all appreciate the extent to which our work reflects our debt to them. Our years studying at Yeshivat Ma'ale Gilboa were particularly precious to us. In that special *beit midrash* on a remote hilltop in northern Israel we encountered a passion for Torah, a thoroughgoing intellectual openness, and a conviction that the eternal word of God must speak to our contemporary challenges. We are particularly thankful to R. David Bigman and R. Elisha Ancselovits, each of whom invested deeply in our education and supported our journeys toward *semikhah* with the Chief Rabbinate of Israel. While our analysis and conclusions are our own, we nonetheless owe them a deep debt for the culture of *talmud Torah* they build and sustain on a daily basis. From R. Bigman we learned to listen carefully to every voice in every layer of our rich tradition. The values-based discourse of *halakhah* that we learned from R. Elisha informs every page of this book. We are proud to call ourselves their students.

We are both proud alumni of the Graduate School of the Jewish Theological Seminary, where we both received doctorates in Talmud and Rabbinics. While this is not an academic work, the reader will see the influence of contemporary scholarship throughout this book. We thank JTS for its investment in our education and for the access we received to outstanding scholars in rabbinics during our years there.

Our colleagues are many. We want to express deep gratitude to the board, faculty, staff, and supporters of the Hadar Institute. This extraordinary institution and the extraordinary people who work there is the living instantiation of the theoretical model we sketch out throughout this book. It is one thing to talk about gender-equal *minyanim* in theory; it is quite another to attempt to make that vision a reality. The *beit midrash* at Hadar has been a central incubator for these ideas. Thank you to our colleagues, R. Elie Kaunfer, R. Shai Held, and R. Avital Hochstein, who have supported this project since its inception. We are also grateful to the full-time faculty of Hadar who have all been critical dialogue partners through the years. Supporters of Hadar have also been passionate about the need for this book and have made its publication possible. We are particularly grateful to David Andorsky, Dov Grossman, David Hiltzik, Yair and Stephanie Listokin, Sally Mendelsohn and David Lowenfeld, David Morris and Elisheva Urbas, Ron Moses, Jeremy Pava, Marc Schiller and Karyn Turecki Schiller, Jorian Schutz, and Yuval Segal, who offered targeted support for this project. Thank you for stepping up and believing in the power of *halakhah* to address our contemporary challenges. Additionally, during the editing and publishing of the first edition, Micha'el was fortunate to work in the wonderfully supportive environment of Hebrew College, a pluralistic setting that honors personal commitments while pushing those who work there to sharpen their thinking. We express thanks to all those colleagues and teachers as well.

The substance of this book is the result of many years of shared learning and discussion. Pride of place goes to our friend and colleague R. Aryeh Bernstein. It is virtually impossible to conceive of this book without him. He worked tirelessly on much of the drafting and redrafting of this discussion, helping us to put oral teachings into written form so that they could reach a larger audience. Aryeh's efforts to turn a set of *shiurim* into prose form helped launch this book and formed its initial kernel. Even as our presentation of the material has changed somewhat over the years, his impact remains throughout. Even more important, Aryeh has been an indispensable thought partner, always pushing us to sharpen our formulations and to be sensitive to hear the truth even when it is hidden. His love for Torah, its cosmic significance, and its stubborn focus on human needs has been a guiding light for us. We are honored to call him a colleague and a friend.

We would also like to thank R. Aryeh Klapper, who has engaged us on these issues over the years, ever since our shared time at Harvard

Hillel. He has always offered sharp critiques and criticisms, while constantly encouraging us to tighten our analysis and follow through the ramifications of every step of the argument. It has been a privilege to learn from him and with him on this and other matters. R. Yossi Slotnik also read drafts of this analysis in its entirety and his critiques led to significant revisions that strengthened our analysis considerably. We are grateful to have him as a colleague, supportive critic, and friend. Friends and mentors who have challenged us, allowing us the chance to sharpen our learning and teaching, are always preferable to those who simply offer support for what we already believe.

We are also deeply grateful to Sally Mendelsohn, Raphael Magarik, and R. Dena Weiss, who read the manuscript in its entirety, reviewing its language and structure. Their insights strengthened it tremendously. No detail was too small to catch their eye; of course, any errors are our own.

Our students, both at Hadar and at Hebrew College, have been constant sources of energy and strength for us. Hundreds of students have learned this material in depth with us over the years; their questions and challenges have left a deep impact on the work. Watching new scholars of Torah emerge is one of the greatest joys of teaching. And it is humbling and rejuvenating to be challenged by those who encounter for the first time sources that we have been turning over for decades. If our Torah has remained fresh, it is thanks to them.

Our families have provided incredible support during this process. Our children have had to tolerate long conversations over Shabbat meals about the Rambam's view of obligation in prayer. Our spouses, Ariela Migdal and R. Miriam-Simma Walfish, have been invaluable conversation partners and have helped the seeds of these ideas flourish into a full presentation. Our own conviction that *halakhah* must address contemporary issues of gender are inspired and guided in no small part by their wisdom and model. We hope our children will all live in a world that affords them a sense of full citizenship in and responsibility for Torah and *mitzvot*. If this book can play a small part in making that world a reality, that is sufficient reward for the work.

Last in word but first in thought—we recognize our debt to the One Who gives Torah, Who has blessed us to be among those who sit in the *beit midrash* so that we may discover the wonders of these teachings. We pray that this book will be a worthy חלק בתורתך.

Ethan Tucker and Micha'el Rosenberg
FEBRUARY 2017 | SHEVAT 5777

INTRODUCTION[1]

SINCE THE MIDDLE of the last century, various communities of Jews, initially in the United States and subsequently in Israel and elsewhere throughout the Jewish world, have questioned, advocated for, argued over, and implemented adoption of equal roles for men and women in Jewish communal prayer services. Different communities have taken on varying degrees of gender-egalitarian practice, some removing gender as a consideration in any aspect of communal ritual, others continuing to count only men for the *minyan* even as women equally read from the Torah, while others have adopted other versions of partial egalitarian practice. Some have incrementally moved toward egalitarian practice over

1 Many have addressed this topic before. In particular, we want to highlight: Broyde and Wolowelsky, "Women as Prayer Leaders"; Frimer, "Nashim u-Minyan"; Frimer, "Women and Minyan"; Frimer and Frimer, "Women's Prayer Services" and "Partnership Minyanim"; Golinkin, "Nashim u-Keri'at ha-Torah" and "Nashim be-Minyan"; Halivni, *Bein ha-Ish la-Ishah*; Hauptman, "Women and Prayer" and "Women and Minyan"; Rabinowitz, "Advocate's Halakhic Responses"; Riskin and Shapiro, "Aliyot for Women"; Roth, "Ordination of Women"; Rothstein, "Women's Aliyot"; Shochetman, "Aliyat Nashim"; Shapiro, "Keri'at ha-Torah" and Henkin's comments in the same issue; Sperber, "Congregational Dignity" and *Darkah shel Halakhah*. We have drawn on much material found in these publications. Our analysis here was significantly influenced by an unpublished article on egalitarian *minyanim* by Wald, "Ha-Ishah bi-Tfillat ha-Tzibbur." While Wald's argument was not fully fleshed out and seems never to have been intended as anything more than a private response to a private inquiry, he suggested several creative new lines of thinking that guided our analysis here.

time. Some communities have instituted these practices in consultation with organized movements and rabbinic bodies, and others have acted independently and with reference to their own grassroots views, sometimes articulated in halakhic language and sometimes not. Though the halakhic questions regarding egalitarian *minyanim* have generated a fair amount of literature, there is still a need for a comprehensive treatment of the issue that seeks to understand the underlying concerns and issues of the different positions taken. This problem is most acutely felt by members of independent prayer communities who care about observing *halakhah* properly but who are not affiliated with an organized denomination whose standards they can adopt or whose central rabbinic body they can trust, even if they do not understand the halakhic issues themselves. Further, many Jews seek a thorough personal understanding of their Jewish lives in their halakhic expression and will be served by an accessible, thorough treatment of this topic, which, though minor in its legal prominence, is quite significant in contemporary personal experience.

Method and Scope

It is our intention here to submit the major questions of gender and public prayer to a thorough, transparent, and accessible analysis. We will aim to survey sources that are relevant to the questions we raise as we identify differing approaches. Our goal will always be to understand the positions we discover on their own terms, as we attempt to articulate the values that underlie various approaches.

Two overarching methodological concerns generally guide us. First, any idea and any position that claims a coherent reading of earlier sources is worthy of being taken seriously and understood. We try to avoid crushing the legitimacy, authority, or viability of rulings based on the nature of their authors or how widely they were accepted when they were proposed. The position of every sage and *posek* is worthy of consideration and is a theoretically viable pathway for thinking about the proper application of *mitzvot* to our lives.

Second, cherry-picking positions in order to make a halakhic argument is not only tendentious; it is also often unwise.[2] As important as it is to understand every possible position, it is equally important to understand the basis of the opposition, particularly when it is broad and reflected among the majority of one's contemporaries. Minority views can be critical for reopening conversations, but they should not be favored at the cost of the wisdom of the majority. Ideally, a halakhic argument inspired by a minority position should make the case as to why conditions have changed such that the erstwhile minority would command majority support in the present moment.

Both of these principles aim to maximize wisdom and they reflect two different messages that emerge from Tosefta Eduyot 1:4:

תוספתא עדויות א:ד
לעולם הלכה כדברי המרובין לא הוזכרו דברי היחיד בין המרובין אלא לבטלן.

ר׳ יהודה אומ׳ לא הוזכרו דברי יחיד בין המרובין אלא שמא תיצרך להן שעה ויסמכו עליהן.

---

2 In the words of Tosefta Eduyot 2:3:

לעולם הלכה כדברי בית הילל והרוצה להחמיר על עצמו לנהוג כחומרי בית שמאי וכחומרי בית הילל על זה נאמ׳ הכסיל בחושך הולך התופס קולי בית שמאי וקולי בית הילל רשע אלא או כדברי בית שמאי כקוליהון וכחומריהון או כדברי בית הלל כקוליהון וכחומריהון.

The *halakhah* is always according to Beit Hillel. But one who wants to be stringent upon themselves to practice according to the stringencies of Beit Shammai and the stringencies of Beit Hillel, about this it is said, "but the fool walks in darkness" (Kohelet 2:14). But one who seizes the leniency of Beit Shammai and the leniencies of Beit Hillel is wicked. Rather, [go] either according to the words of Beit Shammai—according to their leniencies and their stringencies; or according to the words of Beit Hillel—according to their leniencies and their stringencies.

A person should strive for intellectual and religious integrity when studying *halakhah* rather than engaging in a haphazard search for opinions, whether lenient or stringent, on which to hang one's hat.

> **Tosefta Eduyot 1:4**
> The *halakhah* always follows the majority. The words of the individual are only recorded alongside those of the majority in order to reject them.
>
> R. Yehudah says: The words of the minority are recorded alongside those of the majority so that if they are needed at a later time, people can rely on them.

Minority views, says R. Yehudah, are theoretically as valuable as any other and must be studied carefully, since they may prove to be critical religious pathways at a later point in time.[3] But the primary, anonymous voice in the Tosefta reminds us that individual views must be kept in perspective. They were considered and rejected. To the extent one is inspired by the perspective of such a view, one must account for the majority's opposition and explain how that same majority might view things differently through the lens of a later, different experience of the issue.

Our focus on ideas and values also means that we do not claim to cite every potentially relevant source on the topic. We will often be content to cite enough material to outline a basic approach, with a particular focus on earlier sources that lay the groundwork for the contours of all subsequent conversations. In many cases, we examined sources that we felt essentially replayed prior arguments and elected not to engage them in deeper analysis. We welcome the insight and wisdom of readers to add to our framework with other positions we may not have yet fully considered.

Regarding scope, we will address two major questions:

1. The role of gender in selecting a *sheliaḥ tzibbur* (prayer leader or *sha"tz*) for public prayer. The question of Torah reading has been dealt with at length in other articles and responsa;[4] we will build on that literature to consider the more general question of leading rituals that require a *minyan* of ten.

---

3 This is a remarkable passage, in that R. Yehudah's very words seem to be cast as a minority view!

4 See Shapiro, "Keri'at ha-Torah"; Sperber, "Congregational Dignity"; Shochetman, "Aliyat Nashim"; Rothstein, "Women's Aliyot"; Sperber, *Darkah shel Halakhah*; Riskin and Shapiro, "Aliyot for Women."

2. The role of gender in counting the *minyan* for public prayer and other associated rituals.

Our primary goals here are:

1. to clarify misconceptions and dismiss red herrings that often cloud discussions on this topic;
2. to provide a sound basis for understanding the halakhic consequences of various positions related to gender and prayer; and
3. to provide a unifying discourse that can make sense of both egalitarian and non-egalitarian practices in Jewish prayer and enable proponents of both to be able to share a unified halakhic conversation despite their divergent practical conclusions.

There are a range of issues we will **not** address, not for their lack of importance, but in order to focus our discussion. The first group of these are practices that are gendered in classical rabbinic sources, but that do not involve power issues with regard to female participation in parts of the service. For instance, women were classically exempt from reciting the Shema, but individuals in many contemporary congregations never have their obligations fulfilled by the leader in this regard. Nor does the leader perform this function with regard to the blessings surrounding the Shema, where, in many (mostly Ashkenazi) congregations, the leader recites the bulk of the blessing silently, only cueing the congregation regarding pace by reciting the very end of the blessing out loud, which is not sufficient for discharging another's obligation.[5] Similarly, women were classically exempt from Hallel. However, the way we recite Hallel today features all individuals reciting the entire text on their own, including the opening *berakhah*.[6] In both these cases, the character of the leader

5 See Mishnah Berurah 59:15 and Be'ur Halakhah 59 s.v. *be-naḥat* for recognition of the fact that congregants are no longer careful to listen to the *sheliaḥ tzibbur* during the blessings of Shema, instead saying those blessings themselves. As a further extension of this trend, in many communities today not even the leader says the words loudly enough for anyone to follow them. The notion that the leader of the blessings surrounding Shema no longer fulfills the obligations of congregants seems to be assumed by R. Yosef Karo in his defense of minors who lead Arvit on Saturday nights. We will explore this case in depth below, Part One, nn. 125–130.

6 Women's exemption from Hallel seems to flow from Mishnah Sukkah 3:10. That *mishnah* states that when an adult male leads Hallel for others, the respondent only

should not make a difference. Whenever rituals like the Shema and Hallel **are** recited in a way that is intended to enable congregants to fulfill their obligations through the leader, it is not tenable to have someone who is exempt from these rituals fulfill the obligations of others through them. Only a paradigm shift in thinking about gender and ritual obligations—

---

needs to answer *halleluyah* at various intervals, relying on the leader to say the core of the text for him. But when a woman, slave, or minor leads Hallel, adult males must repeat the entire text word-for-word after them. Rashi Sukkah 38a s.v. *makrin* explains this as being based on an early custom, in which the communal prayer leader would fulfill others' obligation in Hallel. He says that women, slaves, and minors are all exempt from Hallel; this exemption is what triggers the respondent's obligation to repeat after them rather than relying on their recitation. Tosafot Sukkah 38a s.v. *mi* also infers from this *mishnah* that women are generally exempt from Hallel. In our settings, where all individuals say all of Hallel personally without being prompted by the *sha"tz* (and the *sha"tz* in most communities does not even say all of Hallel out loud, such that individuals cannot choose to rely on the *sha"tz* even if they wanted to), considerations of obligation would not be relevant. The Mishnah proceeds to curse a man who finds himself in a situation where he needs to be cued by a woman, slave, or minor, even if he says all the words himself. (Rashi and the Tosafot explain the concern behind this curse differently, see there.) When a woman is **not** cueing those present, both because the leader does not say all the words of Hallel aloud and because those present have the text in front of them in the Siddur, there is a strong case to be made that the curse should not apply. For this sort of analysis, see Koren, "Kullam Baki'im ba-Hallel." Frimer and Frimer, "Partnership Minyanim," disagree, arguing that having a leader who is not obligated in Hallel may itself be the source of the curse and/or may produce a problem of *kevod ha-tzibbur*. The notion that someone of lesser obligation might be unfit for leadership of the service even when they are **not** fulfilling the obligations of others is not an argument without merit and is not to be dismissed lightly. Nonetheless, to the extent that is a concern, it is not specific to Hallel and relates to broader issues of honor and dignity we will address below. Note also that it might be possible to read Mishnah Sukkah 3:10 as stemming from concerns other than obligation. The exemption of women from Hallel is not directly noted anywhere in rabbinic sources and it is strikingly absent from Rambam's Mishneh Torah. Rambam codifies Mishnah Sukkah 3:10 at Hilkhot Megillah ve-Hanukkah 3:14, but merely prescribes the Mishnah's protocol without mentioning the curse or even suggesting that there is anything wrong with appointing a woman, slave, or minor as the leader as long as one does not rely on their recitation in place of saying Hallel oneself. He nowhere suggests that these figures are exempt, as is his normal practice. The concern might have to do with social status and the general impropriety of placing oneself in a ritually dependent relationship with such figures.

which we discuss at several points—could alter this analysis with respect to female leadership.[7]

Second, we will not systematically address overarching concerns of sexuality that may or may not recommend gender segregation or integration in the synagogue space (and beyond). These issues are centrally important and also notoriously variable across communities and societies. More to the point, they tend to be comprehensive in ways that overwhelm the details of specific rituals and practices. To the extent that the mixing of genders in a room is improper (whether in the context of sacred spaces or more generally), a broad regime of gender separation is necessary. To the extent that a given community displays no such concerns in mixed-gender settings, those factors may be irrelevant. To the extent that gender segregation heightens sexual energy in a sacred space, such separation may itself be problematic. To the extent that individuals experience mixed-gender prayer settings as inappropriately sexualized, those individuals have an imperative to avoid such settings. These are all serious questions and concerns but are beyond the scope of our analysis.[8] While we engage the possibility of mixed-gender prayer practices and quorums throughout, we also intend our analysis to be sound for communities where full gender segregation during prayer is the norm and perhaps even the recommended ideal. Most concretely, nothing we say in our analysis takes a position one way or the other on the question of *meḥitzah,* the physical barrier between men and women that has also often functioned as an ideological barrier

---

7 Such a paradigm shift is most obviously required in order to argue for a gender-blind practice surrounding the sounding of the *shofar* on Rosh Hashanah. The gender gap in rabbinic sources is clear and power issues are very much in play, given that one person blows the *shofar* for the entire community. In keeping with Mishnah Rosh Hashanah 3:8, the one who blows the *shofar* must be obligated in order to discharge the obligations of others. Validating a woman as an effective *shofar* blower for men would require claiming that contemporary women are maximally obligated in *mitzvot,* including those from which they were traditionally exempt. The notion of such a paradigm shift will periodically resurface throughout our discussion and is most directly addressed in Appendix A; see also Part Two, nn. 76ff.

8 Others have thoughtfully addressed these sorts of issues. See: Berman, "Kol Ishah"; Henkin, *Equality Lost* and *Understanding Tzniut*; Bigman, "Kol Ishah Ervah." See also Responsa Piskei Uzziel bi-Sh'eilot ha-Zeman #44 and Responsa Yeḥaveh Da'at 4:15 for two important responsa on these sorts of issues.

between different segments of the Jewish community.[9] It is our conviction that it is possible to have separate conversations about gender equality on the one hand, and the mixing or separation of the genders in public space, on the other.

Our overarching hope is that the reader will emerge not only wiser, but more committed to the wisdom and richness of *halakhah* as a whole.

---

9 For a treatment of the issue of *meḥitzah* in *halakhah*, see Tucker, "Good Fences."

PART ONE
Serving as *Sheliḥat Tzibbur*

THE COMMUNAL PRAYER leader (*sheliaḥ* or *sheliḥat tzibbur,* or *sha"tz*) performs a number of functions, including helping the community keep a uniform pace. Two functions are particularly critical for determining someone's eligibility to serve as a *sha"tz*:

1. The prayer leader's fulfillment of the obligations of those assembled in some aspect of the service. We will focus on this issue in the context of the public recitation of the Amidah (which occurs during the Shaḥarit, Minḥah, Musaf, and Ne'ilah services).[1]

---

1 The word for Amidah in the sources—especially premodern—is typically *tefillah* (see, e.g., Mishnah Berakhot 4:1, 5:4; Shabbat 1:2; Ta'anit 2:2). But *tefillah* can also mean the concept of "prayer" more generally. We follow the cue of the sources themselves in using the words "prayer," "*tefillah,*" and "Amidah" interchangeably, and hope that it is clear in context if a more general word indicates specifically the Amidah. There are also separate obligations that have nothing to do with the Amidah that relate to our prayer services, most notably the obligation to recite the Shema twice a day; but, reciting the Shema is not covered by the obligation to "pray," which refers in most contexts in this book to specifically the Amidah. The main place of ambiguity is our discussion of the Rambam below, because whatever he thinks constitutes the biblically mandated *tefillah,* it cannot be the formalized Amidah, which is in his view only rabbinically mandated.

2. The leading of those parts of the service known as *devarim shebikdushah*—Kaddish, Barekhu (at Shaḥarit and Arvit), and Kedushah (as part of the public recitation of the Amidah). These elements are only said in the presence of a quorum of ten.

We will devote the first section of our discussion to analyzing both of these modes with respect to gender.

1. Reciting the Amidah Aloud

One of the central roles of the public recitation of the Amidah has traditionally been to enable those in the community who do not know how to pray to have their obligation in saying the Amidah fulfilled, as we see in the ruling of the Shulḥan Arukh:

שולחן ערוך או"ח קכד:א
לאחר שסיימו הצבור תפלתן, יחזור ש"צ התפלה, שאם יש מי שאינו יודע להתפלל יכוין למה שהוא אומר, ויוצא בו; וצריך אותו שיוצא בתפלת ש"צ לכוין לכל מה שאומר ש"צ מראש ועד סוף; ואינו מפסיק; ואינו משיח; ופוסע ג' פסיעות לאחריו, כאדם שמתפלל לעצמו.

Shulḥan Arukh Oraḥ Ḥayyim (= OḤ) 124:1
After the community finishes their Amidah, the *sha"tz* repeats the Amidah, so that if there is someone who does not know how to pray, they may have intention to what the leader is saying, and discharge [their obligation] through them. The one who is discharging [their obligation] through the prayer of the *sha"tz* must have intention for all that the *sha"tz* says, from beginning to end, and may not interrupt, nor speak, and takes three steps backward, like a person who is praying oneself.

The Mishnah establishes the principle that only one who is obligated (in a *mitzvah*) may fulfill another person's obligation in it:

משנה ראש השנה ג:ח
זה הכלל כל שאינו מחויב בדבר אינו מוציא את הרבים ידי חובתן.

Mishnah Rosh Hashanah 3:8
This is the principle: Anyone who is not obligated in a matter cannot discharge the masses of their obligation.

Therefore, since Shaḥarit, Minḥah, Musaf, and Ne'ilah all feature a public recitation of the Amidah, it would seem that one would have to be personally obligated in that prayer in order to serve as a *sha"tz*. In order to allow for gender neutrality around leadership of the Amidah in a mixed-gender space one would minimally have to show that either (a) obligation is no longer relevant for leading the Amidah, or that (b) the obligation in the Amidah is not gendered.

A. THE ARGUMENT THAT FULFILLING OTHERS' OBLIGATIONS IS NO LONGER RELEVANT

One can argue that in most contemporary communities the leader is usually **not** fulfilling the obligations of those unable to pray on their own. It is a well-established principle that one who knows how to pray cannot fulfill one's obligation in prayer by listening to the *sha"tz*.[2] This principle is generally adhered to without exception; those who know how to pray are expected to do so on their own and cannot rely on the leader to discharge this obligation for them.[3] If a community were comprised entirely of knowledgeable Jews, various regulations surrounding the public Amidah might not be in full force. This type of situation and its legal consequences was already highlighted by the Magen Avraham:[4]

---

2 The source for this ruling is found on Talmud Bavli Rosh Hashanah 34b–35a and is incorporated into the conclusions of Shulḥan Arukh OḤ 124.

3 See, for example, Mishnah Berurah 124:1:

אבל הבקי אינו יוצא אפילו בדיעבד בתפלת הש"ץ.

But a literate person does not fulfill [their obligation] even *post facto* with the prayer of the *sha"tz*.

4 The context here is the *halakhah* allowing an individual to prevent another individual from being appointed *sha"tz*. The Magen Avraham argues that this law applied only when the job of the *sha"tz* was to fulfill everyone's obligations, since no one should have to be represented by someone objectionable.

מגן אברהם נג:כ
ונ"ל דדוקא בזמניהם שהיה הש"ץ מוציא הרבים י"ח בתפלתו... משא"כ עתה שכלם בקיאין רק הש"ץ הוא לפיוטים.

Magen Avraham 53:20
It seems to me this was specifically in their times, when the *sha"tz* discharged the masses of their obligation in prayer... which is not the case now, when all are competent, and the *sha"tz* is only for liturgical poems.

Indeed, R. Ben-Tziyyon Meir Ḥai Uzziel affirmed that in any context in which all congregants are praying individually, the *sha"tz*'s sole function is in organizing the service, i.e., keeping everyone together at the same pace. He adds that even people otherwise considered peripheral members of the public prayer community ought to be able to serve in this role, explicitly mentioning children and women:[5]

שו"ת משפטי עוזיאל חלק ג, מילואים ב
במקום שהשומעים אומרים מלה במלה אחרי המברך והקורא אינו אלא מקריא לפניהם הדברים, הרי שהם יוצאים ידי חובתן בברכת עצמם והקורא אינו אלא מסדר הדברים פותח וחותם כל ברכה. וכן בקדושת השם פותח דברי קדושה והקהל עונים אחריו שפיר יכול המקריא להיות קטן או אשה.

Responsa Mishpetei Uzziel III, Miluim 2
In a place where the listeners say each word after the one making the blessings and the reader is only reading the words before them, they fulfill their obligations with their own blessings and the reader only sets the pace by reciting the beginning and end of each blessing. So is it with the Kedushah: [the leader] opens the words of Kedushah and the community answers after him—so the leader could properly be a minor or a woman.

---

5 R. Uzziel's responsum addresses the question of children leading a children's service, e.g., in elementary school, but for which a *minyan* of adults is present.

According to this approach, in communities where all have access to a Siddur and can use it competently, the level of the leader's obligation is no longer relevant.[6] Some have tried to extend this argument further by noting that Siddurim with translations enable even those who do not know Hebrew to pray, rendering them legally "able to pray independently" and thus unable to rely on the *sha"tz* to fulfill their obligations.[7] That would mean that, in any community with abundant Siddurim in translation, the *sha"tz* in no way vicariously fulfills others' obligations in prayer.[8] Questions of obligation would thus be irrelevant for determining who may or may not serve as a *sha"tz* for the Amidah.[9] The public recitation

---

6 R. Uzziel's final conclusion is that allowing minors to lead is inappropriate, not because of concerns about obligation, but on account of *kevod tzibbur*. We will address that issue at length below, nn. 82–113.

7 A straightforward reading of Mishnah Sotah 7:1 yields permission to pray in all languages. The ensuing discussion on Bavli Sotah 33a limits this permission to the case of בצבור and there are at least three interpretive positions that emerge. The Shulḥan Arukh sums it up in OḤ 101:4:

> יכול להתפלל בכל לשון שירצה, וה"מ בצבור, אבל ביחיד לא יתפלל אלא בלשון הקודש; וי"א דה"מ כששואל צרכיו, כגון שהתפלל על חולה או על שום צער שיש לו בביתו, אבל תפלה הקבועה לצבור, אפילו יחיד יכול לאומרה בכל לשון; וי"א דאף יחיד כששואל צרכיו יכול לשאול בכל לשון שירצה, חוץ מלשון ארמי.
>
> One may pray in any language one wants, that is, when in a community, but when alone, one must pray only in Hebrew. But some say that this [restriction to Hebrew] is only when asking for personal needs, such as praying for a sick person or on some other domestic sorrow, but the prayer that is fixed for the community: even an individual may say it in any language. And some say that even an individual asking for personal needs may ask in any language desired, other than Aramaic.

The stringent first position here (derived from Rabbeinu Yonah's reading of the Rif) would only permit prayer in other languages as part of the public Amidah. Following this more stringent reading would obviously cripple this argument.

8 R. Mayer Rabinowitz made this point in his responsum advocating for the ordination of women as rabbis in the Conservative movement: "Today when all of our congregations have prayerbooks with translations for those who cannot read Hebrew, and often with explanatory notes, we are in the category of competent worshippers (*beki'im*), and our obligations cannot be fulfilled by a *sheliaḥ tzibbur*." See Rabinowitz, "Advocate's Halakhic Responses," 117.

9 Obligation would still be a relevant consideration for leading any part of the *tefillah* where one person clearly recites or performs something for others. See Introduction,

of the Amidah would continue merely in order to fulfill the Sages' decree to require a repetition and in order to enable the Kedushah and Priestly Blessing to be said,[10] regardless of the liturgical competence of a given community's members.[11]

---

n. 7. Even with respect to the Amidah, there might, of course, be any number of other restrictions around who can lead; the Magen Avraham clearly would not have permitted Gentiles to lead the Amidah. But other considerations would relate to propriety or definitions of basic membership in the covenantal community, topics we will address below, as opposed to concerns regarding obligation.

10 See, for example, Arokh ha-Shulḥan (124:3):

> ודע דהטור כתב עוד טעם על חזרת הש״ץ משום קדושה ע״ש ונראה שהיה יכול לומר גם משום ברכת כהנים.

> Know that the Tur wrote another reason for the *sha"tz*'s repetition, namely, on account of the Kedushah, see there. And it seems that he could have also added on account of the Priestly Blessing.

The Priestly Blessing is said every morning by the *kohanim* in the repetition of the Shaḥarit Amidah in most communities in the Land of Israel and in most Sefardi communities even in the Diaspora. The dominant Ashkenazi Diaspora custom has been for it to be said by the *kohanim* only in the repetition of the Amidah for Musaf on Yom Tov and on Yom Kippur. However, even where the *kohanim* do not say the Priestly Blessing, the *sha"tz* says a modified form of it. We should note here that it is historically likely that the "repetition" of the Amidah was an original, independent form of public prayer that functions as a model of communal worship. The private Amidah is likely a separate phenomenon, intended to structure the individual's prayer using the communal template. An analysis of this issue is beyond the scope of this discussion but would provide a very different lens through which to view the ongoing importance of the public Amidah, even in a community of literate and competent individuals. See Kaf ha-Ḥayyim OḤ 124:2 for an analysis in keeping with this approach. See also Blidstein, "Sheliaḥ Tzibbur." Sensitivity to these origins is part of what motivates us not to rely solely on a sweeping disqualification of any concern for the public Amidah.

11 Shulḥan Arukh OḤ 124:3:

> קהל שהתפללו וכולם בקיאים בתפלה, אעפ״כ ירד ש״צ וחוזר להתפלל, כדי לקיים תקנת חכמים.

> If a community already prayed and all of them know the Amidah, nevertheless, a *sha"tz* should repeat the Amidah, in order to fulfill the decree of the Sages.

While this line of reasoning can muster some strong support,[12] a number of factors make it a less-than-ideal basis for a gender-blind selection of the *sha"tz*:

1. Sometimes there may be no prayerbooks available to a community, or there may be no translated prayerbooks for attendees who cannot read Hebrew, or some attendees may be unable to read either Hebrew or the language into which the book is translated.
2. Being able to pray in another language might not render someone legally competent in prayer to the point of forbidding them to rely on a public prayer offered in Hebrew. In other words, in communities with many who cannot pray in Hebrew, members might still appropriately choose to have the *sha"tz* fulfill their obligations in Hebrew.
3. Despite R. Uzziel's clear position making clear that concerns about obligation would not prevent a minor or a woman from leading a community where everyone prays individually, it is possible that the Magen Avraham himself would have objected to having a leader **incapable** of fulfilling the obligations of those present, even if there was no need to in the present case. If reciting the public Amidah fulfills the Sages' decree to say it, it might well be necessary to have a person meeting the normal requirements for a *sha"tz*, even when all can pray independently.

Therefore, we will elucidate the question of a *sha"tz* fulfilling others' obligations in prayer, and how gender figures into that equation. We have already seen that the core principle is that only one obligated in a particular *mitzvah* is fit to fulfill other people's obligations in it. There are two perspectives in the Rishonim as to the nature of the obligation of prayer; though there has been some misunderstanding regarding the less dominant of these positions, we will see that, according to both views, men and women are equally obligated in prayer and are therefore, from the perspective of obligation in the Amidah, equally fit to serve as *sha"tz*.

---

12 The position of R. Uzziel as minimally applied to a community fully competent in Hebrew prayer is particularly strong in this regard.

B. THE ARGUMENT FROM EQUALITY OF OBLIGATION

Mishnah Berakhot 3:3 establishes explicitly that men and women are equally obligated in the Amidah prayer:

משנה ברכות ג:ג
נשים ועבדים וקטנים פטורין מקריאת שמע ומן התפילין וחייבין בתפלה ובמזוזה ובברכת המזון.

Mishnah Berakhot 3:3
Women, slaves, and minors are exempt from the recitation of Shema and from *tefillin,* but **are obligated in prayer** and in *mezuzah* and in Birkat ha-Mazon.

This statement effectively summarizes the issue of gender and obligation in *tefillah* and it is the starting point to which all later interpreters must return. The Mishnah, without dissension, makes clear that men and women share an equal obligation in prayer. But in order to understand the complexities of later discussions, more background is needed.

Mishnah Kiddushin 1:7 offers a general rule that women are exempt from positive *mitzvot* caused by time:

משנה קידושין א:ז
וכל מצות עשה שהזמן גרמה אנשים חייבין ונשים פטורות.

Mishnah Kiddushin 1:7
With respect to any positive commandment caused by time, men are obligated and women are exempt.

"Caused by time" classically means that a *mitzvah* comes into force by dint of a certain day or moment coming to pass. For instance, the obligation to sit in a *sukkah* kicks in with the arrival of 15th Tishrei. It is also classically a gendered *mitzvah,* incumbent only upon men and thus aligned with the rule articulated in Mishnah Kiddushin. In keeping with this rule, Talmud Bavli Berakhot 20b asserts that *tefillah* is **not** such a *mitzvah,* placing it instead in the category of positive *mitzvot* **not** caused by time, thus explaining why women are likewise obligated.[13]

---

13 There are two main versions of the text of the Talmud here, one that asserts this point outright, and one that implies it by entertaining a contrary possibility and rejecting

Two core positions exist in the Rishonim to explain women's obligation in prayer: the view of the Rambam, and the view of Rashi, the Ramban, and many others.

1. *The Rambam's View: Biblical and Rabbinic Prayer*

The first view is that of the Rambam, who maintains that prayer is a positive *mitzvah* **not** caused by time, because, on a biblical level, the *mitzvah* to pray is inchoate: neither the frequency, nor the time, nor the content of prayers is legislated by the Torah. That is, a daily utterance of some sort of personal prayer suffices on the level of biblical law, so long as it includes the three main elements of praise, request, and thanks. Here are the relevant words of the Rambam:

ספר המצוות להרמב"ם מצות עשה
(ה) והמצוה החמישית היא שצונו לעבדו יתעלה וכבר נכפל צווי זה פעמים, אמר "ועבדתם את ה' א-להיכם" (שמות כג:כה) ואמר "ואותו תעבודו" (דברים יג:ה), ואמר "ואותו תעבוד" (שם, ו:יג) ואמר "ולעבדו" (שם, יא:יג)...ולשון ספרי "'ולעבדו' זו תפילה" (ספרי דברים מ"א)...

(י)...ולשון התוספתא "כשם שנתנה תורה קבע לקריאת שמע כך נתנו חכמים זמן לתפלה" (ברכות ג:א). כלומר שזמני התפלה אינם מן התורה. אמנם חובת התפלה עצמה היא מן התורה כמו שבארנו (ע' ה) והחכמים סדרו לה זמנים. וזהו ענין אמרם "תפלות כנגד תמידין תקנום" (בבלי ברכות כו:). כלומר סדרו זמניה בזמני ההקרבה.

Rambam, Sefer ha-Mitzvot, Positive Commandments
(5) The fifth commandment is that we are commanded to worship the Elevated One; this commandment has been repeated several times. It says, "And you shall serve the Lord your God" (Shemot 23:25); and it says, "[God] you shall serve" (Devarim 13:5), and it says, "[God] you shall serve" (6:13), and

---

it. This split was already noted by numerous Rishonim, including the Rashba and R. Yehudah he-Ḥasid. See also Ma'adanei Yom Tov, letter *tzadi* on Rosh Berakhot 3:13, and Dikdukei Soferim on Berakhot 20b. The latter version of the Talmud in turn gets emended by Rashi. For a full discussion of the textual history here, see Appendix B and the notes there.

it says, "and serve [God]" (11:13)...In the words of the Sifrei (Devarim #41): "'Serve God'—this is prayer."

(10)...The Tosefta (Berakhot 3:1) says: "Just as the Torah fixed times for the recitation of Shema, so the Sages gave a time for prayer," meaning, the times of prayer are not biblical. Indeed, the obligation of prayer itself is biblical, as we explained (#5) [the previous quoted paragraph], and the Sages assigned it times. This is the sense of the statement, "They established the prayers parallel to the *tamid* sacrifices" (Bavli Berakhot 26b), that is, they established its schedule parallel to the sacrificial schedule.

רמב"ם הלכות תפילה א:א–ב
(א) מצות עשה להתפלל בכל יום שנאמר "ועבדתם את ה' א-להיכם" (שמות כג:כה). מפי השמועה למדו שעבודה זו היא תפלה, שנאמר "ולעבדו בכל לבבכם" (דברים, יא:יג). אמרו חכמים "אי זו היא עבודה שבלב זו תפלה". ואין מנין התפלות מן התורה, ואין משנה התפלה הזאת מן התורה, ואין לתפלה זמן קבוע מן התורה.

(ב) ולפיכך נשים ועבדים חייבין בתפלה, לפי שהיא מצות עשה שלא הזמן גרמא אלא חיוב מצוה זו כך הוא: שיהא אדם מתחנן ומתפלל בכל יום ומגיד שבחו של הקדוש ברוך הוא ואחר כך שואל צרכיו שהוא צריך להם בבקשה ובתחנה ואחר כך נותן שבח והודיה לה' על הטובה שהשפיע לו כל אחד לפי כחו.

Rambam, Hilkhot Tefillah 1:1–2
(1) It is a positive *mitzvah* to pray every day, as it is written: "You shall serve the Lord your God" (Shemot 23:25). By tradition, they learned that this service is prayer, as it says, "and to serve God with all of your heart" (Devarim 11:13). The Sages said, "What is service of the heart? This is prayer." The number of prayers is not biblical, the form of prayer is not biblical, and prayer has no biblically fixed time.

(2) Therefore, women and slaves are obligated in prayer because it is a positive *mitzvah* not caused by time, but the obligation of this *mitzvah* is like this: A person should supplicate and pray

every day and tell of the Holy One's praise, and afterward ask for their needs as a request and a supplication, and afterward give praise and thanks to God for the good that has been bestowed upon them, each person according to their ability.

This view understands biblically mandated prayer to be largely unstructured. The structures of prayer as we know it—specific content at specific times—are rabbinically enacted parameters to formalize that commandment. The details of these requirements fill Rambam's Hilkhot Tefillah from shortly into chapter 1 (*halakhah* 4) all the way through chapter 6. At the conclusion of his elucidation of rabbinic prayer, the Rambam explicitly maintains that these rabbinic requirements are incumbent on women:

רמב״ם הלכות תפילה ו:י
נשים ועבדים וקטנים חייבים בתפלה, וכל איש שפטור מקריאת שמע פטור מן התפלה.

Rambam, Hilkhot Tefillah 6:10
Women, slaves, and minors are obligated in prayer, and any man who is exempt from the recitation of Shema is exempt from prayer.

One way of trying to synthesize these passages would be to argue that the Rambam thinks that women are obligated in prayer (his words in chapter 6), but only in general, unstructured biblical prayer (his words in chapter 1). They would be exempt from the specific rabbinic requirements of prayer, which may constitute a positive (rabbinic) commandment caused by time. Such a position requires reading the *halakhah* in chapter 6 as departing from the local context of rabbinic prayer and returning to recapitulate the ruling stated in 1:1–2 about biblical prayer. Such a reading is unsustainable for three reasons:[14]

1. Context: After five and a half chapters entirely about the details of the rabbinic parameters for prayer, would the Rambam suddenly return to a different, long-completed topic, without giving any

14 R. David Golinkin makes a similar argument in his responsum, Golinkin, "Nashim be-Minyan."

indication about the change? If he were here returning to the earlier biblical parameters of prayer, he would have informed the reader of this.

2. Redundancy: the Rambam already recorded the law about women's and slaves' obligation in biblical prayer, above in 1:1–2; why repeat it here?
3. Content: Above in 1:1–2, when recording the biblical parameters of prayer, the Rambam mentioned that women and slaves are obligated. Here, in 6:10, he mentions women, slaves, **and minors** as being obligated. Minors are never obligated by the Torah in *mitzvot*.[15] They are obligated rabbinically only in that their parents are obligated to train them. To say, therefore, that the reference here to women refers only to the biblical parameters of prayer requires not only understanding the Rambam to be switching topics unannounced and redundantly rerecording a law from chapter 1, but it also requires understanding him to be talking about two different topics within one phrase, making it illogical.

Indeed, R. Yosef Karo explicitly explains the Rambam here to be describing rabbinic prayer.[16] Perhaps most simply: One would never expect the Rambam—or any other post-talmudic commentator—to exempt women from the Amidah, given that no prior source does so!

Rather, the interesting question is not whether, but why: Why are women obligated in rabbinic prayer according to the Rambam? Shouldn't rabbinic prayer be considered a positive commandment caused by time,

---

15 We are aware of Gilat's provocative article challenging this presumption, but it is not relevant for understanding the Rambam's use of the term קטנים. See Gilat, *Hishtalshelut ha-Halakhah*. For the Rambam's approach, see the contrast between Mishnah Sukkah 2:8 and Hilkhot Shofar Sukkah ve-Lulav 6:1.

16 The Kesef Mishneh on the second half of this passage writes:

> וכל איש שפטור וכו׳ – רוב הפטורים מק״ש נאמר בהם שפטורים גם מן התפלה ואף באותן שלא נתפרש פטורים מק״ו דק״ש דאורייתא פטורים **תפלה דרבנן** לא כ״ש.

> Most who are exempt from Shema are also exempt from *tefillah*, and even those who are not explicitly exempted obviously are: if they are exempted from the biblical obligation in Shema, isn't it obvious that they are certainly exempted from *tefillah*, which is only a rabbinic obligation?

from which women are exempt, according to the Mishnah in Kiddushin? The Rambam explains in his commentary on that *mishnah*:[17]

פירוש המשנה להרמב"ם קידושין א:ז
ומצות עשה שהזמן גרמה היא שחובת עשייתה בזמן מסויים, ושלא באותו הזמן אין חיובה חל, כגון הסוכה והלולב והשופר והתפילין והציצית לפי שחובתן ביום ולא בלילה, וכל כיוצא באלו. ומצות עשה שלא הזמן גרמה הן המצות שחובתן חלה בכל הזמנים כגון המזוזה והמעקה והצדקה, וכבר ידעת שכלל הוא אצלינו אין למדים מן הכללות, וְאָמְרוּ "כל", רוצה לומר על הרוב, אבל מצות עשה שהנשים חייבות ומה שאינן חייבות בכל הקפן אין להן כלל אלא נמסרים על פה והם דברים מקובלים. הלא ידעת שאכילת מצה ליל פסח, ושמחה במועדים, והקהל, **ותפלה**, ומקרא מגלה, ונר חנוכה, ונר שבת, וקדוש היום, כל אלו מצות עשה שהזמן גרמה וכל אחת מהן **חיובה לנשים כחיובה לאנשים**.

Rambam, Commentary on Mishnah Kiddushin 1:7
And a positive *mitzvah* caused by time is obligatory at a set time; outside of this time, its obligation does not take effect, such as *sukkah, lulav, shofar, tefillin,* and *tzitzit,* because they are obligatory during the day but not at night... And positive *mitzvot* not caused by time are those *mitzvot* that are always obligatory, such as *mezuzah,* building a railing, and *tzedakah.* You already know that we have a principle that one does not learn from [heuristic] rules,[18] and when [the Mishnah] says "all," it actually means "most." But [the lists of] the positive commandments in which women are obligated or are not fully obligated obey no general rule, rather, they are passed on by tradition. Is it not the case that eating *matzah* on the first night of Pesaḥ, rejoicing on the festivals, the public reading of the Torah every seven years, **prayer**, reading of the *megillah,* Hanukkah candles, Shabbat candles, and reciting Kiddush

17 The Rambam wrote his commentary on the Mishnah in Judeo-Arabic. In this volume when we quote this work we use the standard Hebrew translation by R. Yosef Kapach as it appears in the Mosad ha-Rav Kook edition (1964).

18 Talmud Bavli Eruvin 27a, Kiddushin 34a.

> are all positive *mitzvot* caused by time, yet for each of them **a woman's obligation is the same as a man's obligation**?

The Rambam here discusses laws of biblical authority, such as eating *matzah* on the first night of Pesaḥ and reciting Kiddush, together with rabbinic laws, such as reading *megillah* and lighting Hanukkah candles. The "prayer" he refers to here is clearly rabbinic prayer, since he describes it as caused by time (i.e., happening at fixed times during the day); we have already seen that biblical prayer, for the Rambam, has no fixed times at which it must happen during the day. Nonetheless, the Rambam explains—accounting for Mishnah Berakhot 3:3—that women and men are equally obligated in rabbinic prayer. His larger point is that one should take the Mishnah's rule about women's exemption from *mitzvot* caused by time not as an absolute, but as a non-exhaustive general indicator that describes a number of cases. As we noted, some have argued that the Rambam thinks women are exempt from rabbinic prayer. If such a view is exceedingly difficult given his ruling in Hilkhot Tefillah 6:10, as we explored above, it is impossible in light of this comment in the Rambam's commentary on the Mishnah.[19] The Rambam uses different language in these different texts, but the data all point to a coherent position: there is only one kind of prayer, one that is biblical but whose parameters are rabbinically articulated. Though we have been speaking of "biblical" and "rabbinic" prayer, the Rambam has no notion of a separate entity of

---

19 R. Ovadiah Yosef, in Responsa Yabia Omer OḤ 6:17, opines that the Rambam must have changed his mind between writing his commentary to the Mishnah and writing the Mishneh Torah, which was written later. One could theoretically argue that, in the commentary on the Mishnah, the Rambam had not yet developed his theory of a more amorphous, less scheduled, biblical level of prayer and was therefore forced to posit that women are obligated in thrice-daily prayer. Once the Rambam formulated his more robust theory of *tefillah* in the Mishneh Torah, his final word on the matter was that women are only obligated to pray once a day. While discrepancies between his commentary on the Mishnah and the Mishneh Torah are not uncommon, they are mainly useful when a true contradiction exists. Here, as we argued, there is nothing in the Mishneh Torah indicating any exemption for women, but rather two explicit statements affirming their obligation in both the biblical and rabbinic spheres. R. Ovadiah does not engage Hilkhot Tefillah 6:10 and its relevance to our discussion. R. Ovadiah may be drawn to his explanation of the Rambam in order to implicitly justify the practice of women in his community not to pray multiple times a day. See below, nn. 28–41, for our analysis of the Magen Avraham.

inchoate, biblical prayer that survives beyond the rabbinic structuring of prayer. Moreover, "biblical" and "rabbinic" prayer, for the Rambam, are **not** two conceptually distinct universes. Recall that, for the Rambam, biblical prayer is not totally inchoate. Rather, one must sequentially praise, request, and thank. As is well known, these are in fact the three main sections of the Amidah as formulated by the Sages.[20] Thus, when one recites the rabbinically composed Amidah, one is simply using the Sages' model for fulfilling one's biblical obligation. The biblical *mitzvah* was not gendered, nor was the historical trigger for its rabbinic expansion and codification as described by the Rambam;[21] therefore, the rabbinic parameters of prayer are non-gendered as well. His model explains how the Gemara could refer to prayer as not caused by time (its biblical core possesses this quality), even as it is an obligatory practice multiple times a day, at set times (the rabbinic extension of the biblical core). Women would thus be obligated in the time-bound extension because of their obligation in the non-time-bound core.[22]

---

20 See Talmud Bavli Berakhot 34a.

21 See Rambam, Hilkhot Tefillah 1:4:

> כיון שגלו ישראל בימי נבוכדנצר הרשע נתערבו בפרס ויון ושאר האומות ונולדו להם בנים בארצות הגוים ואותן הבנים נתבלבלו שפתם והיתה שפת כל אחד ואחד מעורבת מלשונות הרבה וכיון שהיה מדבר אינו יכול לדבר כל צורכו בלשון אחת אלא בשיבוש...ואינם מכירים לדבר יהודית...ומפני זה כשהיה אחד מהן מתפלל תקצר לשונו לשאול חפציו או להגיד שבח הקדוש ברוך הוא בלשון הקדש עד שיערבו עמה לשונות אחרות, וכיון שראה עזרא ובית דינו כך עמדו ותקנו להם שמנה עשרה ברכות על הסדר... כדי שיהיו ערוכות בפי הכל וילמדו אותן ותהיה תפלת אלו העלגים תפלה שלימה כתפלת בעלי הלשון הצחה.

> When Israel was exiled in the days of Nebuchadnezzar the Wicked, they assimilated into Persia, Greece, and other nations and children were born to them in Gentile lands, and those children's speech was confused—each one's speech mixed up many languages, and one who would speak was unable to express oneself fully in one language, but only in a confused mix...and they did not know how to speak Hebrew....On account of this, when one of them would pray, they would come up short on Hebrew words for expressing requests and praise for God; other languages would get mixed in. When Ezra and his court saw this, they established a fixed order of eighteen blessings...which would be widely learned and known. Thus the prayer of these inarticulates could be as complete as those with a clear command of the Hebrew language.

22 For an excellent formulation of this point, see Sefer ha-Menuḥah on Hilkhot Tefillah 1:2:

> כלמור כיון שאין לתפלה זמן קבוע מן התורה אבל היא מצוה תמידית שחובה על האדם

The Rambam's model of prayer, though two-tiered, explicitly maintains the Mishnah's ruling that women and men are equally obligated in fixed prayer multiple times a day.

2. *Rashi and the Ramban: Prayer Is Rabbinic*

Rashi reveals a different approach. He explicitly rejects the notion that prayer is commanded by the Torah and explains that the Mishnah's reason for ruling that women and men are equally obligated in prayer is because prayer is a request for mercy, which is necessary for everyone:[23]

לעשותה תמיד נראה שהיא מצוה חביבה עד מאד ומפני זה לא רצו חכמים להפקיע נשים ועבדים ממנה. וכן אתה אומר לכל מצות עשה שאין הזמן גרמ׳.

Meaning: since there is no fixed time for prayer from the Torah, but it is a constant *mitzvah* that is obligatory for a person to do constantly, it seems that it is an extremely beloved *mitzvah*, and because of this, the Sages did not want to remove women and slaves from it. And so too for all positive, time-caused *mitzvot*.

23 Rashi draws this notion of prayer being a request for mercy from two other passages in the Talmud Bavli. After Mishnah Sotah 7:1 lists prayer among the ritual speech acts that may be said in any language, the anonymous voice of the Gemara on Sotah 33a explains that "תפלה רחמי היא, כל היכי דבעי מצלי — prayer is a request for mercy, so however one needs to, one should pray." The second place is Bavli Pesaḥim 117b. After Rava rules that the blessing praising God for redeeming Israel is said in the past tense in Shema and Hallel but in the present tense in the Amidah, the Talmud explains that the reason it is said in the present tense is because "prayer is a request for mercy"

אמר רבא: קריאת שמע והלל, גאל ישראל; דצלותא, גואל ישראל; מאי טעמא – דרחמי נינהו.

It is possible he was also influenced by Yerushalmi Berakhot 3:3 (6b), which comments on our *mishnah*: "כדי שיהא כל אחד ואחד מבקש רחמים על עצמו — In order that everyone should request mercy for themselves." See Appendix B for the fuller textual background for and fallout from Rashi's position here.

רש"י ברכות כ:
"וחייבין בתפלה" — דתפלה רחמי היא, ומדרבנן היא, ותקנוה אף לנשים ולחנוך קטנים.

Rashi Berakhot 20b
"And they are obligated in prayer" — because prayer is [a request for] mercy, and it is from our Rabbis, who established it even for women and for educating children.

Rashi is emphatic (here and elsewhere[24]) that regular *tefillah* has no biblical core. In Rashi's formulation, regular *tefillah* only has one tier: the rabbinic requirement for fixed prayer multiple times a day.

The Ramban expands Rashi's approach, attacking the Rambam and maintaining that there is no biblical requirement of daily prayer; rather, the whole enterprise is a rabbinic enactment:

השגות הרמב"ן לספר המצוות, מצות עשה ה
כתב הרב המצוה החמשית שנצטוינו בעבודתו שנ' ועבדתם את י"י א-להיכם וגו'...ולשון ספרי ולעבדו זו תפלה...ואין הסכמה בזה. שכבר בארו החכמים בגמרא תפלה דרבנן...וכבר ראינו בהלכות תפלה (רפ"א) שאמר שחייב אדם מן התורה בתפלה בכל יום אלא שאין מנין התפלות ולא משנה התפלה מן התורה וכך כתב בזה המאמר במצו' עשירית שזמני התפלה אינם מן התורה אבל חובת התפלה עצמה היא מן התורה. וגם זה איננו נכון בעיני...וכבר אמרו (סוף ר"ה) ברב יהודה דמתלתין יומין לתלתין יומין הוה מצלי, לפי שהיה עוסק בתורה וסומך על מה שאמרו (שבת יא.) חברים שהיו עוסקין בתורה מפסיקין לק"ש ואין מפסיקין לתפלה, שהיא דרבנן לעולם. אלא ודאי כל ענין התפלה אינו חובה כלל אבל הוא ממדות חסד הבורא ית' עלינו ששומע ועונה בכל קראינו אליו...ומה שדרשו בספרי... אסמכתא היא או לומר שמכלל העבודה שנלמוד תורה ושנתפלל אליו בעת הצרות ותהיינה עינינו ולבנו אליו לבדו כעיני עבדים אל יד אדוניהם.

24 Rashi Berakhot 20b s.v. *hakhi garsinan*: דהא לאו דאורייתא היא. See Appendix B for a fuller explication of this passage in Rashi.

> **Ramban's Challenges to Sefer ha-Mitzvot, Positive Commandment #5**
> The master (Rambam) wrote that the fifth commandment is that we must worship God, as it is said, "And you shall worship the Lord your God"...and in the words of the Sifrei, "'Worship'—this is prayer."...This point is not agreed upon. The Sages already clarified in the Gemara that prayer is only rabbinic...We also see that in Hilkhot Tefillah (chapter 1) he said that one is biblically obligated to pray every day, but that neither the number of prayers nor the precise form of the prayers is biblical. So, too, he wrote here in the context of the tenth commandment, where he said that prayer has no biblically fixed time, despite the fact that the obligation to pray is itself biblical. This also seems incorrect to me....It is reported that Rav Yehudah would pray [the Amidah] only every thirty days,[25] since he was constantly learning, and based himself on the view that scholars engaged in Torah must stop for Shema but not for the Amidah,[26] which is always only rabbinic in authority. Rather, prayer is not obligatory at all [on the biblical plane] and it is merely one of the Creator's traits of kindness that the Blessed One listens to us and answers us whenever we call...and the exegesis in the Sifrei...is merely a support [for a rabbinic practice] or means that part of our service to God must be study and prayer in times of need and that our eyes and hearts always be turned to God like those of servants to their masters.

For Rashi, the Ramban, and all others who assume *tefillah* is only rabbinic, the conceptual structure of women's obligation in prayer is even simpler. There is only one level of *tefillah,* and when rabbinic texts speak

---

25 Bavli Rosh Hashanah 35a.

26 Bavli Shabbat 11a.

of women's obligation in prayer, they are obviously speaking about the regular and repeated obligation of daily prayer that is *tefillah*.[27]

27 How did Rashi, Ramban, and others in this school address the fact that the Gemara seems to refer to prayer as not being caused by time? A few approaches were taken:

1. Some argued that even rabbinic prayer is not caused by time, in the sense that there is no time at which prayer is inappropriate. Consider Rabbeinu Yonah on Rif Berakhot 11a, who says:

> ואע״פ שהתפלה יש לה זמן קבוע אפ״ה כיון שאמרו הלואי שיתפלל אדם כל היום כולו כמצוה שאין הזמן גרמא, דיינינן לה ולפיכך נשים חייבות.
>
> Despite the fact that prayer has fixed times, nonetheless, since they said, "Would that people would pray all day long," it is treated like a commandment that is not caused by time. Therefore, women are obligated in it.

The talmudic passage quoted here can be found in various forms at Yerushalmi Berakhot 1:1 (2b), 4:4 (8b) and Shabbat 1:2 (3a); Bavli Berakhot 21a and Pesaḥim 54b. R. Yonah thus explains how we might regard *tefillah* as not caused by time without embracing the Rambam's model of biblical *tefillah*. The ideal of prayer as constant and unlimited is never lost via the Sages' establishment of fixed times, which should be seen merely as the minimum expression of prayer. Unlike eating *matzah* in the month of Tishrei, which is a religiously meaningless act, prayer at any time is meaningful and valued. This approach resonates with the phenomenon of *tefillat nedavah* that was endorsed by many authorities throughout the generations. See Shulḥan Arukh OḤ 107. Speaking less formally, even those opposed to *tefillat nedavah* might concede that prescribed prayers "wallpaper" the daily schedule, such that no time is bereft of such an obligation. See Levush OḤ 106:2. (Even the half-hour after noon that is ineligible for either Shaḥarit or Minḥah is traditionally understood as a precaution to avoid confusion.) Something like this basic approach seems to be behind the analysis of Tosafot Berakhot 20b s.v. *peshita*.

2. Others seized on Rashi's erasure of the passage in the Gemara that speaks about time-boundedness and *tefillah*. See Appendix B for a fuller analysis of Rashi's textual emendation. If the phrase is absent, one can then maintain that **despite** the fact that *tefillah* is indeed caused by time, **nonetheless** women are obligated in it because of its essence as a personal request for mercy. R. Yonah reports this possibility as well, when he continues in the above passage: אי נמי מפני שהיא רחמים.

None of these conceptual and literary debates affect the shared, practical consensus: Women are fully obligated in *tefillah*.

3. The Problem of Women Who Do Not Pray: The Magen Avraham's Defense

Women's and men's equal obligation in prayer remained uncontroversial in halakhic literature until the 17th century. No authority anywhere before that time ever says anything that suggests that women are exempt from any part of the obligation in the Amidah.[28] Commenting on the Shulḥan Arukh's formulation that women are obligated in prayer since it is a positive *mitzvah* not caused by time, the Magen Avraham writes the following:

מגן אברהם קו:ב
"מצות עשה" — כ"כ הרמב"ם דס"ל דתפלה מ"ע דאורייתא היא דכתיב ולעבדו בכל לבבכם וכו'. אך מדאורייתא די בפעם אחד ביום ובכל נוסח שירצה ולכן נהגו רוב נשים שאין מתפללות בתמידות משום דאומרי' מיד בבוקר סמוך לנטילה איזה בקשה ומדאורייתא די בזה ואפשר שגם חכמים לא חייבום יותר. והרמב"ן סובר תפלה דרבנן וכן דעת רוב הפוסקים.

Magen Avraham 106:2
"A positive commandment" — so wrote the Rambam, who thinks that prayer is a positive biblical commandment, as it is written, "and to serve God with all of your heart…" But biblically, it is sufficient to pray once a day, in any formulation that one wishes. Therefore, most women have the practice of not praying regularly, because immediately after washing their hands in the morning they say some request, and this is biblically sufficient,[29] and it is possible that the Sages did not extend their obligation any further. But Ramban thinks that prayer is rabbinic, and this is the opinion of most authorities.

---

28 A way of corroborating this point is to search an electronic database for any conjunction of the words תפילה, אשה, and פטורה in all digitized Jewish literature dating prior to the 17th century. Such a search turns up nothing that suggests exemption for women in prayer on any level.

29 The equation of the practice described here by the Magen Avraham with the Rambam's biblical prayer is somewhat imprecise, since the Rambam thinks that the biblical core requires sequential prayers of praise, request, and thanks.

Some authors have referred to the Magen Avraham as a source for arguing that women are not obligated in prayer, and therefore, to restrict their eligibility to serve as *sha"tz*. But the Magen Avraham does not in fact argue that women are exempt; he confronts a reality in which otherwise pious women are not praying three times a day and attempts to justify this practice as having some basis, even if it is not normative.[30] In so doing, those women can be seen as not sinful, even if their practice is not what one would expect in light of the halakhic sources. This sort of argument, traditionally known as a *limmud zekhut*, aims to stretch the boundaries of legal analysis in order to justify already established religious practices.

We should note a few points in order to maintain a precise understanding of this text:

1. The Magen Avraham does **not** say that the Rambam thinks women are exempt from regular, fixed prayer. As we saw, the Rambam explicitly obligates them in such prayer in Hilkhot Tefillah 6:10 and in his commentary to the Mishnah. Rather, the Magen Avraham notes that, according to the Rambam, there is a biblical core of prayer, which women in his cultural milieu do fulfill in their personal morning petitions, and suggests that maybe the Sages obligated them no further, even though we have no record of such a position: "...immediately after washing their hands in the morning they say some request, and this is biblically sufficient, and **it is possible** that the Sages did not extend their obligation any further." He uses the conceptual model of two-tiered *tefillah* advanced by the Rambam as a way of introducing a new way of reading earlier texts to justify contemporary practice.[31] Since this is incompatible with

30 We should not err in assuming that just because Jewish women in mid-17th century Poland did not apparently regularly pray the Amidah, therefore Jewish women never prayed the Amidah regularly and that their obligation has always been a dead letter. See Golinkin, "Nashim be-Minyan," 63–67, for a nice collection of evidence showing that women did pray regularly in many time periods and places. For one example, see R. Yonah on Rif Berakhot 7a s.v. *gemara*.

31 Note that the Magen Avraham would have to say that the Mishnah's ruling only applies to biblical prayer in order for this reading to cohere, which is an exceedingly difficult claim to make. Though the other *mitzvot* mentioned in Mishnah Berakhot 3:3 (*tefillin*, Shema, *mezuzah*, and Birkat ha-Mazon) **are** all biblical in nature, the term תפילה in Mishnah Berakhot refers to the Amidah when speaking about matters of obligation. See above, n. 1.

the clear equality of obligation assumed in all earlier sources, many later authorities considered this defense to be unsatisfactory, as we will see shortly.

2. Though the Magen Avraham roots his defense of contemporary women in the Rambam, he emphasizes that most authorities reject the Rambam's whole approach and think that prayer is entirely rabbinic, as we saw above in the positions of Rashi and Ramban. According to this view, there is no multi-tiered structure of *tefillah* that could be marshaled to support a gender gap in prayer obligation. The Magen Avraham's concluding words here suggest that he follows the Ramban, ruling that prayer is entirely rabbinic, since he asserts that the majority of authorities rule that way.

Indeed, commenting on the topic of the proper way to end Shabbat before resuming work, the Magen Avraham assumes that women are obligated in the regular Amidah multiple times a day. After the Shulḥan Arukh records the *halakhot* stipulating that one should not work before verbally confirming the ending of Shabbat and that the conventional place to do this is in the Amidah of Saturday night Arvit, the Rema comments regarding the proper way for women to end Shabbat, since they tended in his context not to pray Arvit on Saturday nights:

רמ"א או"ח רצט:י
וכן נשים שאינן מבדילין בתפלה יש ללמדן שיאמרו המבדיל בין קודש לחול קודם שיעשו מלאכה.

Rema on Shulḥan Arukh OḤ 299:10
And one should also teach women who do not make Havdalah in the Amidah to say, "[Blessed is the One] Who separates holy from mundane," before they do any [forbidden] labor.

On this ruling, the Magen Avraham comments as follows:

מגן אברהם רצט:טו
שאין מבדילין — **ואע"ג דחייבות בתפלה כמ"ש סי' ק"ו** מ"מ רובן לא נהגו להתפלל במ"ש. ואפשר לומר כיון דתפלת ערבית רשות אלא דקבלו עלייהו כחובה והנשים לא קבלוהו עלייהו במ"ש.

Magen Avraham 299:16
"Who do not make Havdalah" — **even though they are obligated in the Amidah, as is written in *siman* 106,** nonetheless, most do not have the practice of praying at the end of Shabbat. Perhaps this is because the evening prayer is optional, save for the fact that Jews accepted it upon themselves as obligatory, and women never obligated themselves to pray at the end of Shabbat.

Here, the Magen Avraham explicitly notes that women are obligated in prayer, that this is reflected in *siman* 106 of the Shulḥan Arukh (quoted above), and that any reality of women generally not praying was in tension with the established law. His comment here demonstrates that his comment back in 106 was meant as an attempt to defend a non-ideal practice, and not a principled expression of the law. In both places, confronted with a clash between adjudicated law and popular practice of otherwise pious people, he, like many rabbis throughout history, suggests a conceptual framework in which the legal establishment need not think of those people as transgressors. Regarding Saturday night Arvit in particular, his defense is more modest than his more sweeping pronouncement in *siman* 106: Since Arvit was originally not obligatory and became obligatory only through the power of custom, it is more reasonable to suggest that if the masses of women are not praying, maybe they never participated in the custom that transformed Arvit into a requirement, at least on Saturday nights.[32] This then strongly demonstrates that the Magen Avraham did not truly endorse his suggestion (*limmud zekhut*) in *siman* 106—in part because it would have been impossible for anyone who thinks regular *tefillah* is

32 Note that the Magen Avraham's language here only seeks to justify women who don't pray on Saturday nights, but the conceptual approach opens the door to letting them off the hook for evening prayer in general. This broader justification gained a number of adherents, including Shulḥan Arukh ha-Rav OḤ 106:2 and Mishnah Berurah 106:3. Of course, the status of women's obligation in Arvit has no bearing on the question of their fitness to serve as *sha"tz,* since the whole question of obligation is relevant only for the matter of the *sha"tz* fulfilling others' prayer obligation via the repetition of the Amidah; there is no repetition of the Amidah in Arvit.

entirely rabbinic to get behind it—and that in fact his starting assumption is one of gender equality vis-à-vis obligation in prayer.[33]

Nonetheless, a number of Aḥaronim have maintained the Magen Avraham's defense without challenging the strength of its legal and textual foundations. For example, the Peri Megadim,[34] after citing Rambam, Hilkhot Tefillah 1:1–2 and the Magen Avraham, says: "ולפי זה יצא קולא בנשים די להם בפעם אחד במעת לעת — According to this, a leniency emerged among women to suffice with once a day." Some late Aḥaronim, such as the Arokh ha-Shulḥan[35] and, in our own time, R. Ovadiah Yosef,[36] have tried to strengthen the Magen Avraham's defense of women who do not pray thrice daily by explaining that it was actually the position of the Rambam that women are not obligated in rabbinic—i.e., time-oriented and specifically formulated—prayer. This should be seen as a further attempt to justify ongoing practice, rather than as a principled reading. This is especially true of the Arokh ha-Shulḥan, who also creatively attempts to justify women's non-regular prayer habits even according to Rashi and the Ramban and concludes by openly acknowledging that he is driven to find a generous defense of popular practice:

ערוך השולחן קו:ז

ולפ"ז בדוחק יש ליישב מה שנשים שלנו אינן זהירות בכל הג' תפלות לשיטת רש"י ותוס' ולהרי"ף והרמב"ם א"ש ודו"ק.

33 See also Magen Avraham 70:1, where he cites R. Yonah's language explaining why women are obligated in *tefillah* as a **time-caused mitzvah**. Even more tellingly, he then proceeds to argue that though women are exempt, in his view, from the blessings surrounding Shema, they are obligated to say אמת ויציב, the *berakhah* of גאל ישראל immediately prior to the Amidah, because they should fulfill the obligation to juxtapose the theme of redemption to the Amidah. This is only coherent if he thinks women are obligated to say the Amidah. These points further reveal the Magen Avraham's acceptance of the fact that women are obligated in thrice-daily recitation of the Amidah.

34 Eshel Avraham on OḤ 106:2.

35 OḤ 106:7.

36 Responsa Yabia Omer VI OḤ #6.

Arokh ha-Shulḥan 106:7
And according to this, with great difficulty one may sustain the fact that our women are not meticulous in all three prayers, according to the position of Rashi and the Tosafot, though according to the Rif and the Rambam it makes sense.

As we saw above, any suggestion that the Rambam thought that women were exempt from rabbinic prayer contradicts the evidence of chapter 6 of the Mishneh Torah. The Magen Avraham himself never claimed that the Rambam held this view. Accordingly, a number of Aḥaronim called out this unwarranted expansion and rejected any use of the Rambam to defend women who were not praying regularly. For one example, here are the comments of R. Ben-Tziyyon Lichtman on this passage of the Magen Avraham:

בני ציון או"ח קו:א
ויותר מזה קשה, דהרמב"ם כתב בסוף פ"ו נשים ועבדים וקטנים חייבים בתפילה. ובודאי מיירי בכל התפילות, ולא רק על...פ"א ביום באיזה נוסח שהוא, אלא בסתם תפילה מיירי בכל הפרק, ועוד דומיא דקטנים שחייבין בכל התפילות, והרי נראה ברור שגם הרמב"ם מחייב נשים בכל התפילות ודלא כמ"ש המ"א והפ"ם.

וזה עולה באמת לפי גרסתו בגמרא, "תפילה פשיטא מ"ד הואיל וכתיב...הו"ל מ"ע שהז"ג וכל מ"ע שהז"ג נש' פטורות קמ"ל." ...וזהו כל החידוש שאף בהן נשים חייבות אע"פ שהחיוב דרבנן תלוי בזמן, והטעם הוא דכיון שעיקר חיוב התפלה מדאורייתא אינו תלוי בזמן ונשים חייבות בו אף חכמים לא הוציאו אותן מהחיוב שלהם אע"פ שקבעו לו זמן.

Benei Tziyyon OḤ 106:1
And a further difficulty is that the Rambam wrote in chapter 6, "Women, slaves, and minors are obligated in prayer." And surely he is dealing there with all of the prayers, and not simply with the prayer...of once a day in any form that one wants, but rather with the standard prayer that is the topic of that entire chapter; and furthermore, a comparison is made to minors who are obligated in all of the prayers, and it thus is seen clearly that also

> the Rambam obligated women in all of the prayers, and it is not as was written by Magen Avraham[37] and Peri Megadim.
>
> And this emerges clearly from [the Rambam's] version of the Gemara: "Prayer—that is obvious! What would you have thought? Since it is written... [you might have thought that] it is a positive *mitzvah* caused by time, and from all positive *mitzvot* caused by time women are exempt; therefore, it comes to teach us otherwise."... And this is itself the whole innovation [of the Gemara here], that women are even obligated in [the fixed times for prayer], even though the rabbinic obligation is dependent on time, and the reasoning is that since the core of the obligation for biblical prayer is not dependent on time and women are obligated in it, even the Sages did not exclude them from their obligation, even though they fixed a time for it.

Indeed, other Aḥaronim, such as Maharam ibn Ḥabib,[38] R. Yitzḥak Taib,[39] and R. Shmuel Ehrenfeld,[40] insist that the Rambam mandates that women pray three times daily. R. Yisrael Meir Kagan does not relate to whether the Magen Avraham's passage reflected the correct reading of the Rambam; nevertheless, he expressly states that *halakhah* accords with the Ramban, that prayer is an entirely rabbinic *mitzvah* and unquestionably equal for men and women, and that women should therefore be urged to pray regularly:

---

37 Note that R. Lichtman cites the Magen Avraham as ascribing to the Rambam the view that women are only obligated to pray once a day. We argued above that the Magen Avraham never claimed this, but this text is a good indicator of how powerful a trope it had become to justify women's lack of regular prayer by appealing to the Magen Avraham's use of the Rambam.

38 Kapot Temarim Sukkah 38a.

39 Erekh ha-Shulḥan OḤ 106:1. See also Ben Yedid, the commentary of R. Yedidiah Shmuel Tarica, on Rambam, Hilkhot Tefillah 1:2.

40 Ḥatan Sofer, Tefillah 3:102b.

משנה ברורה קו:ד
אבל דעת הרמב״ן...חייבו אותן בתפילת שחרית ומנחה כמו אנשים הואיל ותפלה היא בקשת רחמים. וכן עיקר כי כן דעת רוב הפוסקים...ע״כ יש להזהיר לנשים שיתפללו י״ח.

Mishnah Berurah 106:4
But the Ramban's view... [is that our Sages] obligated them in Shaḥarit and Minḥah just like men since prayer is a request for mercy. This is the essence of the matter, since it is the view of most authorities.... Therefore, one must impress upon women that they pray the Amidah.[41]

4. *Other Defenses of Pious Women Not Praying*

Other 20th-century Aḥaronim have gone to lengths to emphasize that women are obligated in prayer according to everyone, including the Rambam, yet have offered alternative frameworks for defending contemporary women who do not pray regularly. These defenses have pointed to lifestyle conflicts making it difficult for women in their particular contexts to pray with proper focus. R. Ben-Tziyyon Lichtman wrote as follows:

בני ציון קו:א
ולי נראה ללמד זכות על רוב הנשים שאין מתפללות בתמידות דרוב הנשים מוטל עליהן להתעסק בכל צרכי הבית ובטיפול ילדים והכנת צרכיהם, שמטריד הלב ומבלבל הכונה, ובמצב זה אין להתפלל כמו שכתב הרמב״ם בפ״ד מצא דעתו משובשת ולבו טרוד אסור לו להתפלל עד שתתישב דעתו...ואע״ג שעכשיו אין אנו נזהרי׳ בזה מפני שאין מכונים כ״כ בתפלה, לגבי טרדות הנשי׳ שאני...**אבל אלו הנשי׳ שנמצאות במצב שיכולות להתפלל ודאי צריכות להתפלל כל הג׳ תפלות, כי מדינא נשים חייבות בכל התפלה אליבא דכו״ע.**

41 In fact, the author of the Mishnah Berurah only took up this cause regarding Shaḥarit and Minḥah, having adopted the Magen Avraham's defense of women who do not pray Arvit, a defense we described above.

Benei Tziyyon OḤ 106:1

And it seems to me that the way to justify the practice of those women who do not pray with regularity is that most women are encumbered with dealing with all the needs of the household and taking care of children and preparation of their needs, which distracts the mind and disorients proper focus, and in such a state one should not pray, as the Rambam wrote in chapter 4: "If one's mind is disoriented and one's heart distracted, it is forbidden to pray until the mind gets settled."... And even though nowadays we are not concerned with this, since we are not so focused in our prayer [anyway], regarding the distraction of women [i.e., the raising of children] it is different.... **But those women who find themselves in a situation where they can pray certainly must pray all three prayers, because on the basis of the law they are obligated in all of the prayers according to all authorities.**

In our own day, R. Yehudah Herzl Henkin follows the Benei Tziyyon.[42]

Another Aḥaron, R. Yekutiel Yehudah Halberstam, followed a similar route in explaining that, even according to the Rambam, women are obligated in prayer, and that the Magen Avraham himself understood this. He offered a similar, alternative defense of women who do not pray:

שו"ת דברי יציב או"ח קכא

אך עדיין יש לי להצדיק המנהג שהזכיר המג"א, כיון דבש"ס עירובין ס"ה ע"א יכולני לפטור מדין תפלה שנאמר שכורת ולא מיין עיי"ש... ועכ"פ יש סמך גדול לנשים בזמה"ז שאינן בגדר ימוד את עצמו שיכול לכוון...וק"ו לנשים דטרידי טובא ורשות בעליהם עליהם והטף תלויים בהם, לזה נהגו רוב נשים שאין מתפללות בתמידות, ורק כשימודו בעצמן שיכולים לכוון עכ"פ לפי האפשרות, ולפענ"ד זה אמת...שכיון שבאמת מעיקר התקנתא יהו חייבות בתפלה.

Responsa Divrei Yatziv OḤ #121

But I can still justify the practice described by the Magen Avraham, since in Bavli Eruvin 65a [it is said that] I can

42 Responsa Benei Banim II:6.

> exempt from the law of prayer [one about whom] it is written, "drunk, but not from wine," see there...and there is in any event certainly a sound basis for women today, who are not in the class of those who can assure that they are sufficiently focused... [given that] women are extremely burdened, subject to their husbands' authority and responsible for children. Therefore most women do not pray regularly, and only when they judge themselves to have sufficient focus do they pray, when it is possible. This, in my humble opinion, is correct... since they are in truth included [like men] in the original obligation of prayer.[43]

5. *Summary*

To summarize, the Rambam rules that prayer is commanded in a general way by the Torah, and applies equally to men and women, as it is not caused by time. When the Sages structured that general commandment into specific prayers at specific times, its equal application to women and men remained. Rashi and Ramban argue that there is no such thing as biblically commanded prayer. Prayer—as we know it, thrice daily and with a particular structure—was instituted by the Sages and applied equally to men and women. Both approaches are efforts to explain the same fact, explicitly laid out in the Mishnah, namely, that women and men are equally obligated in prayer.

The Shulḥan Arukh, in codifying this universally agreed upon point, follows a modified version of the Rambam's language in the Mishneh

43 This passage in the Divrei Yatziv is significant for two reasons. First, like the Benei Tziyyon, it rejects the Magen Avraham's suggestion that women are essentially any less obligated than men in daily prayer. Second, and more significant, it actively endorses women's full essential obligation in *tefillah* even in cases where a *berakhah levatalah* is at stake. The responsum here is dealing with the question of whether a woman who lit Shabbat candles may then pray Minḥah—even if she did not explicitly condition her lighting with this in mind. R. Halberstam rules that she may, because her obligation in *tefillah* is identical to men and is thus a standing responsibility that her lighting of the candles and early acceptance of Shabbat cannot eliminate.

Torah, stating that women are obligated in prayer because it is a positive *mitzvah* not caused by time:[44]

שולחן ערוך או"ח קו:ב
נשים ועבדים, שאע"פ שפטורים מק"ש חייבים בתפלה, מפני שהיא מ"ע שלא הזמן גרמא.

Shulḥan Arukh OḤ 106:2
Women and slaves, even though they are exempt from the obligation of reciting the Shema, are obligated in prayer, because it is a positive commandment not caused by time.

Throughout the classical and medieval halakhic literature, the full and equal obligation of women and men in prayer was maintained without controversy. In the period of the Aḥaronim, some authorities, beginning with the Magen Avraham, attempted to defend the religious integrity of pious women who did not pray regularly. The Magen Avraham's defense was far-reaching, but never claimed to be the ideal law. In any event, it met with resistance even as a defense by other authorities and even Magen Avraham himself seems to have abandoned it. A more solid defense argued that the proposed exemption is properly understood as an exemption for women engaged in childcare, **while engaged in childcare,**[45] a defense

---

44 From the Shulḥan Arukh's use of the Rambam's formulation, one might conclude that he also endorses the Rambam's framework of a biblical requirement to pray daily. However, we saw above, in n. 27, R. Yonah's approach that it is possible to consider thrice-daily rabbinic *tefillah* to be the only *tefillah* that there is and nonetheless to describe it as מצות עשה שלא הזמן גרמא. Indeed, R. Yosef Karo cites only Rashi's explanation of the gender-blind nature of the Mishnah (דרחמי נינהו) in Beit Yosef OḤ 106, and Taz OḤ 106:2 took for granted that the Shulḥan Arukh thought *tefillah* was rabbinic without any biblical core. See also Perishah OḤ 106:4, who seems to equate the Shulḥan Arukh's usage of מצות עשה here with the usage of Tosafot Berakhot 20b s.v. *peshita*, which is predicated on *tefillah* being entirely rabbinic.

45 R. Menaḥem Nissel cites R. Yisrael Meir Kagan in Siḥot Ḥafetz Ḥayyim I:27 as also holding the view that women burdened with childrearing may be exempt from *tefillah* on account of these burdens. See Nissel, *Rigshei Lev*, 82–87, along with the notes there. R. Nissel also cites evidence that this was the position of 20th-century luminaries such as R. Shlomo Zalman Auerbach (via oral tradition), R. Ya'akov Kaminetzki in Emet le-Ya'akov OḤ 106:131, the Ḥazon Ish (as cited in Responsa Maḥazeh Eliyahu 19:5), R. Ḥayyim Pinḥas Scheinberg (personal communication

that is dependent on activity conflicts, not on gender, as it would just as reasonably be invoked to defend men who, on account of the pressures of childcare, become less meticulous about prayer than rabbinic law would have them be.[46] The essential equality between men and women regarding prayer thus remains, even as those in caretaker roles may find themselves with a contextual exemption in certain situations. None of this affects a person's ability to discharge others' obligations in prayer by serving as *sha"tz* since, as was already clear in the Mishnah, men and women are equally obligated in prayer.

Women's supposed exemption from prayer cannot serve as a justification for excluding them from serving as *sha"tz*. There is no solid basis for any claim that women are, by dint of the fact that they are women, any less obligated than men in prayer. This is obviously true according to the dominant view of Ramban (without any controversy) and is also true according to Rambam's two-tiered approach to *tefillah*. At most, some of the later uses of Rambam to generate a justification of women who do not pray are at most just that: a justification of a non-ideal situation. They have no place in any discussion surrounding an ideal approach to gender and prayer, nor in the context of a community that is pursuing a more egalitarian approach to *tefillah*. While it is not our place to judge women who rely on the Magen Avraham to justify their own practice, it is important to avoid allowing the justification of pious women who do not pray the Amidah regularly to undermine their fundamental obligation in prayer across halakhic time and space. Those defenses that focus on lifestyle conflicts have proven themselves more legally sound. Thus, gender should not play a central role when it comes to obligation in prayer.[47]

---

with R. Nissel), and R. Moshe Shternbuch in Mo'adim u-Zemanim I:9 and Teshuvot ve-Hanhagot I:74, III:OḤ 36. He also emphasizes that R. Scheinberg, R. Eliyahu Greenblatt, and R. Yosef Shalom Elyashiv stress that a woman who is not in a situation of familial burden is obligated to pray regularly; see Nissel, *Rigshei Lev*, 85–86, nn. 14–15.

46 Indeed, such a basis for exempting men who are primary caregivers is advanced by R. Ben-Tziyyon Abba Shaul in Responsa Or le-Tziyyon II 7:24.

47 Two arguments appear in the Aḥaronim claiming that women are exempt from Musaf:

1. Women are exempt from Musaf because this prayer exists as a memory of the public sacrifices, and women were not obligated to contribute to the pool of funds

set aside for this purpose. (See Mishnah Shekalim 1:3.) This argument first appears in R. Shaul Berlin's collection of responsa, Besamim Rosh. (R. Berlin edited this collection and claimed that it contained lost medieval responsa, including many of the Rosh, R. Asher b. Yeḥiel. Many contemporary rabbis and modern scholars considered the work to be a fraud composed by R. Berlin himself. His work has nonetheless been quoted occasionally by a range of later *poskim*.) Besamim Rosh #89 then goes on to make the interesting claim that women nonetheless have the practice to pray "everything, and have obligated themselves in all the *mitzvot*" (וחייבו את עצמן בכל המצות). A similar argument for exemption is cited in Responsa R. Akiva Eiger I:9. R. Yitzḥak Elḥanan Spector rejects this argument outright in Responsa Be'er Yitzḥak OḤ #20, given that it would imply that no one under twenty is obligated in Musaf. See also Torah Temimah on Shemot 30:22 for a similar critique.

2. Musaf is a time-caused *mitzvah* and therefore, following the rule of the Mishnah in Kiddushin, women are exempt from it. This logic is advanced in R. Yeḥezkel Landau's Tziyyun le-Nefesh Ḥayyah on Berakhot 26a s.v. *ve-shel musafin*. This claim, at first blush, overtly contradicts the Gemara, which already seems to have accounted for the general tension between women's obligation in *tefillah* and the principle of exemption from time-caused *mitzvot*. But R. Landau develops his point by using Rashi's text of the Gemara, which emphasizes that women are obligated in prayer because it is a "request for mercy" (רחמי נינהו). Given that several Rishonim argue that Musaf is not a request for mercy and therefore one cannot make up for a missed Musaf Amidah by repeating the next *tefillah* (תשלומין), it must be that the basis for women's obligation is not present and therefore we revert to the rule in Mishnah Kiddushin. This is a difficult argument on a few counts, not least of which is that it is a debate among commentators as to whether one can make up for a missed Musaf Amidah (see Meiri Berakhot 26a). Furthermore, once women are included in the *mitzvah* of prayer, there is no indication that they are then excluded from any part of it, and it is surprising to think that such a significant exclusion would not have been mentioned anywhere by the *poskim*. Most important, R. Landau's "argument" here is essentially a theoretical analysis of what seems to be an extraneous word in the Tosafot there, and it is unclear whether he ever intended it to have practical halakhic force. In any event, R. Mordekhai Ze'ev Ettinger and R. Yosef Shaul Nathanson (in Magen Gibborim, Elef ha-Magen 106:4) both rejected R. Landau's argument here, claiming that in fact the Musaf Amidah is fundamentally a request for mercy and that the ancient practice in Eretz Yisrael of saying an eighteen-*berakhah* Amidah for Rosh Ḥodesh Musaf confirms this point. Therefore, women are equally obligated in Musaf. In their words, "הדין ברור — the law is clear on this matter." R. Spector also challenges R. Landau here. For a review of the basic positions on this topic, see Responsa Yabia Omer II OḤ 6:4–6.

One can certainly construct out of these dissenting Aḥaronim a justification of those women who do not regularly pray Musaf. There is not, however, enough to work with to claim that communities that assume women have the same obligation as men in Musaf are somehow playing on the legal margins. With

Some recent authors[48] have tried to argue for women's continued exclusion from serving as *sha"tz,* even while acknowledging that such an exclusion cannot be justified on grounds of their not being obligated in prayer. They have argued, instead, that while women are obligated fully in individual prayer, there is a separate "*mitzvah* of public prayer" that is incumbent upon men but not upon women, and that this gap precludes women from serving as *sha"tz*. In Appendix C, we address those concerns, arguing that the nature and contours of public prayer do not generate gender-based distinctions with respect to who may function as its leader.

II. Reciting *Devarim Shebikdushah*

The other main function of the *sha"tz,* in addition to fulfilling the obligation of those who do not know how pray, is to say *devarim shebikdushah,* which are said only in a *minyan*. We will here investigate whether gender affects fitness for leading these uniquely public parts of the prayer service.

Mishnah Megillah 4:3 lists a number of prayers and rituals that are said only in the presence of ten, including public Torah reading, having a *sha"tz* lead prayer, adding God's name to the invitation to Birkat ha-Mazon (*zimmun*), and various occasional rituals:

משנה מגילה ד:ג

אין פורסין את שמע, ואין עוברין לפני התיבה, ואין נושאין את כפיהם, ואין קורין בתורה, ואין מפטירין בנביא, ואין עושין מעמד ומושב, ואין אומרים ברכת אבלים ותנחומי אבלים וברכת חתנים, ואין מזמנין בשם, פחות מעשרה. ובקרקעות, תשעה וכהן. ואדם, כיוצא בהן.

---

respect to Ne'ilah on Yom Kippur, nothing suggests that it is any more gendered than Shaḥarit or Minḥah. Indeed, in Responsa Yabia Omer II OḤ 6:7, R. Ovadiah Yosef states that women are obligated in Ne'ilah, despite the fact that he holds that they are normally exempt from Musaf. We will leave the discussion here with the unambiguous bottom line of R. Spector from the above *teshuvah*: "וכן מוכח מסתימת הפוסקים דנשים חייבות בתפלה ולא חלקו בין מוסף לשארי תפלות—Women are obligated in all types of *tefillah* without any distinction."

48 For example, see Broyde and Wolowelsky, "Women as Prayer Leaders."

Mishnah Megillah 4:3

We do not responsively recite the Shema,[49] nor have a communal prayer leader, nor offer the Priestly Blessing, nor read Torah, nor read from the Prophets, nor perform the standing/sitting [ritual for the dead], nor say the blessing of the mourners, nor the formal comforting the mourners, nor recite the wedding blessings, nor say *zimmun* with the Name in a group of fewer than ten. And when redeeming land we require nine and a *kohen*; and so too with [redeeming] people.

On Talmud Bavli Megillah 23b, R. Yoḥanan bases this on a verse and describes (at least some of) the rituals in this *mishnah* as *devarim shebikdushah*, or sacred rituals:

תלמוד בבלי מגילה כג:

מנא הני מילי? אמר רבי חייא בר אבא אמר רבי יוחנן: דאמר קרא "ונקדשתי בתוך בני ישראל" (ויקרא כב:לב) — כל דבר שבקדושה לא יהא פחות מעשרה.

Talmud Bavli Megillah 23b

How do we know this? Said R. Ḥiyya b. Abba said R. Yoḥanan: The verse says: "And I will be sanctified in the midst of the children of Israel" (Vayikra 22:32)—any *davar shebikdushah* shall not be said with fewer than ten.

On Berakhot 21b, Rav Ada b. Ahavah explicitly includes the Kedushah in this category of prayers that may be said only in the presence of ten:

תלמוד בבלי ברכות כא:

וכן אמר רב אדא בר אהבה: מנין שאין היחיד אומר קדושה — שנאמר "ונקדשתי בתוך בני ישראל" (ויקרא כב:לב). כל דבר שבקדושה לא יהא פחות מעשרה.

49 The exact meaning of *pores al Shema* has been hotly debated. Our translation here follows Tosefta Sotah 6:3 and the analysis of Fleischer, "ha-Pores al Shema." It seems likely that this already assumes some sort of recitation of Barekhu as part of the Shema and its attendant *berakhot*. See Mishnah Tamid 5:1.

Talmud Bavli Berakhot 21b
So said Rav Ada b. Ahavah: From where do we know that an individual does not say the Kedushah? As it says, "And I will be sanctified in the midst of the children of Israel" (Vayikra 22:32)—any *davar shebikdushah* shall not be said with fewer than ten.

In the time of the Geonim, we find explicit statements requiring ten for Kaddish as well:

גאוני מזרח ומערב סימן קכו
עשרה שמתפללין וכיון שהגיעו לאל הקדוש הלך אחד מהן יסיימו את כל הברכות עד שלום רב. אבל יתגדל ויתקדש אי איפשר לומר לו אלא בעשרה.

Geonim of East and West #126
When ten are praying and, upon reaching *ha-El ha-Kadosh* [the conclusion of the third blessing of the Amidah, which includes Kedushah], [if] one of them walks out, they should finish all the blessings until Shalom Rav [the final blessing of the Amidah]. But they cannot say Kaddish unless there are ten [present at that point].[50]

Barekhu is included (along with Kaddish) among the rituals requiring ten for the first time in Massekhet Soferim 10:6:[51]

---

50 The ruling offered here was not wholly accepted in later times. See Shulḥan Arukh OḤ 155:3.

51 Reed Blank has argued that this passage in Massekhet Soferim, particularly the additions of Kaddish and Barekhu to the Mishnah's list, may in fact be a gloss that dates from no earlier than the 13th century. See Reed Blank, "Medieval French Practice." As we noted in n. 49, the practice of including Barkehu as part of the Shema is already attested in some form in Mishnah Tamid 5:1; it also appears as a ritual done specifically in the synagogue in Mishnah Berakhot 7:3, though it is unclear if this is in the context of the Shema or as part of public Torah reading. Either way, the plural grammatical form, the location in the synagogue, and its contextualization in a discussion about *zimmun* indicate an assumed quorum. Kaddish also has early origins; see Bavli Berakhot 3a, 57a, Shabbat 119b, Sukkah 39a, and Sotah 49a. Berakhot 3a sets the Kaddish in public places, like synagogues and houses of study,

מסכת סופרים י:ו
אין פורסין על שמע...ואין עוברין לפני התיבה...ואין נושאין את כפיהן, ואין קורין בתורה, ואין מפטירין בנביא, ואין עושין מעמד ומושב...**ואין אומרין קדיש וברכו** פחות מעשרה.

Massekhet Soferim 10:6
We do not responsively recite the Shema...nor have a communal prayer leader...nor offer the Priestly Blessing, nor read Torah, nor read from the Prophets, nor perform the standing/sitting [ritual for the dead]...**nor say Kaddish or Barekhu** with fewer than ten.

The items mentioned in Mishnah Megillah above, along with other *devarim shebikdushah* such as the recitations of Barekhu, Kaddish, and Kedushah, thus all require a *minyan* of ten. This position is maintained throughout subsequent halakhic literature. One typical formulation is that given in Tur OḤ 55:1:

טור או"ח נה:א
ואומר קדיש ואין אומרים אותו בפחות מעשרה דכל דבר שבקדושה כגון קדיש וברכו וקדושה אין אומרים אותו בפחות מעשרה.

Tur OḤ 55:1
And then [the leader] says Kaddish. And it is not said in the presence of fewer than ten, for any *davar shebikdushah*, such as Kaddish and Barekhu and Kedushah, is not said in the presence of fewer than ten.

We will discuss the criteria for this quorum of ten later, but assuming such an appropriate quorum has been assembled, what role, if any, does gender play in leading these rituals? Rabbinic literature discusses neither the possibility of a woman serving as *sha"tz* nor her saying *devarim*

---

implying some kind of quorum. Sotah 49a associates Kaddish with at least some form of Kedushah. But there is no text in the classical rabbinic corpus that explicitly attaches the requirement for ten to Kaddish and Barekhu, even if this may have been obvious and commonly assumed.

shebikdushah in a general way,[52] but it does discuss women's participation in one of those *devarim shebikdushah*: Torah reading. There is a long literature discussing the ins and outs of the issue of Torah reading in theory and practice.[53] We will only review the most basic outlines of that discussion here, as part of the broader question of leadership of parts of the service that require a *minyan*.

A. GENDER AND TORAH READING

Tosefta Megillah 3:11 and the parallel *baraita* on Talmud Bavli Megillah 23a are the core sources that drive this discussion:

תוספתא מגילה ג:יא
הכל עולין למנין שבעה אפי' אשה אפי' קטן.
אין מביאין את האשה לקרות לרבים.

Tosefta Megillah 3:11
All count toward the total of seven, even a woman, even a minor.
We do not bring a woman to read for the public.

תלמוד בבלי מגילה כג.
תנו רבנן: הכל עולין למנין שבעה, ואפילו קטן ואפילו אשה.
אבל אמרו חכמים: אשה לא תקרא בתורה, מפני כבוד צבור.

Talmud Bavli Megillah 23a
Our Rabbis taught: All may count toward the total of seven, even a minor, even a woman.

---

52 To be sure, talmudic sources in several places discuss the idea of whether women can participate freely with men in various rituals, including the quorum of *zimmun* and the special groups (*ḥavurot*) formed to eat the *pesaḥ* offering. These discussions begin with Mishnah Berakhot 7:2 and Mishnah Pesaḥim 8:7. But these sources do not engage the question of leadership, which might or might not have any connection to one's ability to form a group with the people one is leading. That will become particularly clear as we presently examine the case of Torah reading.

53 In particular, R. Mendel Shapiro and R. Daniel Sperber have treated this subject at length; see Shapiro, "Keri'at ha-Torah," and Sperber, "Congregational Dignity." What follows here is a summary of their main points concerning Torah reading combined with our own analysis and perspective.

> But the Sages said: A woman should not read from the Torah because of the honor of the community.

The "total of seven" spoken of here refers to the seven *aliyot* that are distributed on Shabbat (the same principles would apply to a "total of three" for weekday Torah reading). Today, it is common practice for the Torah reader and the person reciting the blessings over the reading to be two different people. During the time when these texts were composed, however, the person having the *aliyah* and the Torah reader were always one and the same.[54] These two texts each have an opening line that includes more marginal members of the community: women and children.[55] And they both have a second line that scales back or qualifies that inclusion specifically for women. In the Tosefta, there is a simple statement that a woman may not read Torah for the public (*la-rabbim*). In the *baraita* in the Bavli, it is a more general statement that a woman should not read from the Torah, but with an explicit reason given: the honor of the community (*kevod tzibbur*).[56]

Scholars have argued over how to interpret the legal relationship between the first and second lines of these texts:

1. Some have argued that the first lines represent an earlier time in Jewish history when women **were** allowed to read Torah,

---

54 Until the medieval period, there was no appointed Torah reader; in all classical rabbinic texts, having an *aliyah* means that one is reading it as well. See Tosafot Megillah 21b.

55 The expected third member of this group, slaves, is added by R. Yirmiyah on Yerushalmi Megillah 4:3 (75a). It is not clear from that source whether R. Yirmiyah considers the slave to be the same as a woman, subject to the concerns of the *kevod tzibbur* (i.e., he is commenting on the first line of the Tosefta/*baraita*) or whether he is issuing a practical ruling that positions the slave similarly to a minor, who is not subject to such concerns.

56 It is unclear whether the *baraita*'s term כבוד צבור is a restatement of the Tosefta's concern in other language or if it represents a different perspective with different parameters. The term כבוד צבור is otherwise Babylonian amoraic, as it is frequently used by Babylonian Amoraim and never appears in the rabbinic literature of Eretz Yisrael. As such, its use in this *baraita* in the Bavli seems to be by way of Babylonian amoraic influence.

whereas the second lines reflect a later historical development that restricted their participation partially or entirely.[57]

2. Others have read this source as stemming from a single point in time, but laying out a difference between theory and practice.[58] In theory women may read but in practice they do not, and the practical concern on the table is "bringing a woman to read for the public" or violating "the honor of the community."

Either way, an honest assessment of the text will acknowledge that neither of the texts reads "הכל עולין למנין שבעה חוץ מאשה — All count toward the total of seven except **for a woman**," which is the way tannaitic sources would convey a blanket gender-based exclusion. One way or the other, these texts envision a world in which it is at least **theoretically** possible for women to receive *aliyot*. This forces us to address two questions:

1. What would that theoretical inclusion look like? This question will focus on the first lines of the Tosefta and the *baraita*.
2. What practical conditions on the ground would need to be in play in order to turn that theory into practice? This question will focus on the second lines of the Tosefta and the *baraita*.

1. The First Clauses of the Tosefta and the Baraita*: How Gender Blind is Torah Reading in Theory and Why?*

We begin by focusing on a situation where "the honor of the community" does not apply or has been overridden by other concerns. Assuming for a moment that this is possible, does Torah reading then become truly gender blind? For the remainder of this section we will only engage with the first lines of the core texts above. Bracketing the issue of *kevod ha-tzibbur* for a moment, we will make it possible to engage in a legal analysis of the inclusion of women in the first clause.

A number of sources address this question, both as a matter of theory and by way of defining the role of minors in Torah reading. Minors, after

---

57 See Ma'aseh Rokeaḥ on Rambam, Hilkhot Tefillah 12:17 and Safrai and Safrai, "Minyan Shiv'ah."

58 A number of medieval and modern sources to be cited below follow this approach.

all, are never excluded by the second clauses of the Tosefta and the *baraita*, and thus their status with respect to public Torah reading is governed by the first clauses alone. Understanding varying practical approaches to minors and Torah reading is thus also very helpful for understanding the role of gender in Torah reading in situations where *kevod tzibbur* has somehow been addressed. Two main models emerge for how to understand the theory and scope of the inclusion of minors and women in Torah reading in the first clauses of the Tosefta and the *baraita*. We will briefly engage each of them.

a. Identity Is Not Relevant for Torah Reading

The first approach holds that Torah reading is gender-blind in theory and age-blind in practice. The first lines of the Tosefta and *baraita* say simply: Women and children are no different from adult men when it comes to Torah reading. They can have any or all of the *aliyot* in a given reading. The most prominent proponent of this reading is Rabbeinu Tam:

דברי רבינו תם המובאים ברא"ש ברכות ז:כ
והא דסלקי קטן ועבד ואשה, דליתנהו בתלמוד תורה, למנין שבעה, משום דס"ת לשמיעה קאי, וברכה אינה לבטלה, דלא מברכים אשר קדשנו במצותיו וצונו על דברי תורה, אלא אשר בחר בנו ואשר נתן לנו.

Rabbeinu Tam, as quoted in Rosh Berakhot 7:20[59]
And the reason that a minor and a slave and a woman count toward the total of seven, even though they are exempt from the study of Torah, is because the Torah scroll is for hearing. And the blessing is not in vain, because they do not say "Who has sanctified and commanded us regarding words of Torah," but rather "Who has chosen us" and "Who has given us"

R. Tam explains that minors, slaves, and women are not considered obligated in the study of Torah by classical rabbinic sources.[60]

---

59 A version of this passage is also cited in Tosafot R. Yehudah Sirleon on Berakhot 47b.

60 Minors are exempt because they are exempt from all *mitzvot*. Women's connection with the *mitzvah* to study Torah seems to have been more contentious. On the

Nonetheless, this in no way impacts their standing as Torah readers. The *mitzvah* of reading Torah is that the Torah be read—"the Torah scroll is for hearing"—but the identity of the reader (or their obligation in Torah study) is not germane. In fact, Torah reading is not about Torah study at all, as the blessings recited over it refer to the Jewish people's national election through the reception of the Torah, and not about any specific commandment to study or learn it.[61]

This point regarding obligation is stated even more directly by R. Menaḥem ha-Meiri:

בית הבחירה להמאירי מגילה כד.

זה ששנינו קטן קורא בתורה, הטעם לכך משום שאין הכוונה בקריאת התורה אלא להשמיע לעם, ואין זו מצוה גמורה כדי שנאמר בה הכלל שאמרו כל שאינו מחוייב בדבר אינו מוציא את אחרים ידי חובתם.

---

matter of **teaching** one's daughter Torah, Mishnah Sotah 3:4 features a debate between Ben Azzai (who thinks it is mandatory) and R. Eliezer (who thinks it is forbidden or minimally foolish and unnecessary). The idea that a woman **herself** is not expected to study Torah seems taken for granted throughout rabbinic literature (arguably even according to Ben Azzai, who seems only to forcefully advocate for fathers teaching their daughters). Bavli Sotah 21a just assumes this point as a matter of fact. There is no formal text that backs it up until an anonymous *midrash* in Bavli Kiddushin 29b (unparalleled elsewhere) states that the biblical command to teach one's children only applies to sons because of the Torah's use of the (arguably) gendered use of *beneikhem*: "ולמדתם אותם את בניכם – ולא בנותיכם." (Note that the rest of the *sugya*'s logic there holds that those who need not be taught Torah are not expected to learn themselves and that those who must be taught Torah **are** expected to learn themselves. This would then read back into Ben Azzai an obligation for women to learn Torah on their own, something that was unlikely to have been his original perspective.) This seems clearly a *post facto* justification of a gendered approach to Torah study that was a background assumption of rabbinic culture. In any event, the view that women are exempt is dominant if not universal, and it is not challenged as a general principle. Slaves are generally treated as exempt from all obligations from which women are exempt.

61 This last point should clarify why R. Tam would not have accepted a Gentile Torah reader or (more anachronistically) a recorded reading. The reader must be a member of the covenantal community that received the Torah, who can truthfully articulate that in liturgical form.

Beit ha-Beḥirah Megillah 24a

That which we have taught, "A minor reads from the Torah," the reason for this is that the purpose of Torah reading is that the people hear it, and it is not a *bona fide mitzvah* such that we would apply the rule, "Anyone who is not obligated in something cannot fulfill the obligations of others."[62]

One can see how this approach could justify minors, in practice, and women, in cases where *kevod tzibbur* does not preclude it, serving as the sole readers with no *aliyah* being off limits to them. In an unusual case, the Maharam of Rothenberg spells out these practical implications in a case where he determined that *kevod tzibbur* was overwhelmed by other concerns:

שו"ת מהר"ם מרוטנבורג חלק ד סימן קח

ועיר שכולה כהנים ואין בה [אפי'] ישראל אחד נ"ל דכהן קורא פעמים ושוב יקראו נשים דהכל משלימי' למנין ז' אפי' עבד ושפחה וקטן (מגילה כג.). ופי' רבי' שמחה זצ"ל לאו דוקא למנין ז' אלא אפי' לשלשה דתנן סתמא בפ"ג דמגילה (כד.) קטן קורא בתורה [ומתרגם] ונהי דמסיק עלה אבל אמרו חכמי' לא תקרא אשה בתורה מפני כבוד הצבור היכא דלא אפשר ידחה כבוד הצבור מפני פגם כהנים הקוראים שלא יאמרו בני גרושות הם.

Responsa Maharam of Rothenberg IV:108

And in a town whose residents are all *kohanim* and there is not even one *yisrael*,[63] it seems to me that a *kohen* should read twice and then women should read the rest, for all complete

---

62 The Meiri himself did not agree with R. Tam's understanding of the blessings being unrelated to obligation. See n. 118 below, toward the end, for a fuller understanding of his position on this point.

63 This case builds on the ruling of R. Simlai in Yerushalmi Gittin 5:9 (47b), who states that in a city made up (almost) entirely of *kohanim*, a *yisrael* should take the first *aliyah*. While the Maharam is playing out a worthy question even if it was entirely theoretical in his time, it may have been more practical than one would think. Many of the small communities in Northern Europe in his time were made up of just one or two families. If the patriarchs of those two families were *kohanim*, it could then easily be the case that all male residents of the town would be *kohanim*, provided they were all descended from the original patriarchs.

> the total of seven, even male and female slaves and minors. And Rabbeinu Simḥah explained that this refers not only to the total of seven but also to the total of three [the three *aliyot* called up on Monday and Thursday mornings, as well as on Shabbat afternoons], for the Mishnah states simply: "A minor may read from the Torah." And even though the Talmud concludes that the Sages said that a woman should not read because of the honor of the community, in a case where there is no alternative, let the honor of the congregation yield to the concern that we will defame the *kohanim*, so that people will not say they are the children of divorcées.

The Maharam confronts a situation where allowing *kohanim* to take *aliyot* other than the first two will subject them to gossip regarding the legitimacy of their status. He prefers the affront to communal honor of women reading to the potential defamation of *kohanim*. For our purposes, not only does his ruling reveal the possibility of overriding the concern of "the honor of the community," but moreover, once this concern is overridden, he rules that women are eligible for any of the *aliyot*.[64] Many others side with this conceptual approach and permit a minor to serve as the sole Torah reader.[65] According to this approach, the first lines of the Tosefta and the *baraita* are blanket statements of inclusion: If *kevod ha-*

---

64 The first two *aliyot* had to go to a *kohen* for reasons having to do with lineage, not gender.

65 For a brief, but thorough collection of such views, see Responsa Yeḥaveh Da'at 2:15 and 5:25, starting with the second paragraph. Note that the Maharam's specific ruling in the case of the עיר שכולה כהנים was ultimately not accepted. This was not on account of a rejection of the theory of R. Tam that stands behind it, but because many preferred an alternate solution for addressing the honor of *kohanim* without needing to override the concern of *kevod tzibbur* as relates to female Torah readers. Specifically, Responsa Rashba I:13 and I:733 rules that in a community entirely made up of *kohanim*, consecutive *aliyot* for *kohanim* present no problem, since everyone understands the context. Other solutions to the problem are cited in Beit Yosef OḤ 135:12.

tzibbur is not an issue, then women and minors can read and receive any *aliyot,* because the identity of the Torah reader does not matter.[66]

b. Torah Reading Must Be Anchored by Principals, Not Adjuncts

A second approach thinks very differently about the first lines of the Tosefta in the *baraita.* Picking up on the language of "עולין למנין שבעה — count toward the total of seven," this school emphasizes a potentially more limited scope, on two planes:

1. "counting **toward**": women and minors can only have **some** of the *aliyot,* and
2. "the total of **seven**": as opposed to a more limited core of *aliyot,* such as the first three or other possible configurations.

This school's varying opinions share an approach that sees minors and women as theoretically included in public Torah reading, but only as adjuncts, "a supporting cast" to the main anchors: free adult men.

The earliest indication we have of such a view is cited by the Rambam in his commentary to Mishnah Megillah 4:6:[67]

---

66 As we saw, the Maharam of Rothenberg quotes R. Simḥah as saying that the language of למנין שבעה used in the Tosefta and the *baraita* is not intended to be specific, and he appeals to the unqualified inclusion of minors in the language of Mishnah Megillah 4:6. Perhaps he thought that the tannaitic sources refer to the Shabbat morning Torah reading and its seven *aliyot* simply because this is the most prominent form of Torah reading and the most ready reference point. See also the conclusion of Piskei Rid Megillah 23a. R. Yitzḥak b. Moshe of Vienna (in Or Zarua I, Responsa #752) argues that the choice of למנין שבעה is in fact deliberate and intended to clarify just how broad the inclusion is:

> והא דת"ר הכל עולין למנין שבעה אפי' אשה אפי' קטן דסד"א הואיל וכבוד שבת חמירא בינופיא דהכל בטלים ממלאכתם ובאים לבית הכנסת משום כבוד שבת וכבוד ציבור דרבים הם לא יהא קטן עולה קמ"ל, אבל שעולה למנין ג' ל"צ ליה למתני.

> Our Sages [used the number seven when they] taught, "All count toward the total of seven, even a woman, even a minor," because I might have thought that since the honor of Shabbat is a serious matter, and moreover, since a large multitude is present because they do not work and come to the synagogue, the honor of Shabbat and the honor of the community, because so many are present, would preclude a minor from reading. This text teaches us otherwise. But that a minor counts toward the total of three, no one needed to teach.

67 It seems clear that the Rambam himself did not hold this way, at least in cases of need. See his unqualified language in Hilkhot Tefillah 12:16–17 and his direct ruling

פירוש המשניות להרמב"ם מגילה ד:ו
"קטן קורא בתורה", אמר אחד מן הגאונים האחרונים שזה אחר השלישי.

Rambam, Commentary on Mishnah Megillah 4:6
"A minor reads from the Torah." One of the later Geonim reported that this only applies [to *aliyot*] after the third one.

This geonic view clearly sees the permission for minors (and, by extension, women) to apply only to "added" *aliyot* beyond the first three. Since no Torah reading has fewer than three *aliyot*, these represent the core of the reading. Once that core has been completed by free adult men, other adjunct members may fill out the remaining readings.

The Ran (R. Nissim b. Reuven of Gerona), offers a different but similar view:

הר"ן על הרי"ף מגילה יג.
הכל עולין למנין שבעה ואפילו אשה ואפי' קטן. פי' עולין להשלים קאמר ולא שיהו כולם קטנים ולא נשים דכיון דלאו בני חיובא נינהו לא מפקי לגמרי. ולפום עיקר דינא נמי שאינו מברך אלא הפותח והחותם אשה וקטן אין קורין ראשון ולא אחרון משום ברכה לפי שא"א לקורין האחרים שיצאו בברכתם ומיהו השתא דתקון רבנן שיברכו כולם אשה וקטן קורין אפי' ראשון ואחרון.

Ran on Rif Megillah 13a
"All count toward the total of seven, even a woman even a minor." This means: They count to **complete** [this number], but [the *aliyot*] may not **all** go to minors or women; since they are not obligated, they cannot entirely fulfill the obligations of others. According to the original rule, when only the first and last readers said blessings [over the Torah], a woman and a minor could read neither first nor last, on account of the blessing. The other readers could not fulfill their own obligation through the blessings [of a woman or a minor]. But now that

---

in Responsum #184. See also a survey of some later opinions about his views on the matter appearing in Responsa Yeḥaveh Da'at 2:15.

our Rabbis decreed that each reader makes blessings, a woman or minor can read even first or last.[68]

הר״ן על הרי״ף מגילה טו.
קטן קורא בתורה. להשלים למנין ז׳ ולא שיהיו כלם קטנים ולא רובם כמו שכתבתי למעלה אלא על ידי **צירוף** קאמר **דמצטרף** לשבעה.

Ran on Rif Megillah 15a
"A minor reads from the Torah" to complete the total of seven, but they cannot all be minors, nor even the majority, as I have written above, rather by **joining** they can **join** the total of seven.

The Ran's position makes very clear that the identity of the Torah reader matters a great deal. While he rules that, in the present time, there is no restriction on which *aliyot* women or minors can have,[69] they cannot be the exclusive readers. He offers two different formulations in the two passages above, one that insists that women and minors not form **the totality** of the readers[70] and one that insists that they not form **a majority** of the readers.

---

68 The Ran is referring here to the difference between what is assumed in Mishnah Megillah 4:1–2 (namely, that the first reader says an opening blessing and the last reader says a closing blessing) and the practice reported and sanctioned on Bavli Megillah 21b (namely, that each reader says an opening and closing blessing). The latter practice remains in force until the present day.

69 Again, in the case of women, this assumes that the issue of *kevod ha-tzibbur* has been somehow addressed or overridden.

70 A ruling identical to this formulation but with a fuller (and perhaps different) explanation is cited by the Meiri in Beit ha-Beḥirah Megillah 23a:

> יש מי שאומר שמ״מ צריך בכל קריאה קורא אחד גדול והואיל וקרא אחד כבר נשלמה תקנת משה רבינו ואין כאן עוד קריאה אלא מתקנת עזרא שלא היה מנין הקוראים מתקנת משה רבינו אלא גוף הקריאה לבד ויכול להשלים הקריאה על ידי אשה או קטן אבל לא שתעשה כל הקריאה ע״י אשה וקטן.

> There is one who says that nevertheless one needs in every reading one adult reader. And since there is one reader, the decree of Moshe Rabbeinu is fulfilled, after which the reading is only because of the decree of Ezra—because there is no number of readers from the decree of Moshe Rabbeinu, only the actual reading itself; it is [therefore] possible to complete the reading through a woman or a minor, but the entire reading should not be done by a woman or minor.

But essentially, these two formulations boil down to the same point: Women and minors are adjuncts when it comes to Torah reading and they cannot be the main or sole anchors of its public performance.

Why are women and minors adjuncts in this way? What is the theory behind this more restrictive reading of the first lines of the Tosefta and the *baraita*? The Ran spells out his reasoning: "לאו בני חיובא נינהו — They are not obligated," or perhaps better: "They are not members of the obligated class." On account of this, "לא מפקי לגמרי — They cannot be the exclusive agents for fulfilling obligation." This might mean a number of things:

1. Women and minors are not obligated to study Torah. Public Torah reading is connected to this obligation and those who listen to public Torah reading fulfill their individual obligations in this regard. Exempt people cannot therefore anchor this ritual, and at least one or most of the readers need to fulfill the basic obligation of the individuals gathered to study Torah. The Ran would then be in direct conflict with R. Tam's approach to Torah reading outlined above.[71]
2. Women and minors are not obligated to study Torah. Though public Torah reading does not involve vicarious fulfillment of individual obligations, it does involve the fulfillment of a **communal** obligation to read Torah. The Ran would then be saying that a **community** cannot fulfill its obligation to hold a public Torah reading through the exclusive or dominant use of people not obligated in Torah study. This approach could be consistent with R. Tam's theory of Torah reading above. R. Tam speaks about considerations relating to individual obligation, but the Ran would

71 For examples of this reading of the Ran, see Eliyah Rabbah OḤ 282:7 and Shulḥan Arukh ha-Rav OḤ 282:5. This also seems to have been the approach of R. Yaḥya b. Yosef Salah in Responsa Pe'ulat Tzaddik III:194. We know that not everyone accepted R. Tam's view that Torah reading was not an individual obligation. One of the strongest support texts for R. Tam's approach is the Talmud's report on Berakhot 8a that Rav Sheshet paid no attention to Torah reading and would learn other material at that time. This suggests no individual obligation to hear it, in keeping with R. Tam. But R. Yonah, on this passage, reports a view that Rav Sheshet was exempt because he was blind, but that others are individually obligated and thus forbidden from behaving in this way.

be adding a concern regarding the corporate, communal obligation of public Torah reading.[72]

3. Women and minors are generally less obligated in *mitzvot* or obligated in fewer *mitzvot* than are adult men.[73] They can be viewed, in this sense, as adjuncts of the religious community, as opposed to principals.[74] It is thus inappropriate and ineffective for a community to rely on such adjuncts to fulfill its communal obligations. A community should not and cannot fulfill its core obligations by fielding "backbenchers" who are not representative of maximal obligation and responsibility.[75] This interpretation would also be consistent with R. Tam's approach above.

---

72 This approach, which emphasizes public Torah reading as a communal obligation that, while not individualized, nonetheless has real teeth, can be found in Ramban Milḥamot Hashem on Rif Megillah 3a s.v. *ve-od*. This view is cited by the Ran there as well and it clearly influenced him.

73 Again, minors are exempt from *mitzvot* until they come of age. Women are exempt from some positive *mitzvot* classified as time-caused by Mishnah Kiddushin 1:7.

74 The idea that lesser obligation in *mitzvot* impacts a person's standing more generally is found in other medieval sources. The Rambam's commentary on Mishnah Horayot 3:7 explains why that text prioritizes saving a man over a woman when both of their lives are at equal risk:

> כבר ידעת שהמצוות כולן מחויבות לזכרים, ולנקבות מקצתן, כמו שהתבאר בקידושין, והרי הוא מקודש ממנה, ולפיכך קודם להחיות.
>
> You know that all the *mitzvot* are obligatory for men, whereas only some are obligatory for women, as we explained in Kiddushin. Therefore, he is holier than she is and therefore saving him takes priority.

With respect to why it might be inappropriate for women to lead rituals for men, even when they share an equal obligation, Tosafot ha-Rosh Sukkah 38a s.v. *be-emet* offers the following striking formulation:

> אפילו מיחייבי דאורייתא לא חשיבי להוציא אנשים דחשיבי טפי שחייבים בכל המצוות.
>
> Even if women are biblically obligated [in Birkat ha-Mazon] they are still not important enough to fulfill the obligations of men, who are more important on account of their obligation in all *mitzvot*.

75 A number of commentators seem to read the Ran this way. See Responsa Baḥ ha-Yeshanot #158 as well as the slightly different formulation of Levush OḤ 282:3, who emphasizes that there is a dishonor to the Torah scroll to remove it for the sake of women and minors. This reading of the Levush seems to assume the more minimal

However we read the Ran, it should be clear that, according to his approach, those lacking in key obligations (whether they be in *talmud Torah* or more generally) cannot be the sole Torah readers. Other subsequent *poskim* took this approach as well,[76] including the Rema in OḤ 282:3. Thus, even controlling for *kevod tzibbur,* this view allows for women and minors to read only **some** of the *aliyot* in a given Torah reading.

---

reading of the Ran that one can suffice with at least one free adult male reader. (See also Meiri, Kiryat Sefer 5:1.) These last two readings of the Ran focus on the impact of exemption on the community's ability to discharge its obligations with integrity and dignity. Perhaps the best articulation of these approaches can be found in the responsa of R. Avraham b. Mordekhai ha-Levi, Ginat Veradim OḤ 1:36:

> והטעם דבעינן דתיעביד תקנתא דרבנן בבני אדם גדולים...דההקפדה אינה על הספר אלא על הצבור דגנאי הוא לצבור שיהיו כל העולים לחובת היום כולם קטנים המבלי אין גדולים בצבור שיעלו שבעה קטני׳ לס״ת אבל לגבי הס״ת עצמו אין בזה גנאי אם יקרא בו הקטן יחידי לבדו דהא תורה דיליה היא נמי ומפי עוללים ויונקים יסדת עוז דהוי הבל שאין בו חטא.

> The reason that we require the rabbinic ordinance [to read from the Torah] to be fulfilled with adults…is not because of a concern for the scroll, but for the community. It is dishonoring for the community if all those taking *aliyot* as part of the day's obligatory quorum were to be children. Are there no adults in the community such that seven children need to go up to the *sefer Torah*? But there is no dishonor to the Torah scroll when a minor reads from it on their own, for the Torah belongs to them, and [we say of God] "you have laid the foundations of Strength (i.e., Torah) from the mouths of babes and infants," for their speech is devoid of all sin.

According to these readings of the Ran, there is nothing intrinsically or technically problematic about a minor reading Torah, but relying **solely** on minors risks turning the ritual into a disrespectful spectacle.

76 The Rivash followed the Ran's approach and extended it to forbid a minor from reading the *maftir* when a second scroll was removed for this purpose. He felt that the Ran's concern applied to the reading from any given scroll and giving the minor *maftir* would violate the principle that adjuncts should not anchor a reading entirely on their own. See Responsa Rivash 35, 321, and 326. In fact, R. Tam himself is cited as supporting a similar policy regarding minors and *maftir* in Sefer ha-Manhig Hilkhot Shabbat (ed. Mossad ha-Rav Kook), p. 165. As we have seen, R. Tam could not have based this view on the same theory as was proferred by the Rivash, since R. Tam's theory of Torah reading rendered the identity of the reader generally irrelevant. For an attempt to provide a resolution of these two potentially contradictory views, see Responsa Tzitz Eliezer VII:1:23–26. For more on the question of principals and adjuncts in a construction of a *mitzvah* community, see Tucker, "Equality Without Adjuncts?"

c. Applying and Balancing the Two Approaches: R. Tam and the Ran

These two approaches yield divergent consequences.

According to R. Tam's approach, the identity of the reader is irrelevant, paving the way for an essentially gender-blind Torah reading.[77] This is accomplished, of course, without distinguishing in any way between women and minors and would achieve gender-blindness by essentially erasing the identity of the readers, rather than by asserting gender equality.

According to the Ran's approach, those who lack certain core obligations, whether regarding Torah study or *mitzvot* more generally, can only function as adjuncts in public Torah reading and cannot anchor it on their own. For this approach, a gender-blind Torah reading would only be possible by claiming that contemporary women are in fact obligated in Torah study and/or in the full complement of *mitzvot*. This would be a bolder interpretive move, though it would more directly address the growing gender-egalitarianism in the broader society that motivates these conversations. We will encounter a few more positions like the Ran's that would require this sort of paradigm shift in order to be aligned with gender-equal practice. But put simply: the Ran only allows בני חיובא, "members of the obligated class," to anchor a public Torah reading, making Torah reading only **partially** accessible to women and minors. Full gender equality under such a system would require arguing that contemporary women are indeed considered בנות חיובא, equally obligated in *mitzvot* as adult men.[78]

But whose approach should be followed? There is a respectable body of thought that asserts the dominance of the idea that the identity of the Torah readers is irrelevant, or minimally that this approach can be relied on whenever the situation is pressing for one reason or another.[79] Those

---

77 As emphasized throughout this section, this assumes that the concern of *kevod tzibbur* has somehow been addressed or overridden.

78 See our discussion of this sort of argument below, Part Two, nn. 76–81.

79 R. Yoel Sirkes in Responsa Baḥ ha-Yeshanot #158 seems to sideline the Ran; R. David Luria in Responsum #3 dismantles this position entirely and allows minors to read the entire Torah portion without any hesitation. Even R. Yisrael Meir Kagan, who upholds the Rema's ruling like the Ran, says in Sha'ar ha-Tziyyun 282:16 about the view of the Ran and the Rivash, "אינו דין ברור," and rules in Mishnah Berurah 282:13 that one may follow R. Tam's position when there is no other available reader. R.

who base a gender-blind Torah reading on this approach surely have a leg to stand on, particularly if they sense that there is a concrete risk in denying women *aliyot* in an increasingly gender-egalitarian world.[80]

The Ran's approach, however, remains compelling and difficult to dismiss. First, it is risky to ignore the wisdom of an alternate position and to crush it by appealing to later authorities, as if Jewish law is simply a matter of vote-counting to see who has more support. True, it is perfectly respectable and legitimate to claim that R. Tam's approach has many prominent defenders and adherents and that, even though the Rema cites the Ran, R. Yosef Karo himself may not have accepted the Ran's argument.[81] But this in no way addresses the **substance** of the Ran's claim, which is reasonable: How can a community look itself in the mirror when it attempts to fulfill its public obligations relying on ritually marginal members? Moreover, in the present case, relying on R. Tam risks clouding the substance of the specific issue: Is the difficulty with excluding women from Torah reading in the contemporary world that it places too much emphasis on the identity of the reader, or is the difficulty that it excludes **women**? Put another way: R. Tam's position leaves no room for the quite sensible instinct that some might have in the contemporary world, which is that women should be treated as equals to men, but minors should retain the status of adjuncts who should not (at least ideally) anchor a public Torah reading!

We in no way mean to undermine the legitimacy of following R. Tam's model here as a basis for justifying a gender-equal Torah reading. But this is one of a number of points in our analysis where consciousness of halakhic choices and consequences is particularly important. We will reserve more general comments regarding this dynamic for later on.

Ovadiah Yosef rules similarly in Yeḥaveh Da'at, granting the Ran's position only the status of an *ab initio* ideal preference.

80 This sort of fear of the gap between general and ritual expectations and participation is partially what led to the revolution in Jewish learning opportunities for women in the 20th century. It was viewed by some as untenable that women would pursue university degrees and be closed off to learning Torah at high levels, while maintaining respect for and fidelity to Torah in the process.

81 Though the Ran is cited in Beit Yosef OḤ 282, there is no trace of this restriction in the Shulḥan Arukh.

2. *The Second Clauses:* Kevod Tzibbur *(The Honor of the Community)*

We turn now to the second lines of the Tosefta and the *baraita*. In this section, we will first define *kevod ha-tzibbur* and then turn to the question of whether a community may waive its honor.

Using the *baraita*'s terminology of *kevod (ha-)tzibbur*: What is "honor of the community" and why did this consideration lead the Sages to exclude women from going up to bless and read from the Torah? "Honor of the community" appears in four other contexts in the Talmud Bavli, always as a reason to avoid some mode of performing public ritual.[82] The four other unseemly practices are reading Torah from a scroll containing only one of its five books, rolling the Torah scroll in public, allowing a minor to read Torah naked or in tattered clothing, and uncovering the ark in front of the community:[83]

תלמוד בבלי גיטין ס.
רבה ורב יוסף דאמרי תרוייהו: אין קוראין בחומשין בבית הכנסת משום כבוד הצבור.

Talmud Bavli Gittin 60a
Rabbah and Rav Yosef both said: We do not read from *ḥumashim* [Torah scrolls containing only one of the five books] in the synagogue because of the honor of the community.

תלמוד בבלי יומא ע.
ובעשור של חומש הפקודים קורא על פה. אמאי? נגלול ונקרי! אמר רב הונא בריה דרב יהושע אמר רב ששת: לפי שאין גוללין ספר תורה בציבור, מפני כבוד ציבור.

Talmud Bavli Yoma 70a
And [the paragraph about Yom Kippur in Bemidbar] is read from memory [by the High Priest]. Why? Let him roll the scroll and read it from the text! Said Rav Huna b. Rav Yehoshua said

82 All the talmudic cases in one way or another also seem to connect with Torah reading.

83 Our rendition of this last source follows Rashi's interpretation.

Rav Sheshet: We do not roll the Torah scroll in public because of the honor of the community.

תלמוד בבלי מגילה כד:

פוחח פורס על שמע וכו'. בעא מיניה עולא בר רב מאביי: קטן פוחח מהו שיקרא בתורה? אמר ליה: ותיבעי לך ערום? ערום מאי טעמא לא משום כבוד צבור, הכא נמי משום כבוד צבור.

Talmud Bavli Megillah 24b

"A person dressed in tattered clothing may lead the responsive Shema." Ulla b. Rav asked Abaye: May a minor dressed in tatters read from the Torah?[84] He said to him: Would you be in doubt about a naked minor!? Why would a naked minor be forbidden? Because of the honor of the community; here too, because of the honor of the community.

תלמוד בבלי סוטה לט:

ואמר רבי תנחום אמר רבי יהושע בן לוי: אין שליח צבור רשאי להפשיט את התיבה בצבור, מפני כבוד צבור.

Talmud Bavli Sotah 39b

And said R. Tanḥum said R. Yehoshua b. Levi: The prayer leader should not uncover the ark in front of the community because of the honor of the community.

---

84 Rashi explains that the questioner understands that an adult in tattered clothing may not read, on account of the verse, "Let [God] not see in you any nakedness" (Devarim 23:15), but perhaps a minor's nakedness would not be of concern, since Torah prohibitions such as that verse do not apply to them

(קטן פוחח מהו שיקרא בתורה - גדול פוחח הוא דאסור משום "ולא יראה בך ערות דבר", אבל קטן אינו מוזהר, או דלמא לא פליג מתניתין בין קטן לגדול).

Alternatively, a minor's inappropriate exposure may be less disrespectful than that of an adult vis-à-vis the onlooking congregation. The Ritva notes that some versions of the Gemara lack the word קטן here, in which case the question is about whether anyone, adult or minor, may read Torah while wearing tattered clothing. This would seem to depend on having a different version of Mishnah Megillah 4:6. Our version of that text is explicit that an adult in tattered clothing cannot read from the Torah, such that there would be no place for further talmudic discussion.

The phrase *kevod tzibbur* expresses that certain ways of performing ritual actions are disrespectful in a communal context. Reading from an incomplete Torah scroll that only contains one of the five books lacks seriousness. Rolling a Torah scroll in public to get from one section to another is disrespectful of the community's time and creates an awkward pause in the service. Reading Torah while scantily clad is improper and degrading. Removing the adornments from the ark in the presence of the community reduces the grandeur of the sacred space and lessens the awe surrounding the communal ritual. Given the intuitive nature of the consideration, it is not surprising that subsequent authorities apply this term to additional practices. For example, Rashi gives "honor of the community" as a reason to prohibit a minor from performing the Priestly Blessing: It is demeaning for the community to receive the blessing from a minor. The Rambam employs it to explain the preference for a bearded *sha"tz* and for a standing reader of Megillat Esther, both of which imbue the ritual acts with greater gravitas:

רש"י מגילה כד.
ואינו נושא את כפיו — אם כהן הוא, שאין כבוד של צבור להיות כפופין לברכתו.

Rashi Megillah 24a
"[A minor] may not raise his hands" — if he is *a kohen*, for it is not honorable for the community to be subject to his blessing.

רמב"ם הלכות תפילה ח:יא
ומי שלא נתמלא זקנו אע"פ שהוא חכם גדול לא יהא ש"ץ מפני כבוד צבור.

Rambam, Hilkhot Tefillah 8:11
One whose beard has not filled out, even if he is wise and great, should not be a *sha"tz* because of the honor of the community.

רמב"ם הלכות מגילה ב:ז
קראה עומד או יושב יצא ואפילו בצבור, אבל לא יקרא בצבור יושב לכתחלה מפני כבוד הצבור.

Rambam, Hilkhot Megillah 2:7
Whether one read it [i.e., Megillat Esther] standing or sitting, the obligation is fulfilled, and even in the community, but *ab initio* one should not read in a community while seated, because of the honor of the community.

Why has it been considered an affront to communal honor for women to read Torah publicly? Many Rishonim are silent on the issue, apparently taking for granted the reasonableness of the statement. At least two Rishonim connect *kevod tzibbur* to another concept: מאירה, "a curse" that devolves on those who engage in certain kinds of ritual behaviors with social and religious subordinates. The concept of this curse is used in the context of the recitation of Birkat ha-Mazon and Hallel. Let's begin with these background texts:

משנה סוכה ג:י
מי שהיה עבד או אשה או קטן מקרין אותו עונה אחריהן מה שהן אומרין ותהי לו מאירה. אם היה גדול מקרא אותו עונה אחריו הללויה.

Mishnah Sukkah 3:10
One [i.e., a free male adult] being led [in Hallel] by a slave, a woman, or a minor must repeat the words after them and he should be cursed. If it was an adult leading him, then he responds, "*Halleluyah.*"

A full interpretation of this text is beyond the scope of our purpose here. What is clear is that the Mishnah seems to convey two ideas:

1. Hallel is normally or often done in a responsive mode, with a leader chanting the text (מקרא) and with respondents answering with refrains such as *halleluyah*.[85] Free adult men should not rely on a

85 This practice of having a leader and being led in a responsive mode is referred to in a host of tannaitic texts. See Mishnah Rosh Hashanah 4:7, Sotah 5:4; Tosefta Pesaḥim 10:7–8, Sotah 6:2–3.

slave, woman, or minor to say the words of Hallel for them in a responsive form. They should say all of the words themselves.[86]

2. Even if the first concern is addressed and the free adult says Hallel in its entirety, the free adult is worthy of a curse. The function of the curse here is clearly unconnected to any issue of fulfilling one's obligation; the adult free man has said all the words of Hallel himself. But the exact reason for this is not made explicit.

The Talmud Yerushalmi connects this *mishnah* to another matter:

תלמוד ירושלמי סוכה ג:ט, דף נג טור ד
תני אבל אמרו אשה מברכת לבעלה ועבד לרבו וקטן לאביו.

ניחא, אשה מברכת לבעלה עבד לרבו. קטן לאביו? לא כן א"ר אחא בשם ר' יוסי בן נהוריי כל שאמרו בקטן כדי לחנכו?!

תיפתר בעונה אחריהן אמן[87] כהיא דתנינן תמן מי שהיה עבד או אשה או קטן מקרין אותו ועונה אחריהן מה שהן אומרין ותהא לו מאירה.

ועוד אמרו תבוא מאירה לבן עשרים שהוא צריך לבן עשר.

---

86 There is an analogous concern with respect to a father leading small children in Hallel at the Seder: he should not rely on their completion of his opening call (Tosefta Pesaḥim 10:7). Neither that text nor Mishnah Sukkah 3:10 is clear if this is related to matters of obligation (such that, if the preferred protocol were violated, one would need to repeat Hallel).

87 The word אמן is also present in the parallel at Yerushalmi Rosh Hashanah 3:10 (59a), but absent from the parallel at Yerushalmi Berakhot 3:3 (6b). We translate here in accordance with the vast majority of interpreters who, whether or not they have this word in their text, understand it to refer to an adult who repeats all the words of the Birkat ha-Mazon after being cued by a child.

Talmud Yerushalmi Sukkah 3:9 (53d)
It is taught [in a *baraita*]: Indeed,[88] a woman may say Birkat ha-Mazon for her husband, a slave may say it for his master, and a minor[89] for his father.

A woman for her husband and a slave for his master make sense, but a minor for his father? Did not R. Aha say in the name of R. Yose b. Nehorai: [Any obligations] articulated with respect to a minor are [merely] in order to educate him?![90]

[The *baraita*] makes sense if you assume the father repeats the words his son says, just like it says [in Mishnah Sukkah 3:10]: "One being led [in Hallel] by a slave, a woman, or a minor must respond by saying everything they say and he should be cursed."

Furthermore, they said that a twenty-year-old who needs a ten-year-old should be cursed.

This passage in the Yerushalmi begins by quoting a *baraita* that notes that certain figures normally thought of as subordinates are qualified to fulfill the obligations of their superiors in Birkat ha-Mazon. The Yerushalmi accepts this for women and slaves, who share equal obligations with free men in Birkat ha-Mazon, according to Mishnah Berakhot 3:3. But it assumes that children, even if they are obligated in Birkat ha-Mazon, cannot possibly share an equal obligation with adults, so how can the *baraita* allow a minor to say Birkat ha-Mazon for his father? The Yerushalmi proposes that, in this case, the father must be repeating after his minor son, thereby fulfilling all of his obligations on his own. It

---

88 The word אבל here seems to be used in this sense here, as opposed to its other sense of "but." The parallels to this *baraita* in Tosefta Berakhot 5:17, Talmud Bavli Berakhot 20b, and Talmud Bavli Sukkah 38a all read באמת instead of אבל. For this sort of usage of אבל, see Bavli Niddah 3b, and Kaunfer, "Aval Hatanu."

89 In the parallels in the Tosefta and the Talmud Bavli, the text reads בן לאביו, which might well refer to a son who is an adult. With that text, the problem raised here by the Talmud Yerushalmi need not arise.

90 The Yerushalmi's point here is that the minor's obligations are not "real"; they are simply a form of required training for religious adulthood. How can we allow an adult to fulfill his own obligations through the recitation of a minor?

cites Mishnah Sukkah 3:10 as precedent for this kind of behavior.[91] The Yerushalmi then adds a point to the *baraita* on Birkat ha-Mazon, evoking the curse described in Mishnah Sukkah 3:10: A curse should also devolve upon a twenty-year-old who needs the services of a ten-year-old. This seems to suggest that the minor is leading Birkat ha-Mazon for his father on account of the latter's ignorance. The Yerushalmi thus understands the curse to be directed at adult males who have not properly learned something in which they are obligated such that they must rely on those who are not obligated. It seems that no curse is applied to the husband who allows his wife to lead Birkat ha-Mazon for him—she is equally obligated and he need not even repeat after her when she recites the text. How would the Yerushalmi understand the application of the curse to the man who repeats Hallel after women and slaves as well as minors? It would likely assume that women and slaves, though obligated in Birkat ha-Mazon, are exempt from Hallel and are thus similar to the minor who leads Birkat ha-Mazon. An obligated free adult male would thus be subject to the curse if prompted to say Hallel by a woman, slave, or minor.[92]

In the Talmud Bavli, the Yerushalmi's application of the concept of curse to the case of Birkat ha-Mazon is integrated into the *baraita* itself:

תלמוד בבלי סוכה לח.

ת"ר באמת אמרו בן מברך לאביו ועבד מברך לרבו ואשה מברכת לבעלה. אבל אמרו חכמים תבא מאירה לאדם שאשתו ובניו מברכין לו.

---

91 It is not clear if the Yerushalmi assumes that Mishnah Sukkah 3:10 is concerned about matters of obligation as well or if it is just appealing to the possibility that one might allow someone to lead a ritual for them without truly being liturgically dependent on them.

92 Alternatively, one could suggest that the final line in the Yerushalmi is not meant to be limited to minors, but merely gives a minor–adult interaction as an example of an inappropriate inversion of conventional hierarchies. The curse would then not be the result of an obligation difference, but reflective of a difference in social standing. This would render the Yerushalmi's approach identical to that of the Bavli. This reading seems more strained with the Yerushalmi's initial nonchalant acceptance of women and slaves leading Birkat ha-Mazon for free adult men, and would have to read the second part of the passage as backing away from this initial approach.

Talmud Bavli Sukkah 38a

Our Sages taught [in a *baraita*]: In fact, they said: A son may say Birkat ha-Mazon for his father, a slave for his master, and a woman for her husband. But the Sages said: A curse should come upon a person whose wife and sons say Birkat ha-Mazon for him.

Here we have a striking difference from the Yerushalmi: The curse is applied to the case of the woman and her husband as well (and presumably the slave-master case also). Whereas in the Yerushalmi the concern triggering the curse seems to have centered around relying on a non-obligated person for prompting, in the Bavli the problem may be one of social status. Even though a woman and a man share an equal obligation in Birkat ha-Mazon,[93] the Bavli's version of the *baraita* condemns a man who is either dependent on his wife to bless for him or perhaps allows someone of subordinate social status to perform this ritual for him. This, in turn, means that perhaps Mishnah Sukkah 3:10's application of the curse to those who have Hallel recited for them by a woman need not be understood as stemming from an obligation gap. The function of the curse may be grounded in notions of social hierarchy alone.

The Ritva[94] and R. Avraham min ha-Har equate the concern conveyed by the term *kevod tzibbur* with the notion of *me'eirah* as understood in the Talmud Bavli. The latter's formulation is as follows:

ר' אברהם מן ההר, מגילה יט:

והכי איתא בהדיא בריש ערכין (ב.), הכל חייבין [במגילה], הכל לאתויי נשים, וכדר' יהושע וכו'. מיהו ודאי לכתחילא לא תוציא אחרים, כדאמרינן במי שמתו (ברכות כ:), תבא מארה לאדם שאשתו ובניו מברכין לו. ואמרינן בפרק עומד יושב (מגילה כג.), הכל עולין למנין שבעה אפילו אשה או קטן, אבל אמרו חכמים אשה לא תקרא בצבור מפני כבוד הצבור וכו'.

93 On Bavli Berakhot 20b, Ravina wonders whether men and women in fact share an equal obligation in Birkat ha-Mazon, but the Bavli itself assumes that the *baraita* we are discussing here would normally be understood as assuming that women are in fact biblically obligated in Birkat ha-Mazon just like men.

94 See his comments on Bavli Megillah 4a.

R. Avraham min ha-Har, Megillah 19b

And so do we have it explicitly at the beginning of Arakhin: "'Everyone is obligated [in the *megillah*]—"everyone" includes women, following R. Yehoshua [b. Levi, who ruled that women are obligated in the reading of the *megillah*].' However, of course, *ab initio*, she should not discharge others of their obligation, as we said on Berakhot 20b: "May a curse come to a man whose wife or sons bless [Birkat ha-Mazon] for him." And we said on Megillah 23a, "Everyone counts toward the total of seven, but the Sages said that a woman should not read for the community because of the honor of the community…"

R. Avraham min ha-Har asserts that women and men have an equal obligation in *megillah* reading, such that, in terms of obligation, women would be permitted to read the *megillah* for men. Nonetheless, he says that women should **not** read for men, invoking the concerns of *kevod tzibbur* and comparing it to the case of *me'eirah*. This is precisely the notion of *me'eirah* as used in the Talmud Bavli: Even when obligations are equal or irrelevant, there is something shameful about a man having his wife or his son lead him in a ritual. Whether this is because the man would be presumed to be liturgically illiterate or simply because his wife and children are his social and educational inferiors, he is worthy of condemnation. R. Avraham min ha-Har clearly sees this in play in the context of female Torah readers as well: A woman's reading would unsettle the social order and suggest ignorance on the part of the male congregants.[95] According to this line of thought, women are not a part of the educated class and are not expected to be able to read Torah.

95 Note that the man is condemned for allowing his son (in the Talmud Bavli, almost certainly even his adult son) from saying Birkat ha-Mazon for him, whereas minors do not pose a concern for *kevod tzibbur*. This is likely because Birkat ha-Mazon is an individualized obligation that every man was expected to be able to perform, whereas Torah reading was a more specialized skill performed by a select few in front of the whole congregation. This underscores even more why it would have been surprising and unusual for a woman to have the skill to read when not even all men were expected to have this skill.

Contemporary *poskim*, such as R. Yehudah Herzl Henkin, follow this line of reasoning,[96] explaining that the curse refers to the embarrassment of being made to look as if one is illiterate or otherwise unable to fulfill one's own obligations:

שו"ת בני בנים ב:ב
אמנם, מהו באמת פרוש כבוד הצבור לענין עליות נשים, לע"ד כיון שהריטב"א...וביותר בירור ברבנו אברהם מן ההר...מבואר שהוא ענין של מאירה פי' שבזיון הוא לצבור שנראה כאילו אין די גברים היודעים לקרוא בתורה ולכן הביאו נשים, וכן פרש בפתח הדביר סימן רפ"ב אות ט', ולא נמצא בראשונים מי שחולק על זה. לכן בוודאי הכי נקטינן.

Responsa Benei Banim 2:2
Indeed, what is truly the meaning of "honor of the community" vis-à-vis *aliyot* for women? In my humble opinion, [in] the Ritva... and even more clearly, in R. Avraham min ha-Har... it is explained to be the matter of a curse, i.e., that it is insulting to the community for it to seem as though there are not enough men who know how to read Torah, and that is why they summoned women; and this is also how Petaḥ ha-Devir (282:9) interpreted it, and there is no Rishon who disputes this. Therefore, of course, this is how we hold.

R. Henkin's words speak for themselves. Most attempts to redefine *kevod tzibbur* to refer to something other than concerns about social honor and shame depart from the plain sense of these words and how they are used in other contexts. The concern of *kevod tzibbur* does not relate to matters of obligation and exemption, nor is it even connected to gender *per se*.[97] Like the other areas where it is invoked, *kevod tzibbur* is a halakhic concern rooted in social realities and protocols.

---

96 See also D. Sperber, *Darkah*, 24–28.

97 Matters of obligation and exemption were already addressed in our analysis of the first clauses of the Tosefta and the *baraita*; see above, nn. 59–81. Despite what we have argued here, Frimer and Frimer, "Partnership Minyanim," argue that *kevod tzibbur* is **entirely** about either an obligation gap or concerns relating to sexual impropriety.

Having explored the concerns at play in the notion of *kevod ha-tzibbur*, we will now consider whether these types of concerns are designed to protect people from involuntary violations of their honor, or whether

---

They construct two "schools" corresponding to these concerns. Their analysis of the "schools" they posit is problematic:

1. They correctly cite a number of medieval authorities as being concerned about appointing leaders for parts of the service in which they are not obligated. Tosafot Sukkah 38a s.v. *u-tehi* and Tosafot ha-Rosh Sukkah 38a s.v. *tavo* both state that the מאירה in Mishnah Sukkah 3:10 is focused on the fact that someone not obligated in Hallel is leading the man in that liturgy, even if he repeats after them. This is inspired by a Yerushalmi-type reading of the problem of מאירה. But those Rishonim never apply that concern to Torah reading, which does not follow the same rules as other rituals. This is both in light of the fact that a minor may read Torah despite presenting a problem of מאירה in the context of Hallel, and because the "obligation" involved in Torah reading is somewhere on the spectrum of non-existent to unique. We believe the Frimers' attempt to exclude women from Torah reading via an obligation-based *kevod tzibbur* while justifying the inclusion of minors based on an educational agenda (חינוך) is a dodge and unsupported by the sources. Again, see our analysis above, nn. 59–81. In any event, there is no indication that any Rishon maps this understanding of מאירה back onto *kevod tzibbur*. The Frimers cite a number of Aḥaronim who take this position—though not all of them obviously say what is claimed. Even if one follows these Aḥaronim over the explicit positions of the Rishonim—precisely what R. Henkin argues against above—matters of obligation would only be relevant for those (a) following the Ran's model and (b) wishing to provide an occasional woman with a minority of the *aliyot*. Any fully egalitarian Torah reading claiming the support of the Ran would need to address questions of obligation raised by the first clause of the *baraita* independent of any ancillary ones that arise via *kevod tzibbur*. We will return to more plausible applications of concerns surrounding obligation below, when considering leadership of the service more broadly; see n. 154.

2. As for attempts to read sexuality into *kevod tzibbur*, the term itself militates against such a reading. Tannaitic sources know well how to speak about sexual impropriety and they would have said something like אשה לא תקרא בתורה מפני הרגל עבירה. R. Henkin has been among the most vocal in denying this as a plausible reading. Indeed, a number of medieval and modern authorities explicitly reject this interpretation (which is in any event untenable when applied to the other instances of the term in talmudic literature). Consider, for example, Sefer ha-Me'orot Berakhot 45a:

> וליכא משום פריצות הגדול עם הנשים...ועוד ראיה מדאמרינן בעלמא אשה לא תקרא בצבור משום כבוד צבור, **טעמא משום כבוד צבור אבל פריצותא ליכא.**
>
> There is no sexual impropriety when an adult male [ritually joins in a *zimmun*] with women...A further proof of this is from the general statement that a women may not read from the Torah in public because of the honor of the

they come to prescriptively assign this honor even for those who might not be concerned with it. This leads directly to a consideration whether a community may elect to waive its honor—and if so, under what circumstances. When a restriction motivated by *kevod tzibbur* is in place, how does it function? Specifically, what if a given community decides that it is willing to forgo its honor in order to serve another need? Are the restrictions we saw above merely protections for the community, such that the community has the ability to waive its honor when it so chooses? Or are these restrictions in fact prescriptive and binding, such that communities are forbidden from electing to forgo their own honor? This

---

> community; **the reason is because of the honor of the community, but not because of sexual impropriety.**

Sefer ha-Menuḥah on Hilkhot Berakhot 5:7 has a similar formulation. Responsa Piskei Uzziel bi-She'ilot ha-Zeman #44 states:

> ופירוש כבוד הצבור הוא שלא יאמרו: שאין בין האנשים מי שיודע לקרא בתורה אבל לא אמרו משום פריצות.

> The explanation of *kevod ha-tzibbur* is that people should not say that there are none among the men who know how to read the Torah, but they did not say this because of *peritzut*.

See also Responsa Benei Banim 2:10. The Frimers cite a host of Aḥaronim who prevent women from reading Torah on account of sexual impropriety. The vast majority of them are in fact clear that this is **an entirely separate concern** than *kevod tzibbur*. As such, it may be a real issue worthy of consideration, but one that applies to any sort of public leadership by women. This sort of concern might be addressed by telling men who experience female Torah reading as sexually improper to stay away from such services rather than by excluding women from Torah reading. In any event, this is the sort of general, overarching issue that we are not addressing here and already referred to above, Introduction, n. 8.

3. The Frimers are also overzealous in the prosecution of their cause to exclude women from Torah reading. They accuse R. Shapiro and R. Henkin of ignoring Rishonim and Aḥaronim who supposedly contradict their theses. As we noted, some of the Rishonim and Aḥaronim the Frimers cite do not say what they claim they say. But more to the point, the Frimers ignore the very Rishonim and Aḥaronim who contradict their own thesis! Sefer ha-Batim, R. Ya'akov Emden, and R. Ben-Tziyyon Abba Shaul all offer analyses that only make sense if one outright **rejects** the considerations the Frimers posit as central and embrace *kevod tzibbur* as being a *halakhah* rooted in sociology. See below, n. 107 and onward.

crucial question has produced a rich literature.[98] We will only draw out the core dispute and its consequences.

a. *Kevod Tzibbur* Is a Protection for the Community that Can be Waived

R. Yosef Karo, in a number of places in his Beit Yosef, cites rulings that involve *kevod tzibbur* and indicates that when this is the central concern, the community is indeed allowed to waive its honor and set aside the restriction. We saw above the Talmud's objection to reading from a partial Torah scroll on the grounds of *kevod tzibbur*. As the world gradually shifted from the use of scrolls to codices, it became more common to have manuscripts of the five books of the Torah bound as a book. The question arose: In a situation where no valid Torah scroll is available, is it possible for the community to forgo its honor and read from a codex? R. Karo writes:

בית יוסף או"ח סימן קמג
וכן כתב רבינו ירוחם (נ"ב חג כ.) דספרים שלנו שאינם עשויים כתיקון ס"ת אסור לקרות בציבור ולא שייך הכא טעמא דמפני כבוד הציבור שיוכלו למחול על כבודם. ומיהו משמע מדבריו שבחומשים העשויים כתיקון ס"ת אם מחלו הציבור על כבודם קורים בו.

Beit Yosef OḤ 143
And so wrote Rabbeinu Yeroḥam, that we may not publicly read from our books, which are not made in the form of a Torah scroll [i.e., they are codices, not scrolls]. The reason of "the honor of the community" is not germane here, such that the community would be able to waive its honor. But implied in [R. Yeroḥam's] words is the claim that in the case of a scroll of a single book of the Torah, if the community waived its honor, it would be allowed to read from it.[99]

---

98 Shapiro, "Keri'at ha-Torah," and Sperber, "Congregational Dignity," treat this question at greater length.

99 See also Mordekhai Menaḥot #968 for a similar approach.

R. Yosef Karo assumes in this passage that when the only issue on the table is *kevod tzibbur,* the community can elect to waive the concern.[100] A similar dynamic is at work when he cites the Rambam's explanation of the Talmud Bavli's prohibition on not having a bearded *sha"tz* as being on account of *kevod tzibbur*: "ולפי זה אם רצו הצבור למחול על כבודם נראה שהרשות בידו — According to this explanation [of the problem], if the community wishes to waive its honor, it seems that it is permitted to do so."[101]

Finally, in Beit Yosef OḤ 53, R. Karo struggles to defend a practice of allowing a minor to lead Arvit on Saturday nights[102] in the face of the explicit ruling of Mishnah Megillah 4:6 that a minor may not lead the community in prayer. He cites the view of the Ra'avad, who holds that the sole reason for the Mishnah's ruling is because it would be dishonorable for the community to have a minor lead them.[103] On this, the Beit Yosef

---

100 On the practical matter of this case, the Beit Yosef cites the view of the Ra'aviah and others who argue that there are other issues besides congregational dignity at stake, such as a desire to drive the community to invest in a complete Torah scroll.

101 Again, in this case, the Beit Yosef proceeds to cite a conflicting view of the Rosh, who seems to have disagreed with the Rambam that the issue at stake with a non-bearded *sha"tz* was indeed *kevod ha-tzibbur* alone.

102 This practice was instituted to let minors who were in mourning recite the prayers at this time, as the end of Shabbat was commonly regarded as a time when the souls of the recently dead return to Gehenom (Hell). If a child led the prayers, however, the soul of their deceased parent could be protected. This mourning practice (not with respect to minors in particular) is mentioned in the Kol Bo #114:

> ויש שמתפללין כל מוצאי שבת תפלת ערבית לפי שבאותה שעה חוזרין לגיהנם הרשעים ששבתו בשבת ואפשר שתגן עליהם אותה תפלה.
>
> And there are those who pray Arvit every Saturday night because at that time the wicked that rested on Shabbat return to Hell, and perhaps that *tefillah* will protect them.

103 The Ra'avad, cited in Responsa Rashba I:239, reasons that minors are rabbinically obligated to pray (see Mishnah Berakhot 3:3) and as such are no different from adults, who also have a rabbinic obligation (in keeping with the non-Maimonidean views we saw earlier in our discussion of the nature of obligation in prayer). Therefore, lack of obligation cannot be the basis for forbidding a minor from leading. We will return to this text below. Many others felt that the rabbinic obligation of minors was of a lesser level than the rabbinic obligation of adults and would not have accepted the Ra'avad's logic here.

comments: "ולפי טעם זה יש מקום למנהג לומר שהצבור מוחלים על כבודם — If this is the reason [for the exclusion], then we can justify the practice by saying that the community waives its honor." Again, when *kevod tzibbur* is the sole concern, a community can forgo its honor and proceed with the otherwise problematic practice.

According to the Beit Yosef, *kevod tzibbur* is invoked to restrict certain practices that do the community dishonor, but ultimately the community may waive the concern for its honor and perform that practice. To this view, the thrust of the Gemara's restrictions seem to be that a minority interest may not impose its will on everyone if the main body of the community would be offended. However, if everyone thinks that it is acceptable or justified to violate their honor in this way, then it is permitted. Alternatively, the point could be that a community may not waive its honor consistently and regularly, but for occasional needs they may choose to do so. Either way, the priority of this honor is determined by the subjective decision of the community in whose name it is invoked.

The ramifications for gender and Torah reading should be clear. Following the Beit Yosef's position, a community that desires to forgo its honor and allow women to read Torah would be properly exercising their right to waive *kevod tzibbur.* This is then one strong basis for permitting a more gender-equal Torah reading.[104]

b. *Kevod Tzibbur* Is an Objective Standard of Dignity

Against this, the Baḥ insists that the whole point of the *kevod tzibbur* restrictions is to prevent the community from undermining its dignity in the face of competing interests. He also cites the Rambam's view that the prohibition on having a non-bearded *sha"tz* is due to *kevod tzibbur* but strongly objects that this implies any kind of waiver:

ב"ח או"ח סימן נג

ולפע"ד נראה דאף להרמב"ם...לא מהני מחילת הצבור דאין פירוש
מפני כבוד הצבור שהוא כנגד כבודם לפני בני אדם שתועיל בו
מחילת הצבור, אלא פירושו שאין זה כבוד הצבור שישלחו לפניו
יתעלה מי שאין לו הדרת פנים להליץ על הצבור דאף לפני מלך בשר

---

104 Addressing *kevod tzibbur* returns us to our discussion in the previous section. Whether women participate as equals or as adjuncts would be driven by the R. Tam-Ran divide we explored above.

ודם אין שולחין להליץ על הצבור אפילו אם הוא חכם גדול אלא אם כן שהוא בעל צורה ויש לו הדרת פנים שנתמלא זקנו כל שכן לפני מלך מלכי המלכים הקדוש ברוך הוא. דלפי זה אין מקום כלל לומר דמהני למנותו כשרצו הצבור למחול על כבודם...אלא הדבר פשוט כיון שכך תקנו חכמים דחששו לכבוד צבור אין ביד הצבור למחול ותו דאם כן כל הני תקנות שתקנו חכמים מפני כבוד צבור, שלא לגלול ספר תורה בצבור וכן אשה לא תקרא בצבור מפני כבוד הצבור ופוחח לא ישא כפיו...אם אתה אומר דרשאין למחול א"כ לא הועילו בתקנתם כלום דכל צבור יהיו מוחלים!

Baḥ OḤ 53

In my humble opinion, even according to the Rambam…the community cannot waive its honor, because the meaning of "on account of the honor of the community" is not because it is disrespectful to the people present, such that they could waive the concern. Rather, it means that it is not fitting for the community that they should send before the Exalted One a person lacking an impressive countenance to intercede on behalf of the community. Even a very wise person does not intercede on behalf of the community before a human king unless he is of striking appearance and has an impressive countenance with a full beard. All the more so with the Supreme King of Kings! In keeping with this, there is no place whatsoever to say that the community could appoint [a young man as the (permanent) prayer leader] when the community wishes to waive its honor…Rather, the matter is simple: Once the Sages legislated because of their concern for the honor of the community, a community has no license to waive it. Further, if it were the case [that the community could waive it], all these enactments that the Sages legislated because of the honor of the community, such as not rolling the Torah scroll before the community, or that a woman not read in public because of the honor of the community, or that a person in tattered clothing may not offer the Priestly Blessing…if you say that the community may waive [its honor], then the legislation has accomplished nothing, because every community will then waive it!

Communities may wish to cut corners because of expedience (rolling the Torah in front of everyone rather than preparing ahead of time, coming to *shul* in tattered work clothes rather than changing), or for other reasons. Against this impulse, the Sages assert that Torah reading and public prayer are serious, communal acts that require the highest levels of dignity. According to the Baḥ, the *kevod tzibbur* restrictions were enacted precisely to **prevent** communities from waiving their dignity. Even when the community is not concerned for its own dignity, the Sages are.

For the Baḥ, the honor of the community is about the community taking itself seriously. *Kevod tzibbur* is not a prerogative to be either exercised or waived; rather it is a charge to keep, an expectation that communities live up to the standards of dignity and seriousness that they know they are capable of. *Kevod tzibbur* indeed refers to the dignity of the congregation, but not as viewed subjectively from within. Instead, the Baḥ's *kevod tzibbur* is the objective assessment of communal action when viewed from afar: Is the act in question something one would do when presenting oneself to an earthly sovereign? Would it meet our standards for seriousness in other realms of life? If not, then it is inappropriate to settle for something less in a communal, ritual context. Drawing the Baḥ's support for a gender-equal Torah reading would require the bolder and more direct claim that, at least in some pockets of the contemporary world, the concerns of specific issues of *kevod tzibbur* no longer apply or are overridden by other factors. Short of such a claim, individual communities cannot, according to the Baḥ, circumvent the concerns of the Tosefta and the *baraita*.

c. Applying and Balancing the Two Approaches

Poskim over the past few centuries have split in their rulings on whether to follow the Beit Yosef or the Baḥ.[105] Some argue that a greater number of prominent authorities accord with the Beit Yosef's ruling that *kevod ha-tzibbur* may be waived,[106] and therefore communities should be able

---

105 See Shapiro, "Keri'at ha-Torah," 35–36, for citations to a number of these authorities.

106 Peri Ḥadash strongly rejects the Baḥ's approach in the former's comments on OḤ 53, 143, and 144. See also R. Ḥayyim Palache in Responsa Nishmat Kol Ḥai OḤ #9. This voice includes, in our own time, R. Ovadiah Yosef in Responsa Yabia Omer OḤ VI:23, as well as, probably, other strongly authoritative modern *poskim*, such as the Mishnah Berurah and the Arokh ha-Shulḥan. See Sperber, "Congregational Dignity," nn. 203–204.

to waive their honor and allow women to read Torah. However, let it be noted that the Beit Yosef's approach to such a waiver implies that a real offense is occurring, but that the community is willing to allow it in the name of other priorities. In other words, even if one concedes that it is dishonorable to allow women to read Torah in public, one might be willing to suffer this indignity in order to give women a greater sense of inclusion and connection. This approach is similar to those who would advocate for allowing adolescents to regularly lead parts of the service. No one would deny that their gravitas is considerably less than other, older candidates. But it might be worth suffering their less impressive appearance and demeanor in order to more deeply entwine them with communal prayer.

The advantage of the Beit Yosef's approach is plain: It requires no radical reimagining of *kevod tzibbur* and it need not attempt to translate the gender revolution taking place in society into halakhic language. It simply states that the potential dishonor involved in a gender-equal Torah reading is not that big a deal and can be addressed through an elective waiver of the community. Its disadvantage is also plain: It engages assumptions about honor and dignity around gender that are increasingly foreign to contemporary social experience and does not acknowledge that possible discomfort with male-only Torah reading is generally grounded in something deeper than just wanting to give women a few chances to approach a Torah scroll.

The road to gender-equal Torah reading through the Baḥ is simultaneously bolder and more honest. Communities with egalitarian social norms are not claiming that women should be able to read Torah and lead **even though** it is undignified; they are claiming that there is no less dignity in a woman reading than in a man reading. Perhaps they are even claiming that all-male Torah readings in a socially egalitarian context are themselves degrading.

As above in our discussion of R. Tam versus the Ran, we in no way intend to undermine the legitimacy of relying on the Beit Yosef's approach to *kevod tzibbur* as a basis for communities adopting or maintaining an egalitarian practice around Torah reading. But we also do not want to lose the wisdom of the Baḥ; maintaining high communal standards of dignity—even when the community wants to waive them—makes just as much sense today as it did in the 17th century. It is therefore also important to ask not just whether *kevod tzibbur* can be circumvented, but whether it has been sufficiently redefined in our world around gender so as to produce a different ruling in practice.[107]

This notion, that the concern of *kevod tzibbur* spelled out in the *baraita* might not apply in all times and places, is not new. We find prominent voices among generations of *poskim* suggesting that, if communal honor is not violated or if the available alternatives are worse, it would be appropriate for women to read.

R. David b. R. Shmuel Kokhavi recorded the following:

> **ספר הבתים, בית תפילה, שערי קריאת התורה, שער שני, סימן ו**
> יש מן הגדולים שכתב שהמתפללין בבתיהם בעשרה אשה קוראה שם בתורה, שלא נקרא ציבור אלא כשמתפללין בבית הכנסת.
>
> **Sefer ha-Batim, Beit Tefillah, Sha'arei Keri'at ha-Torah 2:6**
> There is one among the great ones who wrote that when people pray with ten in their homes, a woman may read from the Torah there, for it is not called a "community" unless they are praying in a synagogue.

Sefer ha-Batim recognized that the concern of *kevod tzibbur* was grounded in social context: the same Torah reading in a private home might not share the concerns of the highly public space of the synagogue.

Later, in a different context, R. Ya'akov Emden produced similar reasoning:

---

107 Shapiro, "Keri'at ha-Torah," articulates this basic line of reasoning. He writes: "[The Baḥ says that] just as a community should choose the imposing figure over the wise man to represent it before God, so the congregation should not denigrate *keri'at ha-Torah* by performing it through women. This line of thought is out of tune with modern perceptions...Jewish women are widely represented in the professions, including those, such as law and public office, which demand that they act as representatives and advocates for others" (27). R. Shapiro's conclusion blends giving prominence to the Beit Yosef over the Baḥ with a willingness to think differently about how the Baḥ may apply to contemporary settings: "To recapitulate, there appears to be sound halakhic basis for the argument that...in synagogues where there is a consensus that a **woman's Torah reading does not violate community standards of dignity** [emphasis ours], women may be permitted to read Torah (or at least portions of it) as well. The only serious objection to *keri'at ha-Torah* by women is the one raised by the *baraita*, namely that women's Torah reading violates *kevod ha-tzibbur,* and *kevod ha-tzibbur* should be regarded as a relative, waivable objection that is not universally applicable" (51–52).

מגדל עז, הלכות יולדת, שוקת ב, דף יב עמוד ג
ונראה דכשתמפללין וקורין עשרה בצמצום בבית היולדת ואין בעלה כאן, יש להעמיד הדבר על הדין שאשה עולה וקוראה בתורה כהאי גוונא. אע"ג שאמרו חכמים לא תקרא בציבור מפני הכבוד, לא אמרו אלא בקהל רב, ושלא לעשות תדיר, אבל בהאי גוונא דהויא מילתא דלא שכיחא ומשום תקנתא דידה, איכא למימר לא גזרו. עכ"פ הרי בפירוש אמרו שעולה למניין ז', ואם לא עכשיו אימתי. אלה הדברים איפוא הם אמורים, ובודאי לא יפול שום דבר מדבריהם ארצה שלא יהא לו מקום, ובאופן זה כדיעבד דמי. כך דעתי נוטה אם יסכימו עמי חברי.

Migdal Oz, Hilkhot Yoledet, Shoket B, 12c
It seems that when ten pray and read Torah in a small group in the house of the new mother, and her husband is not there, one may restore the basic principle that a woman may go up and read Torah. Even though the Sages said that she should not read in the community because of honor, they said that only with reference to a large congregation, and not to do so regularly, but in this situation, which is an irregular occurrence, and it is for her sake, one can say that they did not decree. In any event, they explicitly said that she goes up among the seven, and if not for now [= this sort of case], for when were these words intended? Certainly, everything the Sages said must have some applicable context, and in this sort of case, it is similar to a *post facto* case. So inclines my opinion if my colleagues will agree with me.

In our own time, R. Ben-Tziyyon Abba Shaul reasoned similarly, though he expressed practical reservations:

אור לציון, שו"ת חלק ב, הלכות פסוקות, או"ח א, עמוד ח
ואגב יש להעיר במה שכתב מרן בשו"ע...הכל עולים למנין שבעה, אפילו אשה וקטן שיודע למי מברכין, אבל אמרו חכמים אשה לא תקרא בציבור מפני כבוד הציבור. וצריך עיון, שאם עכ"פ אין אשה עולה מפני כבוד הציבור, מאי נפק"מ שאשה עולה למנין שבעה, ולשם מה כתב מרן הלכה זו. **ולכן היה נראה לומר שנפק"מ במקום שאין חשש משום כבוד הציבור**, כגון במקום שהמתפללים הם בני משפחה אחת, והאשה היא ראש הבית וכל שאר המתפללים הם בניה ונכדיה,

שאז אין חסרון כבוד הציבור במה שתעלה לתורה, **בכה"ג שפיר יכולה לעלות לתורה ולהצטרף למנין שבעה.** ולמעשה צ"ע.

Or le-Tziyyon, Responsa II, Halakhot Pesukot, OḤ I, p. 8
We should consider that which our master wrote in the Shulḥan Arukh…"All may count for the total of seven, even a woman or a minor who knows to whom we bless, but the Sages said that a woman should not read in public because of the honor of the community." More investigation is required. If a woman cannot go up because of the honor of the community, what difference does it make that she can [theoretically] count for the total of seven, and why did our master bother to write this *halakhah*? **Therefore, it seems that there is practical relevance in a case where there is no concern for the honor of the community,** such as in a place where all those praying are members of a single family and the woman is the head of household and all the others praying are her children and grandchildren. **In that case, there is no diminishment of the honor of the community by her going up to the Torah, in which case she would be able to go up to the Torah and count toward the total of seven.** But regarding practice, more investigation is required.

Note that none of these views claims that the honor of the community has been **waived**. Instead, they each reason that, in the case they are discussing, it does not **apply**.[108] Calculations of communal honor play out differently in different social arrangements. That might be because of the more private nature of the ritual, its *ad hoc* nature, or the social context in which the woman having the *aliyah* quite obviously possesses as much gravitas as anyone else in the room.[109] The Or le-Tziyyon's analysis is

---

108 For another intriguing example of this sort, see Ḥashukei Ḥemed Gittin 60a, where R. Yitzḥak Silberstein addresses a case of prisoners who only have separate scrolls of the five parts of the Torah. He concludes that none of the reasons for demanding a complete *sefer Torah* apply and therefore permits reading in this context.

109 One remarkable historical instance of this dynamic is provided by Sperber, *Darkah shel Halakhah*, 32–33, n. 37. In 1901, Flora Sassoon, the famed business woman and

perhaps most helpful here: In many pockets of the contemporary world, society in its entirety has become like his small laboratory of gender equality. Just as the matriarch in his thought experiment poses no clear affront to the dignity of those in the room, it is now broadly true in many settings that women are not taken less seriously than men just because they are women, nor is their knowledge of ritual matters experienced as a slight to men or to the community as a whole. The Or le-Tziyyon's hesitancy regarding practice is understandable, as it should be in any case grappling with a new and still unfolding social dynamic. But the years that have passed since he penned these words have only moved society more forcefully in the direction of gender equality, making less hesitance in this regard not only justifiable but quite plausibly wise. When women are fully educated, hold public office, and run corporations, female leadership in the synagogue is no longer disrespectful to the community. Faithfulness to the concept of *kevod tzibbur* itself demands that it be reevaluated in light of women's relationship to the broader cultural context. In communities where men and women are educated equally in Torah and general studies, where women and men increasingly share the corridors of power and enjoy electoral success, it can be claimed that no shame or dishonor would any longer follow from having women read Torah in the presence of men.

Perhaps even more dramatic are the claims that *kevod tzibbur* is at times overridden by other concerns. We saw above the view of the Maharam of Rothenberg, who countenanced the idea that the risk of a greater indignity—to the *kohanim*—can justify overriding the normal concern regarding indignity surrounding gender. Similarly, in his glosses on our passage in the Talmud, R. Ya'akov Emden concisely explained that the Gemara's restriction on women reading is not absolute. If excluding women from reading will cancel the Torah reading altogether for lack of competent men, then women may read all of the *aliyot*:

ר' יעקב עמדין, הגהות וחדושים, מגילה כג.
"אבל אמרו חכמים אשה לא וכו'": נראה דהיינו היכא דאפשר,
ורישא מיירי בדליכא שבעה (בהני עשרה דמצטרפי לדבר שבקדושה)
דבקיאי למקרי ואיכא אשה בקיאה דלא סגי בלא דידה.

Torah scholar, visited Baghdad. The community, which was at that time under the religious leadership of R. Yosef Ḥayyim Al-Ḥakham (the Ben Ish Ḥai), honored her by calling her to read Torah in the synagogue.

R. Ya'akov Emden, Hagahot ve-Ḥiddushim, Megillah 23a
"But the Sages said that a woman should not..." It seems that this means where possible, but the beginning [of the text, which stated that in principle women may read] is referring to when there are not seven who know how to read, but there is a woman who knows how, such that they cannot suffice without her.

Along these lines, R. Daniel Sperber has argued for another overriding factor: the human dignity of women (*kevod ha-beriyot*), which can be deeply harmed in the contemporary world when women are excluded from rituals. He argues that just as the Maharam's concern for *kohanim* led him to override *kevod tzibbur*, so too contemporary practice should grant the human dignity of women no less weight.[110]

We are less certain as to whether *kevod ha-beriyot* is an appropriate legal concept on which to base gender-equal Torah reading. *Kevod ha-beriyot*, while highly evocative, is generally invoked for *ad hoc* situations and not because of a critique as to how a given *mitzvah* or rabbinic expectation makes a person feel.[111] We would translate the instinct behind this legal move differently: As the Baḥ emphasized, the restrictions around *kevod tzibbur* may not just be reflecting reality, but supporting and creating a reality of greater dignity and seriousness. To the extent that adhering to the restriction in question begins to **undermine** that dignity and seriousness, it is not clear that the earlier prohibition could even possibly be in place.

Specifically, it might be that, in our world, *kevod tzibbur* itself is what leads many people to want to have gender-equal Torah reading! We live in a world in which there are almost no all-male institutions left that are taken seriously at all. Other than in a few specific arenas, all major institutions of Western society allow women access as equals, at least in theory. One might reasonably claim that maintaining the exclusion of women from Torah reading in fact **denigrates** its status as a serious activity in communities that expect gender equality in other areas of their

---

110 Sperber, "Congregational Dignity."

111 The core talmudic passage is on Bavli Berakhot 19b–20a.

lives.[112] Given that maximizing communal honor was the driving internal halakhic consideration for gendering Torah reading in the first place, it is particularly compelling—in the name of halakhic values themselves—to revisit a gendered regime, to the extent it threatens communal honor and dignity. An argument of this sort for egalitarian Torah reading would fill out the tradition above that reassesses socio-halakhic factors like *kevod tzibbur* and fully engage the Baḥ's concern for robust and objective standards of communal dignity.[113]

3. *Summary*

As the first clauses of Tosefta Megillah 3:11 and the *baraita* on Talmud Bavli Megillah 23a indicate, Torah reading is at least theoretically inclusive of women. R. Tam's theory of Torah reading supports the idea that this equality was total, whereas the Ran felt it was only permissible to include women as adjunct participants.

The second clauses of the Tosefta and the *baraita* point to a practical ban on letting women read Torah. In the *baraita,* this is formulated as *kevod tzibbur,* "the honor of the community." *Kevod tzibbur* can be engaged either through the prism of waiver or reassessment.

Torah readings only open to adult males are coherent on the grounds that *kevod tzibbur* remains an obstacle to female participation. In communities where women are not educated equally to men, or where women do not

---

112 Noam, "la-Meḥitzah ha-Penimit," has reflected on this point:

> סילוק הנשים מן העשייה הדתית הציבורית מסלק את העשייה הזאת עצמה מן החיים אל המוזיאון.

> Removing women from public religious acts removes the act itself from life into the museum.

113 We should also note the explicit statements of a number of *poskim* that the prohibition of calling women to read is only *ab initio,* but that *post facto,* having read, the reading is valid, or even just having been called up, they may go ahead and read. This view is seen not only from those sages mentioned above, such as the Maharam, who allowed women to read in certain circumstances, but also from a number of others who never specifically discussed allowing it, yet said that it is valid *post facto,* including two commentators to Tosefta Megillah 3:11: R. David Pardo (Ḥasdei David), and R. Meir Friedman (Tekhelet Mordekhai).

in general serve in public capacities, the injury done to communal honor by allowing women to read Torah may remain intact. Communities with similar gender roles to those of the ancient and medieval world ought to be expected to have similar concerns on this front.

A fully egalitarian Torah reading can justify itself without reevaluating assumptions and categories by simply endorsing the approach of R. Tam and the approach that allows communities to waive *kevod tzibbur.* A more robust formulation of the gender-specific motivations for equality would need to articulate a redefinition of *kevod tzibbur* as described above and not suffice with a waiver alone. Finally, any effort to bring the Ran on board with a fully egalitarian Torah reading would have to reevaluate notions of gender and obligation more broadly, with regard to Torah study and potentially all *mitzvot.* Communities for which that broader reevaluation is not on the table, but for whom the Ran's approach is compelling, might well include women as adjunct participants without having them be fully equal to men.

B. ARE OTHER *DEVARIM SHEBIKDUSHAH* THE SAME AS TORAH READING?

Our investigation of Torah reading has also established another important, and more general, point: Controlling for *kevod tzibbur,* there is nothing about a ritual's status as a *davar shebikdushah* that genders its leadership requirements in the presence of a valid *minyan.*[114] This flows from a simple reading of Mishnah Megillah 4:3, cited here again:

משנה מגילה ד:ג

אין פורסין את שמע, ואין עוברין לפני התיבה, ואין נושאין את כפיהם, ואין קורין בתורה, ואין מפטירין בנביא, ואין עושין מעמד ומושב, ואין אומרים ברכת אבלים ותנחומי אבלים וברכת חתנים, ואין מזמנין בשם, פחות מעשרה. ובקרקעות, תשעה וכהן. ואדם, כיוצא בהן.

---

114 We will explore the criteria for *minyan* in greater depth below. Our conclusions here hold even if the reader assumes a *minyan* of ten adult men.

Mishnah Megillah 4:3

We do not responsively recite the Shema, nor have a communal prayer leader, nor offer the Priestly Blessing, nor read from the Torah, nor read from the Prophets, nor perform the standing/sitting [ritual for the dead], nor say the blessing of the mourners, nor the formal comforting the mourners, nor recite the wedding blessings, nor say *zimmun* with the Name in a group of fewer than ten. And when redeeming land we require nine and a *kohen*; and so too with [redeeming] people.

The Mishnah lists Torah reading in the midst of a host of other rituals requiring a quorum of ten. As we saw above, the Gemara then explains the Mishnah's requirement of ten with the statement that any *davar shebikdushah* requires ten. The straightforward conclusion is that Torah reading is itself among the *devarim shebikdushah* referred to by the Talmud Bavli.[115] This is implied by the structure of Rambam, Hilkhot Tefillah 8:4–6, which groups the first five rituals in our *mishnah* together with Kaddish and Kedushah and describes them all as *devarim shebikdushah*:

רמב"ם הלכות תפילה ח:ד-ו

וכיצד היא תפלת הציבור? יהיה אחד מתפלל בקול רם והכל שומעים, ואין עושין כן בפחות מעשרה גדולים ובני חורין...וכן אין אומרים קדושה ולא קוראין בתורה ומברכין לפניה ולאחריה ולא מפטירין בנביאים אלא בעשרה. וכן לא יהיה אחד מברך ברכת שמע והכל שומעים ועונין אחריו אמן אלא בעשרה, וזה הוא הנקרא פורס על שמע. ואין אומרים קדיש אלא בעשרה, ואין הכהנים נושאים ידיהם אלא בעשרה והכהנים מן המנין, שכל עשרה מישראל הם הנקראים עדה...וכל דבר קדושה לא יהא אלא בתוך העדה מישראל שנאמר "ונקדשתי בתוך בני ישראל."

Rambam, Hilkhot Tefillah 8:4–6

What is public prayer? One person prays aloud and the others listen. We do not do that with fewer than ten free adults... We also do not say Kedushah, nor read from the Torah with

115 See also Bavli Gittin 59b, where the language of דבר שבקדושה is used in the context of *aliyot* to the Torah, among other rituals.

> blessings before and after, nor read a final portion from the Prophets unless there are ten. One should also not say the blessing over the Shema while others listen and respond unless there are ten—this is what is known as *pores al Shema*.[116] And we do not say Kaddish unless there are ten, and the priests do not offer the Priestly Blessing unless there are ten. The priests count toward this ten, for any ten Jews are called an *eidah*.... And any *davar kedushah* should not be done except in the presence of an *eidah* of the Jewish people, as it says, "I shall be sanctified in the midst of the children of Israel."

Many later authorities and interpreters therefore assert that Torah reading is a *davar shebikdushah*. R. Mordekhai Jaffe states this directly in Levush 143:1: "קריאת התורה היא דבר שבקדושה — Torah reading is a *davar shebikdushah*." Other prominent authorities who explicitly articulate this view include R. Ovadiah of Bartenura, R. Yisrael Lifshitz, R. Yisrael Meir Kagan, R. Yeḥiel Mikhel Epstein, R. Barukh ha-Levi Epstein, and R. Moshe Feinstein.[117] This would seem to settle the matter: the fact that a ritual act is a *davar shebikdushah* reveals nothing about whether it is gendered. It would then stand to reason that, controlling for concerns of *kevod tzibbur*, the recitation of Kedushah, Kaddish, and Barekhu would be similarly non-gendered.

However, matters are not so simple. First, not all authorities accepted the notion that Torah reading is a *davar shebikdushah*.[118] The views of this camp may cut against the plain sense of the Mishnah and may be generally underrepresented among later *poskim*, but any argument should

---

116 Note that Rambam's definition of this term is different from our translation above. This is one of a number of medieval interpretations of the phrase פורס על שמע. See above, n. 49. See also Introduction, n. 5 above, which discusses how many contemporary communities have abandoned even practicing Rambam's definition of פורס על שמע, rendering it practically irrelevant for our discussion.

117 R. Ovadiah of Bartenura and Tiferet Yisrael on Mishnah Megillah 4:3; Mishnah Berurah 143:1; Arokh ha-Shulḥan Yoreh Deah 334:7; Torah Temimah Vayikra 22:32, n. 195; Iggerot Moshe OḤ I:23.

118 The most prominent source in this regard is Eliyah Rabbah 128:1, who cites the Ran as demurring from the Levush's conclusion that the Priestly Blessing and Torah reading are considered *devarim shebikdushah*. Eliyah Rabbah is referring to the following passage in the Ran:

ר"ן על הרי"ף מגילה יג:

ואין נושאין את כפיהם פחות מי' דכתיב וישא אהרן את ידיו אל העם ויברכם וכתיב כה תברכו את בני ישראל אמור להם. ובני ישראל עשרה משמע כדילפינן בגמרא לענין דבר שבקדושה מדכתיב ונקדשתי בתוך בני ישראל...ומיהו הני מילי כולהו אסמכתא דרבנן נינהו דסדר תפלה גופה דרבנן.

ואין קורין בתורה ואין מפטירין בנביא בפחות מעשרה. דתקנתא דרבנן הוא ולא תקון אלא בצבור...

מנא הני מילי וכו'. וכל דבר שבקדושה לא יהיה פחות מעשרה...והאי טעמא סגי לאין פורסין על שמע ואין עוברין לפני התיבה משום קדושה דאית בהו ולאין נושאין את כפיהם מטעמא דכתיבנא במתניתין.

Ran on Rif Megillah 13b

"And they may not offer the Priestly Blessing with fewer than ten"—for it is written, "Aharon raised up his hands toward the people and blessed them," and it is also written, "So you must bless *benei yisrael*, say to them." And *benei yisrael* signifies ten, as we learn here in the Gemara with respect to a *davar shebikdushah*, deriving this from the verse: "And I will be sanctified in the midst of *benei yisrael*."...But these are all only rabbinic laws and the verses are here for symbolic support, because all the laws of prayer are themselves rabbinic.

"And they may not read from the Torah nor add from the Prophets with fewer than ten" because these are rabbinic enactments and they were only enacted to be done in public....

"Any *davar shebikdushah* shall not be said with fewer than ten."...This reasoning is sufficient to explain [why we require ten] for the blessings of Shema and to have a communal prayer leader, since both of those rituals contain Kedushah, but [the basis for requiring ten] for the Priestly Blessing is what I wrote in explaining the Mishnah.

The Ran here clearly states that the Priestly Blessing does **not** require ten because it is a *davar shebikdushah*, but rather because the term בני ישראל—already associated with ten in the context of *devarim shebikdushah*—is used to describe the object of the blessing. (This point was already made by the Rashba on Megillah 23b.) Whether the Ran feels the same way about Torah reading is less clear, and depends on one's reading of two clauses in the above passage: (1) When the Ran says that Torah and Haftarah reading require ten because they are rabbinic ordinances that must be done in a communal setting, this gives the impression that he is distinguishing them from the first items in the list (אין פורסין על שמע and אין עוברין לפני התיבה), to which he explicitly applied the Gemara's grounding of the quorum of ten in their nature as a *davar shebikdushah*. One might thus read him as saying that Torah reading is **not** a *davar shebikdushah*. On the other hand, he might simply be explaining that Torah reading follows the rules of *devarim shebikdushah* because it was given holiness by the Sages as a public ritual and given the same status as the other initial items in the

Mishnah's list. (2) In the last clause above, the Ran seems to say that the rationale of *devarim shebikdushah* only applies to the first two items on the list, excluding Torah reading. But the continuation of the sentence suggests that this formulation may only be intended to buttress his claim that the Priestly Blessing is not *a davar shebikdushah*, but conceding that Torah reading is indeed in this category.

In other words, the Ran's precise position on the status of Torah reading as a *davar shebikdushah* like any other is unclear, and this lack of clarity is reflected in the interpretations of him in later Aḥaronim. While Eliyah Rabbah reads him in conflict with the Levush on the question of Torah reading, others resisted this reading. See Mishpetei Uzziel III OḤ #14 for one such example. See also R. Aryeh Leib Ginzburg, in Turei Even on Megillah 23b, who takes issue with the view of the Rashba—cited by the Ran—that the Priestly Blessing is not *a davar shebikdushah*. He asks:

> ולדידי ק״ל הא אין קורין בתורה דתנא אחריו וודאי טעמא דצריך י׳ משום דדבר שבקדושה הוי וה״ט דריש׳ דאין פורסין ועוברין לפני התיבה. ואם איתא דטעמא דאין נושאין לאו מש״ה הוא אלא מפני הזכרת השם אמאי נקט לה באמצע בין הני דטעמא משום דבר שבקדושה.
>
> I myself find this difficult [the Ran's claim that the Priestly Blessing is not a *davar shebikdushah*]. The phrase "We do not read from the Torah [without a quorum of ten]" immediately follows [the Mishnah's stipulation that the Priestly Blessing is not said without a quorum of ten], and the reason for [Torah reading] requiring a quorum of ten is obviously because it is a *davar shebikdushah,* and this is also the reason that we do not responsively recite the Shema nor publicly recite the Amidah [without a quorum]. If it were the case that the reason for not saying the Priestly Blessing [without a quorum] is only because of the mentioning of God's Name [in the blessing], then why would it be placed between these other rulings, which are all on account of each of them being a *davar shebikdushah*?

The Turei Even clearly never imagined that anyone—including the Rashba—might think that Torah reading was not a *davar shebikdushah*. He would clearly have read the Ran in the alternate ways suggested above. Note also that while the Peri Megadim and the Be'ur Halakhah cite the Ran's dissent on characterizing the Priestly Blessing as *a davar shebikdushah* in OḤ 128, they make no mention of such a position of his with regard to Torah reading.

One other view worth noting is that of the Meiri on Megillah 23b:

> שאין הכהנים נושאין את כפיהם אלא בעשרה אף זו דבר שבקדושה היא וכן בקריאת התורה שהרי צריך לומר ברכו.
>
> Torah reading is *a davar shebikdushah* because it includes the recitation of Barekhu.

The formulation here indicates that the Meiri did not consider the reading of Torah **itself** to be a *davar shebikdushah,* but rather that Torah reading had this status on account of the Barekhu recited by each reader. In fact, a similar point was made

take their approach into account as well.[119] If Torah reading is not a *davar*

---

explicitly by R. Menaḥem Azariah of Fano in Responsum #91, where he says that while it is possible to debate whether the reading of the Torah is a *davar shebikdushah*, it is obvious that the recitation of Barekhu as part of having an *aliyah* is considered a *davar shebikdushah*:

> מ"מ אפי' לפי דעת החולקים בזה יש לנו דברים ברורים ושל טעם הם יחוייב השומע ומבין להודות בהם: הנה לדברי הכל ברכו את ה' המבורך הוא דבר שבקדושה.

> Nevertheless, even according to those who disagree about this, we have clear and reasonable words that the person who hears understands, which is that according to everyone, *Barekhu et Adonai ha-mevorakh* is a *davar shebikdushah*.

This point is then cited in Magen Avraham 146:6.

One might think that this insight would conclusively show that *devarim shebikdushah* are in no way gendered, since, controlling for *kevod tzibbur*, women would have said the blessings over their *aliyot*. But one would still have to contend with the view, cited in Meiri Megillah 23a, that negates the idea that women could ever have said the blessings over the Torah:

> ויש מי שמפרש שלא נאמרו הדברים אלא בזמן בהיו קוראין אמצעיים בלא ברכה ואשה יכולה לקרות באמצע אבל עכשו שכלן מברכין אין אשה קוראה כלל וכן הדין נותן שהרי היאך תברך והיא פטורה.

> Some explain that these words [the *baraita*'s permission, in principle, for women to read Torah] only applied at the time when the intermediate readers [of any given set of Torah readers] said no blessing, such that a woman could be an intermediate reader. But now that all say a blessing, a woman cannot read at all. And this makes sense: How can she say a blessing when she is exempt?

A similar ruling is cited by R. David b. R. Shmuel Kokhavi in Sefer ha-Batim, Sha'arei Keri'at ha-Torah 2:6. This view is far from unanimous or authoritative and invites many layers of analysis; the interested reader can see Shapiro, "Keri'at ha-Torah," 12–15. In addition to R. Tam's explicit rejection of this approach, see the Ran on Rif Megillah 13a s.v. *ha-kol* for another clear disagreement. Accommodating the view cited in the Meiri and Sefer ha-Batim would indeed mean that a woman could not have any *aliyot* even if one controlled for *kevod tzibbur*, though perhaps she could read Torah in contexts where the reader and *oleh* are separate functions. Addressing this view would require engaging the analysis we offered regarding justifying a gender-equal Torah reading under the Ran's rubric of בני חיובא. For our purposes here, this view cited in the Meiri merely demonstrates further that there are important voices that would not consider women's participation in Torah reading to be useful data for a more general conclusion regarding their ability to lead *devarim shebikdushah* such as Kedushah, Kaddish, and Barekhu.

119 In the words of R. Uzziel in Mishpetei Uzziel III OḤ #14:

shebikdushah, it can no longer function as evidence for a gender-blind approach to such rituals. Even if there is no particular reason to think that rituals such as Kedushah, Kaddish, and Barekhu are gendered,[120] satisfying this camp of interpreters demands grounding that claim in sources unrelated to Torah reading.

Second, and more important: Even if *devarim shebikdushah* are not *ipso facto* gendered (whether or not Torah reading is appropriate evidence for this), they might be gendered due to other concerns, such as a gender gap in obligation. In fact, Mishnah Megillah 4:5–6 makes abundantly clear that one cannot necessarily extrapolate from one type of *davar shebikdushah* to another:

משנה מגילה ד:ה–ו

המפטיר בנביא הוא פורס על שמע והוא עובר לפני התיבה והוא נושא את כפיו ואם היה קטן אביו או רבו עוברין על ידו.

קטן קורא בתורה ומתרגם אבל אינו פורס על שמע ואינו עובר לפני התיבה ואינו נושא את כפיו. פוחח פורס את שמע ומתרגם אבל אינו קורא בתורה ואינו עובר לפני התיבה ואינו נושא את כפיו.

לפום ריהטא דסוגיא משמע דפורסין על שמע וקורין בתורה ומפטירין בנביא חד טעמא וחד דינא הוא.

The flow of the *sugya* implies that *porsin al Shema* and reading the Torah and Haftarah are all based on one reason and one law.

120 Indeed, R. Mendel Shapiro explicitly says that he knows of no objection to women saying *devarim shebikdushah* in general: "I have heard the argument put forward that women may not say *birkhot ha-Torah* of *keri'at ha-Torah* because they are *davar shebikdushah*...which women may not recite, but I have found no evidence to support this conclusion. *Devarim shebikdushah* require an appropriate *minyan*. Absent such a *minyan*, they may not be said by men or women. **Where there is such a minyan, there is no reason to suppose that women may not say *devarim shebikdushah*** (emphasis ours). I have also heard it argued that women are precluded from saying the Barekhu that precedes the *birkhot ha-Torah* said by those called to the Torah. I have found no basis for this position and can only speculate that its origin may be in the perception of Barekhu as a *davar shebikdushah* that women may not say. Again, there is no reason to believe that women may not say *devarim shebikdushah* in the presence of a *minyan* of ten men..." Shapiro, "Keri'at ha-Torah," n. 90.

Mishnah Megillah 4:5–6
The one who reads from the Prophets leads the responsive reading of the Shema and publicly recites the Amidah and says the Priestly Blessing. If [the one who said the Haftarah] was a minor, then his father or teacher goes in his place.

A minor reads from the Torah and translates but does not lead the responsive reading of the Shema, nor publicly recites the Amidah, nor says the Priestly Blessing. A person dressed in tattered clothing does lead the responsive reading of the Shema and translates, but does not read Torah, nor publicly recites the Amidah nor says the Priestly Blessing.

This *mishnah* shows that a person can be included in Torah reading and still be excluded from other rituals. Whatever the reason for the minor's exclusion from leading the rituals of *pores al Shema* and the public Amidah,[121] it is clear that these exclusions coexist with his inclusion in Torah reading. There are strong reasons to assume that Torah reading would indeed function the same as Kedushah, Kaddish, and Barekhu. After all, having an *aliyah* to the Torah involves the recitation of Barekhu! Nonetheless, we have seen that extrapolating from one category to another can be unsound. Specifically, perhaps one who leads *devarim shebikdushah* is fulfilling the individual obligations of others in these parts of the liturgy and perhaps women are exempt from these requirements and thus unable to lead. Therefore, we must turn to a more piecemeal examination of Kedushah, Kaddish, and Barekhu to see if the requirements for leading them are gendered in any way.

---

121 Rashi thinks the issue with *pores al Shema* relates entirely to obligation. See Rashi Megillah 24a s.v. *katan* and s.v. *pores et Shema*. He thinks that the issue with the Priestly Blessing is the indignity done to the congregation by having a minor bless them; see s.v. *ve-eino nosei et kapav*. With regard to a minor's inability to recite the public Amidah, the Ran on Rif Megillah 15a thinks this is an issue of obligation gap as well. By contrast, the Ra'avad, cited in Responsa Rashba I:239, feels the issue is one of congregational indignity (גנאי לציבור).

C. OTHER *DEVARIM SHEBIKDUSHAH*: KEDUSHAH, KADDISH, AND BAREKHU

In this section, we will explore three central questions:

1. Are individuals obligated in *devarim shebikdushah*? If not, then the ability for a given person to lead them should in no way depend on the level of their obligation.
2. If there is some sort of individual obligation in *devarim shebikdushah*, is this obligation fulfilled vicariously through the prayer leader? If, instead, the obligation is fulfilled by congregants on their own, then level of obligation would similarly be irrelevant when choosing a leader.
3. If the obligation is fulfilled vicariously through the leader, is the obligation in *devarim shebikdushah* gendered?

Only if the answer to all three questions is "yes" would there be any sense to gendering leadership of *devarim shebikdushah* based on concerns surrounding obligation. If the answer to any of the questions is "no," we would expect the conversation to return to considerations of *kevod tzibbur*, already highlighted and discussed in our treatment of Torah reading above.

1. Is There Individual Obligation in Kedushah, Kaddish, and Barekhu?

As was the case with public Torah reading, we would not naturally expect there to be an individual obligation with regard to *devarim shebikdushah*, given that these liturgical elements can **only** be said in a communal context. Not surprisingly, there is a strong strand of the tradition that denies that an individual obligation exists at all. With respect to Kedushah, Rashi is a good exemplar of this view:

מחזור ויטרי סימן מד

ועל עשרה שהתפללו כולו ושמעו קדוש׳ וברכו וסדר תפילה, שיכולין להימנות להמניין אחר בשביל אחד שלא התפלל...ואפילו אחד מאותן שהתפללו כבר יכול לחזור ולהתפלל להוציא את החייב. וסומך ר׳ ומראה פנים מן הציבור שמתפללין י״ח כל אחד לעצמו, וחוזר וכופלו השליח ציבור בשביל קדושה. נמצא שהמתפללין נימנין לסדר המניין על הקדושה לבדה. נענה מאן דהו וא׳ שמא בשביל הקדושה שלא

אמרו כל אחד לעצמו הן נימנין, נמצאו עדיין מחוייבין בדבר. והשיב ר׳ **לא מצינו בכל התלמוד חיוב קדושה אלא חביבה היא לנו ואינה בפחות מעשרה.**

Maḥzor Vitry 44[122]
Regarding ten people who have prayed everything and have heard Kedushah and Barekhu and the full order of prayer: They can count toward another quorum for one who has not yet prayed…and even one of those who has prayed already can repeat the Amidah to fulfill the obligation of the one still obligated. And my master [i.e., Rashi] provides support for this ruling from the fact that though the community prays the Amidah individually, the leader repeats it in order to say Kedushah. We see, therefore, that those who have already prayed count toward the quorum on account of the Kedushah alone. Someone challenged this and said: Perhaps, in your example, they are counted toward the quorum only because they have not yet heard Kedushah? They are therefore still obligated and can therefore count in the *minyan*! My master responded: **We do not find anywhere in the Talmud an obligation to hear Kedushah; rather, it is dear to us and it cannot be said in a group of fewer than ten.**

Rashi argues that our deep attachment to Kedushah is essentially performative and emotional. Categorizing Kedushah as an obligation to be fulfilled misses the point. The same logic (and the same absence of talmudic evidence to the contrary) would seem to extend to Kaddish and Barekhu as well.[123] A clear practical corollary to this approach is assumed

---

122 For parallels to this text, see Responsa Rashi #92, Sefer ha-Orah II:1129, Siddur Rashi #59, and Issur ve-Heter le-Rashi #124. In the responsum, the argument is explicitly connected to the Massekhet Soferim text we analyzed above, n. 51.

123 The notion that these parts of the service are "dear" and not to be missed is reflected in a range of practices designed to enable latecomers who missed these parts to find a way to get a second chance to hear or say them. The earliest source of this sort is Seder Rav Amram Gaon, Siyyum ha-Tefillah (near the end of that section), which allows for saying Barekhu at the end of the service for those who come late to Shaḥarit and even allows interrupting between the final blessing after Shema before

by the Mordekhai. He comments on Talmud Yerushalmi Megillah 4:4 (75a), which condemns those who leave a *minyan* of exactly ten people that has begun one of the rituals that requires a *minyan*. He includes an important additional clause:

מרדכי מגילה רמז תתי
ועל היוצאין **שאין מניחין שם י'** נאמר ועוזבי ה' יכלו (ישעיה א:כח).

Mordekhai Megillah #810
And regarding those who leave **and do not leave behind ten,** it is said: "Those who abandon God shall be consumed" (Yeshayahu 1:28).

The Mordekhai goes out of his way to clarify that no opprobrium is attached to one who leaves a *minyan* as long as the *minyan* remains intact. Rema OḤ 55:2 later clarifies the implications of this approach: "אבל אם נשארו י' מותר לצאת — But if ten remain, it is permitted to leave." This is true even though the rituals to which this discussion applies include Kedushah, Kaddish, and Barekhu.[124] This is essentially a claim that the only obligation here is on the community as a whole, but it does not devolve on specific individuals in any way.

The practical corollary of this approach to *devarim shebikdushah* is that questions of obligation are beside the point when thinking about who is qualified to lead these parts of the service. This notion achieves clear expression in R. Yosef Karo's treatment of the question of a minor leading Arvit, which we briefly explored above. Many communities had the practice of allowing boys under the age of thirteen to lead the evening prayer on Saturday night.[125] R. Karo in his Beit Yosef grapples with the

---

the Arvit Amidah to do the same! This later develops into an even more robust set of practices of this sort, sometimes used to accommodate even a single straggler. For a fuller history, see Reed Blank, "Medieval French Practice."

124 Be'ur Halakhah 55 s.v. *aval* argues that neither the Mordekhai nor the Rema allow for walking out in the middle of Kedushah and that their discussion is not meant to refer to that ritual. But his concern relates to the impropriety of walking out in the middle of this particularly focused ritual and is not addressing the question of walking out in advance of its recitation, which the Mordekhai would clearly permit.

125 As noted above, these boys were mourners, and their prayers were understood to be particularly effective for protecting the souls of the deceased. See above, n. 102.

validity of this common practice in the face of sources, starting with Mishnah Megillah 4:6, that unambiguously forbid a minor from serving as a *sha"tz*.[126] Here is his analysis:

בית יוסף או"ח סימן נג

ומדברי רבינו ודברי המפרשים שכתבתי משמע בהדיא שקטן אינו רשאי לירד לפני התיבה אפילו באקראי בעלמא, ויש לתמוה על מה שנהגו שקטן יורד לפני התיבה במוצאי שבתות להתפלל תפלת ערבית.

ואפשר לומר דלא הקפידו חכמים אלא בתפלת שחרית שיש בברכת יוצר ובתפלה קדושה וגם שצריך שליח ציבור לחזור התפלה להוציא הרבים ידי חובתן, וקטן כיון דלאו בר חיובא הוא אינו מוציאם כדתנן: כל שאינו מחוייב בדבר אינו מוציא את הרבים ידי חובתן.

ושמעתי שהרב ה"ר יוסף אבודרהם קרא תגר על מנהג זה שנהגו הקטנים לירד לפני התיבה במוצאי שבתות והסכים על ידו הרב הגדול מה"ר יצחק די ליאון ז"ל לבטל המנהג.

ומצאתי להרשב"א שכתב בתשובה (ח"א סי' רלט) בשם הראב"ד דטעמא דתנן דקטן אינו פורס על שמע ואינו עובר לפני התיבה דכיון דברכות ותפלות דרבנן נינהו וקטן שהגיע לחינוך דרבנן הוי אמינא אתי דרבנן ומפיק דרבנן קמ"ל דמשום כבוד הצבור לא עבדינן גנאי הוא לצבור שהקטן מוציאן עכ"ל. ולפי טעם זה יש מקום למנהג לומר שהצבור מוחלים על כבודם ואפילו למאי דפירש רש"י דטעמא דמתניתין משום דכל שאינו מחוייב בדבר אינו מוציא את הרבים ידי חובתן איכא למימר דתפלת ערבית שאני דרשות היא.

Beit Yosef OḤ 53

From the words of our master [the Tur] and the words of the commentators that I have recorded, it seems blatantly clear that a minor cannot lead the community in prayer, even on a happenstance basis. Therefore, the practice of having a minor lead the community in prayer at the end of Shabbat by leading Arvit is surprising.

---

126 The various sources that prohibit someone whose beard has not filled in from serving as *sha"tz* only make the assumption that a minor is invalid all the more obvious. See Tosefta Ḥagigah 1:3 and Bavli Ḥullin 24b.

> But it is possible to argue that the Sages were only particular [about banning a minor from leading] regarding Shaḥarit, which has Kedushah in the first blessing before the Shema and in the Amidah, and during which the leader must also repeat the Amidah to fulfill the obligations of others. Since a minor is not obligated, he would be unable to fulfill their obligations, as it is taught, "One who is not obligated in something cannot fulfill the obligations of others."
>
> I have heard that R. Yosef Abudraham attacked this practice of allowing minors to lead the evening prayers on Saturday night and our teacher R. Yitzḥak de Leon *z"l* agreed with him that the practice should be stopped.
>
> But I found that the Rashba wrote in a responsum in the name of the Ra'avad that the reason that it was taught that a minor cannot lead the responsive reading of the Shema nor lead the community in prayer is because it would be disgraceful for the community to have a minor fulfill their obligations. Given that all blessings and prayers are only rabbinic in status and a minor who is capable of praying is also rabbinically obligated, I might have thought that one rabbinically obligated person [the minor] can fulfill the obligations of another rabbinically obligated person [an adult member of the congregation]. The Mishnah comes to teach us that we do not do this on account of *kevod tzibbur*. According to [the Ra'avad's] reason, we can justify the practice by saying that the community waives its honor. And even according to Rashi, who explained the Mishnah as being based in an obligation gap, one can say that Arvit is different, because it is optional [and therefore no obligations need to be fulfilled].

The Beit Yosef's argument here has a number of steps. He notes the apparently problematic nature of the practice and cites several contemporary authorities who try to stop it. He nonetheless attempts to justify it in the following two ways:

1. Perhaps the Mishnah's statement of קטן...אינו יורד לפני התיבה only applies to Shaḥarit,[127] where Kedushah is said, and where the Amidah is said aloud and the one saying it must be able to fulfill the obligations of others. This resolution rests on the assumption that a minor is not obligated in *tefillah* at the same level as an adult. In this justification, the Mishnah is primarily concerned about this obligation gap in the Amidah (Rashi is quoted to this effect at the end of the passage),[128] and some other concern about Kedushah (הקפידו חכמים), which does **not** have to do with obligation, but seems to be a matter of dignity or gravitas that makes it inappropriate for a minor to say Kedushah for the community. The concerns would then not apply to Arvit, where there is neither Kedushah nor a public Amidah recitation, and the communities' practice makes sense.
2. Perhaps the Mishnah's statement of קטן...אינו יורד לפני התיבה has nothing to do with obligations. In principle, the Ra'avad argues that a minor who knows enough is just as obligated in all the blessings and prayers as any adult, since the common source of their obligations is rabbinic authority. Therefore, the Ra'avad argues that the Mishnah's concern—with respect to leading all services, not just Arvit—is one of congregational dignity. In keeping with this analysis, the Beit Yosef suggests that a community might waive its dignity, which these communities elected to do for Saturday night Arvit.

The Beit Yosef does not seem to side wholly with the Ra'avad's analysis at the end, but a combination of Rashi and the Ra'avad's frames can justify

---

127 The concerns here would apply to Minḥah as well, but the Beit Yosef is simply contrasting Arvit with the most problematic alternative, which is Shaḥarit—where, unlike in Arvit, Kedushah appears in both the blessings of Shema and the Amidah.

128 It is worth noting that in our version of Rashi, he explicitly invokes the obligation gap only as the reason why a minor cannot be פורס על שמע. The Beit Yosef understood this to be the reason for both ואינו פורס על שמע and the following phrase, אין עוברין לפני התיבה. Support for this reading can be found in the Ran on Rif Megillah 15a, who explicitly applies the concern about obligation to both clauses.

the specific practice he is trying to defend.[129] Two points are salient for our conversation. First, in his initial line of defense, the Beit Yosef does **not** use the language of obligation to describe the obstacle to a minor leading Kedushah. Second, the Beit Yosef never imagines that leading Barekhu and Kaddish present any concern grounded in obligation. Indeed, in his quest to justify the practice of a minor leading Arvit, the Beit Yosef is **only** concerned about obligations relating to the Amidah and issues of propriety surrounding having a minor in a leadership position. For him, there is nothing to address with respect to Barekhu and Kaddish, because no individual obligation is being fulfilled. There is no individual obligation in *devarim shebikdushah*; rather, the community performs these rituals as part of public prayer and must do so in the presence of a valid *minyan*.

In the Shulḥan Arukh, R. Karo delivers his verdict:

שולחן ערוך או"ח נג:י
יש ללמוד זכות על מקומות שהקטנים יורדין לפני התיבה להתפלל תפלת ערבית במוצאי שבתות.

Shulḥan Arukh OḤ 53:10
There is room to justify those places where the custom is for minors to lead the congregation in prayer at the end of Shabbat.

The Magen Avraham clarifies what lies behind this ruling when he says,

מגן אברהם או"ח נג:יב
דהא אינו מוציא הרבים ידי חובתן דהא אין מחזירין התפלה רק שאומר קדיש וברכו.

Magen Avraham OḤ 53:12
For the minor does not fulfill the obligations of the congregants, because the Amidah is not recited publicly; he only says Kaddish and Barekhu.[130]

---

129 See R. Ovadiah Yosef in Responsa Yabia Omer IX OḤ #100, 4 who criticizes someone for trying to claim that the Beit Yosef is justifying communities where minors lead Shaḥarit, based on his use of the Ra'avad. R. Ovadiah argues that the Beit Yosef only accepted the Ra'avad as a supplemental justification that could coexist with Rashi and thus would only apply to Arvit, where no public Amidah is recited.

130 Note also the carefully chosen language of the Meiri in Beit ha-Beḥirah Megillah 23b to describe the nature of Kaddish and Kedushah: בעין חובה. The Meiri, in that passage,

The ramifications of this view for leadership of *devarim shebikdushah* are clear: Questions of obligation are irrelevant, since the leader does not fulfill any obligations for others when leading them in rituals like Kaddish and Barekhu. The only potential concerns are those that relate to issues of dignity and seriousness. Following this approach would essentially return us to the discussion of *kevod tzibbur* that we explored above in the context of Torah reading. Determining whether a person could lead *devarim shebikdushah* would be no different from analyzing their effect on communal honor as a Torah reader, and the practical conclusions would be the same.

However, not all authorities seem to have thought about *devarim shebikdushah* in this way. Specifically, some voices have a more nuanced approach to the question of individual obligation and *devarim shebikdushah*. Consider the following passage from the Ramban, who argues that *devarim shebikdushah* are **communal** obligations, rather than individual ones:[131]

מלחמות ה׳ על הרי״ף מגילה ג.
השנויים במשנתינו כולם חובות הצבור הן ואינן אלא במחויבים בדבר,
אבל מגילה כשם שהצבור חייב כך כל יחיד ויחיד חייב.

Milḥamot Hashem on Rif Megillah 3a
Those things mentioned in our Mishnah [Megillah 4:3] are all communal obligations, and they apply only to groups obligated in them,[132] but *megillah*, just as the community is obligated, so too each and every individual is obligated.

---

is invested in giving some obligatory status to *devarim shebikdushah* such that they will be immune from restrictions surrounding *tefillat nedavah*. Nonetheless, he does not or will not make the case that a *bona fide* obligation is at stake when reciting them, suggesting his agreement with the approach that individualized obligation is not in play here.

131 The Ran on the Rif here cites the view of Ramban approvingly as well.

132 This follows the reading of the Ran, who interprets the phrase מחוייבים בדבר to mean a group of people who have not yet performed the ritual in question, such as Kaddish or Kedushah.

The Ramban here is responding to a claim made by R. Zeraḥiah ha-Levi, who suggested that the exclusion of the reading of the *megillah* from Mishnah Megillah 4:3 proved that it did not require a *minyan*. Ramban disagrees, arguing that the reason that act is left out of this list is not because it does not require a *minyan*, but because of the nature of its obligation. Acts such as Torah reading and the leading of communal prayer (which includes saying the *devarim shebikdushah*, i.e., Barekhu, Kaddish, and Kedushah) are not obligatory on individuals—as opposed to the reading of the *megillah*, which, even though it should be read with a *minyan*, remains obligatory on each individual. This seems to accord well with the approach we saw in the Beit Yosef, which leaves no room for individual obligation in *devarim shebikdushah*.

But Ramban also uses the phrase מחוייבים בדבר, which suggests that those gathered **do** have some sort of obligation in *devarim shebikdushah*. The phrase clearly cannot refer to individuals being obligated in this particular act from the moment they wake up in the morning, since Ramban's entire point in this passage is to deny that such an individual obligation exists with respect to the rituals being discussed here in the Mishnah.[133] And Ramban may here mean nothing more than an obligated **community**, in the sense of a *minyan* of people who have "not yet heard" these things said, who have not yet gone through the paces of these rituals. Perhaps the language of "obligated" does not indicate an obligation that must be checked off, but rather a sense that the person has not yet completed the action in question.[134]

---

133 Ramban here seems to be paraphrasing an earlier formulation of this idea expressed by R. Meshullam b. Moshe in Sefer ha-Hashlamah on Megillah 5a in the following clear language:

> דכל הני דקתני במתניתין אין פורסין על שמע ליכא חיובא כלל בציר מעשרה אבל במגילה איכא ביחיד.
>
> For all of these that are taught in our Mishnah that one should not *porsin al Shema* are not obligations at all [if there are] fewer than ten, but regarding the *megillah* there is [an obligation even] in [the case of] an individual.

134 In a similar fashion, R. Ḥayyim Yosef David Azulai and the Arokh ha-Shulḥan both interpret Massekhet Soferim's statement that women are חייבות בקריאת ספר as merely indicating that it is appropriate for them to hear the reading (Kisei ha-Raḥamim on Soferim 18:4; Arokh ha-Shulḥan Yoreh Deah 282:11). R. Shlomo Riskin cites these sources in his article, Riskin and Shapiro, "Aliyot

Also possible, however, is that we are dealing with the sort of obligation that devolves upon the individual **only when in an appropriate group.**[135] Consider the paradigm of *zimmun*. No individual is obligated to search out a group of three with whom to eat a meal.[136] But once a group of three has formed, each individual possesses an obligation to participate in the communal invitation and blessing.[137] Ramban may be imagining that *devarim shebikdushah* work the same way: There is no individual obligation to participate in them—unlike the reading of the *megillah*, for example—but once in a group of ten that has not yet performed these rituals, the individuals in the group all become obligated.

Whatever Ramban's plain meaning, there is clearly a strand running through halakhic literature that speaks about some sort of obligation in *devarim shebikdushah*.[138] Here are a few examples:

רש"י מגילה כד.
הוא עובר לפני התיבה – **להוציא את הצבור** בקדושה שבתפלה.

Rashi Megillah 24a
"[The one who recites the Haftarah should also be the one] who recites the public Amidah"—**in order to fulfill the obligations of the community** in Kedushah in the Amidah.

רש"י ברכות מז:
מצוה דרבים – **להוציא רבים ידי חובתם בקדושה.**

---

for Women," to claim that women lack an individual obligation in Torah reading. Nonetheless, he problematically and inconsistently insists that Ramban's similar language here **does** signal an individual obligation.

135 We are grateful to R. Yossi Slotnik for suggesting this line of analysis.

136 Indeed, in the case of the last meal before Tisha B'Av, Shulḥan Arukh OḤ 552:8 counsels against sitting in a group of three so as to avoid the creation of this *zimmun* obligation.

137 Mishnah Berakhot 7:1.

138 This strand might plausibly have drawn support from Bavli Berakhot 21b, where the Talmud entertains (and rejects) a view that even individuals might say Kedushah, and cites (and rejects) a view that explicitly allows for interrupting the Amidah in order to respond to Kaddish. While none of this requires positing an individual obligation, it certainly underscores the power of these rituals and makes their later interpretation as obligations even more intelligible.

Rashi Berakhot 47b
"A *mitzvah* for multiple people/a community"—**to fulfill the obligations of multiple people/a community in Kedushah.**

תוספות מגילה כד.
אבל אינו פורס על שמע – ואפילו לרבי יהודה דמכשיר ליה במגילה לעיל (דף יט:) הכא מודה **שלא יוציא אחרים ידי חובתן בדבר שבקדושה.**

Tosafot Megillah 24a
"[A minor] may not be *pores al Shema*"[139]—Even R. Yehudah, who validates a minor for the reading of the *megillah*, would concede here that **he should not discharge the obligations of others in a *davar shebikdushah*.**

חידושי הרשב"א מגילה כד.
אבל אין פורס על שמע. דכיון דאיכא דבר שבקדושה אינו בדין **שיוציא בו את הרבים ידי חובתן.**

Rashba Megillah 24a
"[A minor] may not *pores al Shema*"—Given that there is a *davar shebikdushah*, it is not right for him **to fulfill the obligations of others.**

The plain sense of these sources is not entirely clear. In particular, Rashi here uses the language of obligation to speak about Kedushah, whereas the

139 Above, we translated this term as "responsively reading the Shema," in keeping with what seems like the best interpretation of rabbinic sources. For Rashi and the Tosafot, however, this term already referred to something different. When latecomers arrived at the synagogue toward the end of the service, one person would get up and say Kaddish, Barekhu, and the first blessing prior to the Shema (which included its own form of Kedushah). See Rashi Megillah 23b s.v. *ein porsin*. Rashi Megillah 24a s.v. *katan* states that a minor cannot be *pores al Shema* because he is exempt and cannot fulfill the obligations of the assembled congregants. This almost certainly refers to his lack of obligation in Shema, as opposed to obligations in Kaddish and Barekhu; see Rashi s.v. *poḥeaḥ* where Rashi justifies a person in tattered clothing as *pores al Shema* because he is מחויב בברכה, indicating that the concern regarding obligation is focused on the blessing before Shema, not on Kaddish or Barekhu.

citation of him in Maḥzor Vitry was adamant that no such obligation exists. One might resolve this apparent contradiction by saying that Rashi here is using להוציא imprecisely, as we suggested with Ramban above. One might make the same claim for the Tosafot and the Rashba as well.[140] However

---

140 The Tosafot's language might not be referring to *devarim shebikdushah* as a class of things obligatory for individuals **on account of their being** *devarim shebikdushah*. Rather, it might merely be using the phrase to refer to some of the specific items in this list—i.e., the Shema and the Amidah—which present a problem for the minor because he is not obligated **in those specific practices**. Indeed, note the language of the Meiri in Beit ha-Beḥirah Megillah 24a, which might even be a paraphrase of the Tosafot: "ואם הוא קטן ואינו ראוי להוציא את הרבים בפריסת שמע ותפלה — And if he is a minor and not fit to discharge the public['s obligation] for *porsin et Shema* and Amidah." No mention is made of a separate problem regarding fulfilling obligations in *devarim shebikdushah* on account of them having that status. For a reading of the Tosafot in this way, see Responsa Mishpetei Uzziel III OḤ #14. The Rashba's language here and in the following part of the passage sounds as if it is about the **impropriety** of allowing a minor to fulfill the obligations of others in **something else** (like the blessings of Shema) when a *davar shebikdushah* is involved (seemingly the Kedushah embedded within the first blessing of the Shema). This would then be opposed to a statement that it is **impossible** for a minor to fulfill another's obligation in a *davar shebikdushah*. Note also that R. Yosef Karo, despite his clear stance above that there are no issues of obligation with regard to Barekhu, does not hesitate to use the language of להוציא the context of Barekhu in Shulḥan Arukh OḤ 236:2. This might also be evidence for the notion that the language of להוציא could be read as "giving others the opportunity to respond" such that they can, **through their response**, fulfill the *mitzvah* of sanctifying God's name publicly. See our analysis of a passage from Shibbolei ha-Leket below, at n. 142. Another interesting text comes from R. Eliezer b. Natan in Ra'avan #73:

שו"ת ראב"ן עג

שאלני אחי ר' חזקיה: הקורא בתורה למה אומר לציבור ברכו את ה' המבורך, יברך ברכת התורה ודיו. והשבתי לו לפי שעזרא תיקן לישראל שיהו קורין בתורה בב' וה' ובשבת והקורא בתורה מוציא את הציבור ידי חובתן מקריאה, לפיכך הרי הוא אומר לציבור אתם צריכין לברך ולקרות כמוני תסכימו לקריאתי ולברכתי ותברכו עמי והם עונין ומברכין. וכן ש"ץ אומר ביוצר ומעריב, **לפי שהוא מוציא את הציבור ידי חובתן ואומר להם תסכימו לקריאתי ולברכתי ותברכוהו עמי והם עונין ומברכין ויוצאין ידי חובתן.**

Responsa Ra'avan #73

The brother of R. Ḥizkiyah asked me: The one who reads the Torah, why does he say for the community, "*barekhu et Adonai ha-mevorakh*"? He should bless the Birkat ha-Torah and it should be enough! And I responded to him: Because Ezra decreed for Israel that they should read the Torah on Mondays, Thursdays, and Shabbat, and the one who reads the Torah discharges the community of their obligations to read. Therefore, he says to the community, "You need to bless and read like me. Agree to my reading and to my blessing and bless with

one deals with the precise interpretation here, we see that minimally the **language** of obligation has begun to surface for *devarim shebikdushah* and therefore the concept, even if not fully developed here, would not be far behind.[141] Indeed, one can even see how a strong desire to say *devarim shebikdushah* might have morphed—perhaps first anthropologically and later halakhically—into a more formal sense of individual obligation.

One can see this sort of thinking at work in later reinterpretations of some of the sources we looked at above. For instance, we cited above the Mordekhai's position that one may leave a *minyan* as long as ten are left behind, which seemingly indicates indifference to whether a given individual participates in *devarim shebikdushah*. This is glossed by R. Ya'akov Lorberbaum (Derekh ha-Ḥayyim, Laws of Kaddish #9):

> me," and they answer and bless. And so too the *sha"tz* says in Yotzer Or and in Maariv Aravim, **since he discharges the community of their obligation and says to them, "Agree to my reading and to my blessing and bless with me," and they answer and bless and discharge their obligation.**

The Ra'avan here discusses the function of Barekhu and *zimmun* as setting up the conditions for one person to fulfill the obligations of others in a ritual that is no more the leader's responsibility than it is the congregants' responsibility. In Torah reading, the designated reader is essentially an emissary for all members of the community and thus they must participate in part—by answering to Barekhu—in order to have their obligation fulfilled in the Torah reading itself. (This accords with the views we saw above that posit some kind of individual obligation in Torah reading.) The same is true, writes the Ra'avan, for the Barekhu that introduces the blessings of Shema, where the leader—in a configuration most services no longer have today—is fulfilling the obligations of the group in those blessings. But note that the obligation spoken of here is not Barekhu itself, but rather some other obligation that follows. The call-and-response quality of the *devarim shebikdushah* themselves is not something described as being vicariously fulfilled. Rather, it requires participation in order to be realized. General caution is thus warranted in interpreting a phrase such as להוציא את הרבים בקדושה (or some similar variant). Such phrasing **might** refer to an individual obligation to hear *devarim shebikdushah*, it might refer to an obligation that devolves upon the individual once a group has been formed, or it might simply be language capturing the idea that the leader enables the community to fulfill its **corporate** obligation in *devarim shebikdushah*.

141 Massekhet Soferim 10:6 uses the language of individual obligation as well in the context of Kaddish and Barekhu (יצא ידי חובתו). We do not cite this text again here, however, since that passage seems to be a later addition to Soferim based on the very traditions we see emerging here in Rashi and the Tosafot. See Reed Blank, "French Medieval Practice."

"יכולין הנשארים לצאת אם כבר שמעו קדושה וברכו והקדישין עד אחר עלינו — The extras [above the quorum of ten] may leave if they have already heard Kedushah, Barekhu, and the Kaddishes up until Aleinu."[142] This eviscerates much of the force of the Mordekhai's ruling, but gives a clear sense of the culmination of a discourse that thinks about *devarim shebikdushah* as liturgical pieces that are obligatory on the individual. This school of thought provides a contrast to the model of R. Yosef Karo that we saw above, which sees an individual obligation to participate in *devarim shebikdushah.*

2. *The* Sha"tz *as Agent for Kedushah, Kaddish, and Barekhu?*

Even according to this view, however, we must ask how the individual obligation is actually fulfilled. For instance, when a person hears a *berakhah* made by someone else, the individual listener has an individual obligation to respond *"amen,"* but in no sense is the one who makes the *berakhah* fulfilling the listener's obligation to answer *"amen"* just by saying the blessing. The individual obligation is fulfilled by answering *"amen,"* not vicariously by the person who said the blessing, nor by the *amen* of another congregant. Similarly, even if there is an individual obligation to sanctify God's name through *devarim shebikdushah,* this might well be accomplished by the individual's recitation of various phrases—such as ברוך ה׳ המבורך לעולם ועד or קדוש קדוש קדוש or יהא שמיה רבא מברך—and not about having the *sha"tz* perform these rituals on their behalf.

Indeed, consider the following passage from R. Tzidkiyah b. Avraham ha-Rofei:

> **שבלי הלקט ענין תפילה סימן כ**
> וכן מצאתי לרבינו ישעיה זצ"ל אע"ג דאמרינן שומע כעונה הני מילי בברכות אבל בקדוש ומודים ואמן יהא שמיה רבא שהן קלוסין חשובין לפני הקב"ה אינו יוצא ידי חובתו בשמיעה עד שמוציא בפיו עם הצבור.

142 The Kaddishes after Aleinu were generally treated as less serious and "optional."

> **Shibbolei ha-Leket Tefillah #20**
> And so too I found in the name of R. Yeshayah [di-Trani]: Even though we normally say that one who listens [to the *berakhah* made by another] is considered as if they said it themselves, that only applies to *berakhot*. But with regard to Kedushah... and Kaddish, which are lofty expressions of praise for God, one does not fulfill one's obligation just by listening; rather, one must actively voice the words along with the community.

This source uses the language of individual obligation to talk about Kedushah and Kaddish, but it denies that the leader can vicariously fulfill this obligation for anyone else. Indeed, this is the most straightforward way to understand the essence of the rituals of Kedushah, Kaddish, and Barekhu. The function of the leader of these rituals is to prompt the community to sanctify God publicly together. The leader either calls on the community to bless God (in the case of Barekhu: ברכו את ה' המבורך) or to sanctify God (in the case of Kedushah and Kaddish: נקדש/נקדישך/יתגדל ויתקדש). The truly significant work of blessing and sanctification happens through the communal response (ברוך ה' המבורך/קדוש קדוש קדוש/יהא שמיה רבא מברך), which is **not** delegated to the leader. Even if one chooses to see part of the obligation to sanctify God's name as playing out in an individual obligation in *devarim shebikdushah*, that obligation might well be about **participation** in those rituals, rather than simply being present for them while another leads, which is not the way they are structured. Among later authorities, this point was emphasized by R. Yeḥiel Mikhel Epstein. He engages with a ruling of the Rema that if a *sha"tz* deliberately intends **not** to fulfill the obligations of someone in the community whom he hates, then no one's obligations are fulfilled. R. Epstein claims this law no longer applies in a community where everyone knows how to pray on their own, because the *sha"tz* then no longer functions as an agent of individuals in the community.[143] He then addresses the objection that the *sha"tz* would still be necessary as an agent for *devarim shebikdushah* such as Kedushah, Kaddish, and Barekhu:

---

143 This claim originates with the Magen Avraham, cited above, n. 4.

ערוך השלחן או״ח תקפא:ה
ואי משום קדיש וקדושה וברכו אין זה יציאת חובה דכל עשרה מישראל עונין דבר שבקדושה ומי שיש בשעת מעשה עונה עמהם וכן בעניית אמן.

Arokh ha-Shulḥan OḤ 581:5
And if [you are concerned] on account of Kaddish, Kedushah, and Barekhu, there is no fulfillment of obligation involved. Any group of ten Jews answers to a *davar shebikdushah*. Whoever is there answers with them. And so it is with answering "*amen*."

This same line of thinking is advanced by R. Uzziel, who also notes its practical ramifications for our question. He notes that the very structure of Kedushah is such that questions of obligation play no role in determining who is fit to lead this *davar shebikdushah*. Accordingly, controlling for issues of *kevod tzibbur*, in principle a minor or woman can lead Kedushah, and serve as *sha"tz* in general:

שו״ת משפטי עוזיאל חלק ג, מילואים ב
במקום שהשומעים אומרים מלה במלה אחרי המברך והקורא אינו אלא מקריא לפניהם הדברים, הרי שהם יוצאים ידי חובתן בברכת עצמם והקורא אינו אלא מסדר הדברים פותח וחותם כל ברכה. **וכן בקדושת השם פותח דברי קדושה והקהל עונים אחריו שפיר יכול המקריא להיות קטן או אשה.**

Responsa Mishpetei Uzziel III, Miluim 2
In a place where the listeners say each word after the one making the blessings and the reader is only reading the words before them, they fulfill their obligations with their own blessings and the reader only sets the pace by reciting the beginning and end of each blessing. **So is it with the Kedushah: they open the words of Kedushah and the community answers after them—so the reader could properly be a minor or a woman.**[144]

---

144 The logic he employs here applies equally to Kaddish and Barekhu, which have congregational responses that are structured similarly.

In a later section of this responsum, R. Uzziel objects to following through on this suggestion in practice, because he feels that letting a minor (and presumably a woman) lead would violate the Baḥ's notion of *kevod tzibbur* and cannot be addressed through a simple communal waiver of that concern. That would once again return our conversation to the playing field of *kevod tzibbur* discussed in the context of Torah reading. According to the approach represented by R. Yeshayah di-Trani and R. Uzziel, the individual obligation in *devarim shebikdushah* is fulfilled by each and every congregant, such that there is no need to ascertain that the leader is equally obligated. The only potentially relevant concerns are those related to congregational dignity and propriety.

Nonetheless, there are other voices that clearly advance the idea that individuals are obligated in *devarim shebikdushah* and that see a critical role for the *sha"tz* in fulfilling this obligation. R. Natan b. Yehudah writes that any Kaddish said by minors must not be an "obligatory" one, since otherwise, these children, not being "obligated," would not be able to fulfill the obligations of other individuals, based on the rule discussed above in Mishnah Rosh Hashanah 3:8:

> **ספר המחכים ד"ה הקורא**
> נר[אה] שכל אותם קדישים שאומרים קטנים לא נתקנו אלא לחנכן במצות דאי הוו חובה האיך מוציאין את הקהל, שכל שאינו מחוייב בדבר אינו מוציא אחר ידי חובתו.
>
> **Sefer ha-Maḥkim s.v. *ha-korei***
> It seems that all the Kaddishes that minors say were only instituted in order to educate them in *mitzvot*. If they were obligatory, how could they fulfill the obligations of the community? Anyone who is not obligated in something cannot fulfill another person's obligation.

But these claims are rare in the Rishonim,[145] and the topic receives more attention from the Aḥaronim. For example, in the passage below, R. Shneur Zalman of Liady expands on the discussion of a minor leading

---

145 Agur #334, quoting the Maharil, is another example:

> נשאל גדול הדור מוהר"ר יעקב מולן. איך המנהג בקדיש יתום...ולמה הקטנים אומרים זה הקדיש הואיל והוא דבר שבקדושה. והשיב הרב...ונקרא זה הקדיש קדיש יתום בשביל

Arvit on Saturday night. The Shulḥan Arukh had justified this practice and the Magen Avraham had clarified that this justification was bound up with a theory of obligation being irrelevant for Kaddish and Barekhu. The Rema, on Shulḥan Arukh OḤ 55:10, says that places that do not already have such a practice on Saturday nights should not take the initiative to institute it. The following text, after quoting the Shulḥan Arukh with the Magen Avraham's clarification, spells out one possible interpretation of this hesitation to fully embrace the practice:

שולחן ערוך הרב או״ח נג:יג
יש ללמד זכות על מקומות שנוהגין שהקטנים יורדים לפני התיבה להתפלל ערבית במוצאי שבתות לפי שאין מוציאין את הרבים ידי חובתן שהרי אינן מחזירין את התפלה רק שאומרים ברכו וקדיש ובמקומות שלא נהגו כן אין לקטן לעבור לפני התיבה אפילו בתפלת ערבית (משום ברכו שבה...ואין ברכו של תפלת שחרית וערבית דומה לברכו של קריאת התורה שקטן יכול לאמרה לפי שאינה חובה כל כך...אבל אלו הן חובה על כל צבור לשמען שחרית וערבית) וקטן שאינו חייב אינו מוציאם ידי חובתן.

שהקטנים שאינם יכולים להתפלל בצבור יכולים לומר קדיש זה כי נתקן בשביל המתים ולכן הקטנים יכולין לאומרו כי איננו חובה כשאר הקדישות של תפלה.

The great one of the generation, the Maharil, was asked: What about the custom of Mourner's Kaddish...and why do minors say this Kaddish since it is a *davar shebikdushah*? And the rabbi answered:...This Kaddish is called "Mourner's Kaddish" because minors, who are unable to pray in the community, are able to say this Kaddish, because it was established for those who are deceased. And so minors are able to say it, because it is not an obligation like the other Kaddishes of *tefillah*.

One source sometimes inaccurately cited as evidence of an obligation in *devarim shebikdushah* is that of the Meiri on Berakhot 45a. In discussing the difference between women's participation in *zimmun* and their participation in the reading of *megillah* and Torah, the Meiri discusses a gender gap between men and women regarding obligation. However, he is discussing there the difference between men and women with regard to obligation in *zimmun* (cf. Rashi on Berakhot 45b s.v. *de-afilu*), **not** with regard to any "obligation" in *devarim shebikdushah*. See Appendix D on *zimmun* for our full analysis of the passage in Sefer ha-Mikhtam on which this Meiri is based.

Shulḥan Arukh ha-Rav OḤ 53:13

There is room to justify those places where the custom is for minors to lead Arvit at the end of Shabbat, because they do not fulfill the obligations of others, seeing as they do not repeat the Amidah and merely say Barekhu and Kaddish. But in places that do not already have this practice, a minor should never lead, not even Arvit (because of Barekhu…and the Barekhu of Shaḥarit and Arvit is different in this regard from the Barekhu of Torah reading, which a minor may say, for the latter is not really an obligation, whereas the entire community is obligated to hear the former), and a minor, not being obligated, cannot fulfill their obligations.[146]

The last part of this passage clearly approaches *devarim shebikdushah* as individual obligations that require an obligated individual to lead them on behalf of congregants. As we have noted throughout this section, this approach is hardly universal among later authorities. R. Ovadiah Yosef surveys the views of Aḥaronim who see an individual obligation in *devarim shebikdushah* but rejects them.[147] Nonetheless, for those following this line of reasoning, we would then need to ask: Do men and women have an obligation gap when it comes to *devarim shebikdushah*?

---

146 Note that the Rema himself gives no reason for his desire to limit the practice, which in fact just seems to flow from R. Yosef Karo's own ambivalence, despite the fact that the latter ends up justifying it. The Rema might simply be filling in what he felt was implicit in the Beit Yosef, or he might prefer a less convoluted reading of the Mishnah's seemingly comprehensive ban on allowing minors to lead, or he might be toeing the line on issues related to *kevod tzibbur*, cited in the Beit Yosef as the Ra'avad's reason why a minor cannot lead any of the *tefillot*. Shulḥan Arukh ha-Rav is the first to suggest that one would oppose the practice because of issues related to obligations grounded in Kaddish and Barekhu, though this is a plausible continuation of the discussion we saw in Sefer ha-Mikhtam and, possibly, Massekhet Soferim, cited at n. 51 above. Note, however, that the distinction between different kinds of Barekhu posited here is explicitly rejected by the Or le-Tziyyon II 5:14, who says that a minor may say Barekhu following the Mourner's Kaddish based on the fact that he is already permitted to do so in the context of Torah reading.

147 Responsa Yabia Omer VIII OḤ 14:3–4.

3. *Are Kedushah, Kaddish, and Barekhu Gendered?*

We have already seen several views that are concerned that minors do not have the appropriate level of obligation to fulfill the obligations of others (such as they are) in *devarim shebikdushah*. Does this concern related to age map onto gender as well? The simple answer is that there is no direct evidence suggesting that it does, even as there is no concrete record of a woman serving as a *sha"tz* in any of the classical sources either. To the extent that Kedushah, Kaddish, and Barekhu do devolve as individual obligations, they would seem to be located under the rubric of the controlling *mitzvah* of *kiddush hashem*, the sanctification of God's name in public. Indeed, the verse "ונקדשתי בתוך בני ישראל — I shall be sanctified in the midst of the Jewish people" (Vayikra 22:32) is the scriptural anchor for these various parts of the liturgy. Rabbinic sources assume women are obligated to sanctify God's name in public in the same way that men are.[148] Minors might be unfit agents for this *mitzvah* because they are **generally** unfit as agents, because **they are minors**. There is no evidence that the blanket concern regarding obligation and maturity would translate to gender.[149]

In fact, R. Yair Ḥayyim Bacharach makes explicit that there is nothing gendered about Kaddish, arguing that the only obstacle to women saying it is custom. Women in theory can say Kaddish, he says, since there is universal agreement that they are obligated in martyrdom (called *kiddush hashem*), which falls under the same controlling idea of sanctifying God's name (a literal translation of *kiddush hashem*) as do *devarim shebikdushah* and is attached to the same set of verses:

> **שו"ת חות יאיר סימן רכב**
> שאלה דבר זר נעשה באמשטרדם ומפורסם שם. שאחד נעדר בלי בן וצוה לפני פטירתו שילמדו עשרה כל יום תוך י"ב חודש בביתו בשכרם ואחר הלימוד תאמר הבת קדיש...ולא מיחו בידה חכמי

148 More to the point: There is no reason one would ever have assumed that this sort of *mitzvah* was gendered. Talmud Bavli Sanhedrin 74b assumes that Esther was obligated in this *mitzvah*.

149 Put simply, no one prior to contemporary opponents of egalitarian *minyanim* suggests that women are "exempt" from Kedushah, Kaddish, and Barekhu.

הקהילה והפרנסים. ואף כי אין ראיה לסתור הדבר כי גם אשה מצוות על קידוש השם גם יש מנין זכרים מקרי בני ישראל...מ"מ יש לחוש שע"י כך יחלשו כח המנהגים של בני ישראל שגם כן תורה הם ויהיה כל אחד בונה במה לעצמו ע"פ סברתו...ולכן בנדון זה שיש אסיפה ופרסום יש למחות.

Responsa Ḥavvot Yair #222

Question: A strange thing happened in Amsterdam and was well publicized there. A man died without a son and he ordered before his death that ten men learn every day in his house for twelve months and after their learning his daughter should say Kaddish…and the sages and leaders of the community did not object. And even though there is no evidence to contradict them in this matter, for women are also commanded to sanctify the Name and there is also a quorum of males who are called *benei yisrael*…nonetheless, we should worry that by such an act Jewish customs will be weakened…and everyone will build an altar of their own according to their own theories…Therefore in this case, where the act is public we should protest.

The logic here is clear: On the axis of obligation, there is no reason why gender should be a factor in determining who says Kaddish. Other factors, such as communal stability and religious propriety, loomed large in the Ḥavvot Yair's time, as they do today. But these factors should not be confused with matters of obligation and exemption.[150] This logic would

150 Some try to deflect the relevance of the Ḥavvot Yair here by suggesting that his entire discussion is about a "non-obligatory" Kaddish being said in a private home. (See our citation of Sefer ha-Maḥkim above, at n. 145, for one example of this distinction. Some later *poskim* make this distinction as well; see Responsa Beit Yehudah #22 for one example.) They read the Ḥavvot Yair as if there is an introductory passage saying, "Given that this is not one of the obligatory Kaddishes said in the synagogue and no issues of obligation are at stake, women's obligation in *kiddush hashem* is sufficient to establish the theoretical legitimacy for them to say Kaddish." Suffice it to say that this is not what the Ḥavvot Yair says. In fact, it would have been much simpler for him to have made this claim, but he did not, recognizing that there is no real basis for positing a gendered obligation gap with respect to Kaddish. Indeed, the concern that there is no real gendered difference with regard to Kaddish has led some later authorities to prevent women from even saying the Mourner's Kaddish,

seem to extend to all other *devarim shebikdushah*—such as Barekhu—which are also just manifestations of the same gender-blind command to sanctify the Divine Name in public.

The responsum of R. Uzziel cited earlier clarifies the non-gendered nature of Kedushah. Responding to a question about minors in a school

---

for fear that once this door is opened, there will be no real grounds for claiming that women cannot recite the other Kaddishes in the service as well. If one assumes that such an egalitarian approach to Kaddish is unwise and dangerous on the grounds of *kevod tzibbur* and general religious destabilization, then this is a reasonable fear. The most poignant and passionate articulation of this fear can be found in R. Ya'akov Emden's Mor u-Ketziah #55:

> ואין צריך לומר שאין הבת הקטנה מוציאה את הרבים בקדיש ואע״פ שאין צריך לצירופה מכל מקום פשיטא דאפילו גדולה לדברי הכל אינה מוציאה את הרבים ידי חובתן אף לדברי האומר שמצטרפת (ולא דמי לקטן מטעמים דאמרן) וזה אין צריך לפנים. והרי גדולה מזו אמרו אפילו בברכת הזמון דחייבת בה התנו בפירוש ובלבד שלא יזמנו בשם...על אחת כמה וכמה שלא יעלה על הדעת שתעמוד בת קטנה...בצבור להוציאן בדבר שבקדושה שאין למעלה ממנו מה שאפילו גדולה אינה רשאה לעשות בשום אופן ישתקע הדבר ומי שחידש מנהגים כאלו...עתיד ליתן את הדין ואם לא תוגדר פרצה זו תמה אני אם לא תקרב אשה גדולה לעבור לפני התיבה גם להיות שליח צבור תבקש בכח גדול שהרי ודאי יפה כחה מקטנה (שהורע כחה בקריאת התורה ובזמון).
>
> Obviously, a daughter who is a minor cannot fulfill the obligations of the community in Kaddish, even if she is not going to be counted toward the *minyan*. But it is also true that even if the daughter had reached the age of majority, everyone would agree that she cannot fulfill the obligations of the community, even according to the view [R. Simḥah] that she [in principle] counts toward the *minyan* (a woman being unlike a minor for the reasons we stated above [and thus more eligible to count in a *minyan*]) and this requires no further thought. Even in the case of Birkat ha-Mazon, in which women are obligated, they explicitly specify that women may not say the Name in *zimmun*...all the more so one cannot entertain the idea that a minor girl would get up in public to fulfill the community's obligation in something as lofty as a *davar shebikdushah*—indeed, even with a minor boy, who will eventually come to full obligation in *mitzvot* and is more connected [to the full obligation], nonetheless we have serious doubts [as we see from the discussion in the Ra'avad and the Rashba and the Beit Yosef]—we would not even allow an adult woman to do this under any circumstances. Perish the thought and anyone who innovates practices like these...will face a reckoning in the future. And if this breach is not repaired [and minor daughters are allowed to continue to say Kaddish for their deceased fathers in the presence of a *minyan* of men], I would be shocked if an adult woman will not lead the public Amidah and demand to serve as a *sha"tz*, given that she has even more status than a minor (whose status is diminished [by lack of obligation] in Torah reading and *zimmun*).

See also Responsa Yaḥel Yisrael #84.

leading a *minyan* that includes ten adults, R. Uzziel makes the point that the text of Kedushah is simply an expansion of the third *berakhah* of the Amidah, known as Kedushat Hashem. Given that a woman is obligated in this *berakhah*, as she is in all other *berakhot* of the Amidah, how could it be that she is unable to fulfill the expanded version of this *berakhah* recited in public?

R. Uzziel argues that minors cannot so obviously fulfill the obligations of adult males in Kedushah (or any other part of the Amidah), but implies that women, since they are fully obligated in *tefillah*, may:

שו״ת משפטי עוזיאל חלק ג, מילואים ב
ואל תשיבני מדתנן: נשים ועבדים וקטנים פטורין מק״ש ומן התפילין וחייבים בתפלה ומזוזה...הא למדת שקטנים חייבים בתפלה ובכלל תפלה הוא גם קדושת ה׳, וכיון שכך מוציאים את הרבים ידי חובתם.

ואין זו תשובה. שהרי פירש רש״י: דתפלה רחמי ומדרבנן היא, ותקנוה אף לנשים ולחנוך קטנים. דוק ותשכח דחובת קטנים אינה אלא ממצות חנוך ואינה כחובת הנשים שחייבות כאנשים מתקנת רבנן.

Responsa Mishpetei Uzziel III, Miluim 2
And do not respond to me from that which is taught in a *mishnah*: "Women, slaves, and minors are exempt from the reciting of Shema and from *tefillin*, but are obligated in the Amidah and *mezuzah*"—[and say based on this text:] You have learned that minors are obligated in the Amidah and included in the Amidah is Kedushah. And therefore, they may fulfill the obligations of others.

For that is not a good response. After all, Rashi explained: "Prayer is a request for mercy, and it is rabbinic, and they declared it also for women and for the education of minors." You see from here that the obligation of minors is only a derivative of the general obligation in education, and it is not like the obligation of women, who are obligated like men according to the decree of the Rabbis.

Though R. Uzziel in this passage rejects this proof for minors, he does not reject the assumption on which it is based, namely, that the Kedushah is subsumed as part of the general obligation of prayer.[151] Given that the obligation in the Amidah is gender-blind, so would be any obligation in the Kedushah that is simply an elaboration on its third blessing. The sources we have seen provide solid grounding for egalitarian practice in this area, **even if** we assume that the leader is vicariously fulfilling the individual obligations of the assembled congregants.

Again, there is no strong textual or conceptual background to any claim that tries to make *devarim shebikdushah* gendered. Is there any way to ground an insistence on non-egalitarian practice in this area in anything other than the concerns of dignity, propriety, and religious stability that we have affirmed as relevant throughout?

We suppose it would be possible to make one of the following three claims:

1. In the Ran's model of Torah reading, we explored one reading of his position that might claim that only members of the fully obligated class (free adult men) should anchor the community's responsibility of Torah reading.[152] In the case of Torah reading, the Ran saw the possibility of including women and children among the readers as dependent on their adjunct role in the proceedings. In the case of *devarim shebikdushah,* one could argue that each ritual item stands on its own, unlike the case of a subdivided, single Torah reading. One could then claim that having a female leader for any *davar shebikdushah* would put the community in the position of

151 A similar idea seems to lie behind the view of Arokh ha-Shulḥan OḤ 69:14, cited in Yabia Omer 8:14 discussed above. The Arokh ha-Shulḥan argues that, while one may not read Torah unless there are ten individuals who have not yet heard it read, one may still say Barekhu and Kedushah so long as there are six present who have not yet participated in those rituals, because the latter are ענייני תפילה שכל יחיד חייב בזה ("issues related to prayer in which individuals have a distinct obligation")—presumably resulting from their obligations in prayer more generally. R. Ovadiah contrasts the view of the Arokh ha-Shulḥan with that of Ramban, showing that the latter clearly rejects the former's distinction between Torah reading on the one hand and Barekhu and Kedushah on the other. To the extent that Kedushah makes a claim on the individual, it is only because of its connection to prayer more generally; therefore, just as in the case of *tefillah,* there is nothing essentially gendered about Kedushah *per se.*

152 Note that the reading of the Ran that sees the focus on the gender obligation gap in Torah study would not be relevant here, as women are obligated in *kiddush hashem.*

being represented by an adjunct member in an unacceptable way.[153] Gender equality would only follow upon making a broader claim of gender equality in *mitzvah* obligation in the contemporary world.[154]

2. Perhaps, like *zimmun*, the obligation in *devarim shebikdushah* indeed devolves upon individuals once they form a group. But perhaps this obligation only devolves upon those who are constitutive of the group in the first place. As such, if one assumes that women and minors do not count toward the *minyan*, perhaps this obligation never devolves upon them. If one couples this assumption with the idea that the *sha"tz* then vicariously fulfills this obligation for the congregants—as opposed to prompting them to do it for themselves—one could construct a system whereby obligation plays some sort of role in barring women from leading *devarim shebikdushah*. Gender equality in this regard would then depend on the question of gender equality in the formation of a *minyan*.[155]

---

153 One could imagine an approach that would make a more modest claim and allow women to lead a minority (or at least not all) of the *devarim shebikdushah* in any given service, parallel to the distribution the Ran allows in Torah reading.

154 In fact, as we noted above, n. 74, Tosafot ha-Rosh Sukkah 38a s.v. *be-emet* argues that even when women share an equal obligation with men in a specific ritual, the fact that they are not maximally obligated in general makes them unfit, outside of the intimate circle of family, to serve as public communal emissaries: "אפילו מיחייב דאורייתא לא חשיבי להוציא אנשים דחשיבי טפי שחייבים בכל המצות—Even if women are biblically obligated [in Birkat ha-Mazon], they are still not important enough to fulfill the obligations of men, who are more important on account of their obligation in all *mitzvot*." This approach essentially argues that the scope of one's religious obligation, not one's social standing, ultimately determines a person's capacity for communal ritual leadership. (Whether it is tenable or coherent for there to be a gap between those two is a worthy question in its own right. See below, Part Two, nn. 76–81). One could easily imagine applying this concern to minors leading parts of the service, even if issues of obligation were addressed.

155 If one followed all the (uncertain) assumptions needed to get this sort of argument off the ground, one might draw further support from views on מאירה that we explored above in our discussion of Mishnah Sukkah 3:10 in nn. 85–97. Various passages of the Tosafot reveal an understanding of מאירה as focused on the indignity of an obligation gap, even when the congregants are not relying on the leader to fulfill their obligations. If the person leading is not religiously accountable for the ritual they are performing, the dignity of the proceedings suffers. Perhaps one could

3. One could take a piecemeal approach to *devarim shebikdushah* and claim that some are gender equal and some are not. Specifically, one could make the claim that *devarim shebikdushah* follow the status of the rituals in which they are embedded. Kedushah in the Amidah, which is itself gender equal, would be gender-blind. The Barekhu of Torah reading might be theoretically gender-blind, but the Barekhu introducing the blessings of Shema—which are themselves gendered—might itself be gendered.[156] This position is somewhat awkward and requires introducing distinctions among things that seem very much the same.

We offer these thoughts not by way of undermining our arguments above, but in an effort to make sense of as wide a range of approaches as possible. In particular, there is some sense to the first possibility suggested here, which is that communities should only allow themselves to be publicly represented and led in *devarim shebikdushah* by those who bear a maximal load of ritual responsibility. We confess to not finding the second and third suggestions here very convincing. Such theories are also not truly necessary. There is a very solid basis for maintaining non-egalitarian practice with respect to leadership of the parts of the service that require a *minyan* of ten: *kevod tzibbur*. While we discussed the solid ground for waiving or reassessing this concern in the contemporary world, it is surely intelligible (aside from whether it is plausible or objectionable) that a community would maintain that *kevod tzibbur* remains a live concern with gendered ramifications today. There is no need to run away from that conversation by forcing the creation of gender obligation gaps in *devarim shebikdushah* that are not clearly supported by traditional sources.

---

argue that this would extend to allowing someone to lead who is not able (and not responsible) to make up the *minyan*. That would hardly be a position commanding wide agreement; we saw many sources in our discussion that quite clearly rejected such a correlation between *minyan* membership and the ability to lead the *minyan*.

156 Such a position might make a bit more sense of Shulḥan Arukh ha-Rav's claim that one cannot extrapolate from the Barekhu of Torah reading to the Barekhu of Shema, though his language does not sound like he is advancing this sort of argument.

D. SUMMARY

Devarim shebikdushah, such as Torah reading, Barekhu, Kaddish, and Kedushah, need to be said in a *minyan.* There is no explicit discussion in classic sources over who is fit to lead most of these rituals, such as Barekhu, Kaddish, and Kedushah. There is discussion over who is fit to perform one of the items on the Mishnah's list, namely, Torah reading. The Talmud Bavli states that in principle women may do so, but adds that the Sages said that women should not read because of "the honor of the community," understood by several Rishonim to mean that men would be dishonored by the implication that they are incapable and must rely on a woman. Authorities split over whether individual communities may waive concern for their honor. There is solid basis for endorsing such a waiver. Even those who think such honor is objective and not subject to communal discretion might reassess whether it applies in contemporary society. If there is no longer any affront to communal honor via women's public performance of important communal duties, this concern may simply no longer be in play, such that the question of its potential waiver is no longer relevant.

We also explored the specific cases of Kedushah, Kaddish, and Barekhu. We demonstrated the viability of a position that denies that obligation is relevant at all, as codified in the Shulḥan Arukh and the Magen Avraham's explanation thereof. Even among those who spoke of individualized obligation, we demonstrated the strand of thought that sees this obligation as being fulfilled through the participation of each individual in these communal rituals. Finally, even working with a model of vicarious fulfillment, there is no reason to assume a gender gap with respect to these rituals. As the Ḥavvot Yair and Mishpetei Uzziel make clear, these rituals are rooted in the obligations to sanctify God's name (*kiddush hashem*) and to pray (*tefillah*), in which women have equal obligation.

Nonetheless, the Ran's approach to Torah reading might provide useful insight into those who are firmly committed to non-egalitarian leadership of the service. One might claim that until there is broader equality between men and women in *mitzvot* more generally, having a gender-blind practice is no different from opening up the *bimah* to children in a way that might well be forbidden and inappropriate. As we have said repeatedly, we by no means see this as a **necessary** reading of the sources, and many great authorities (R. Tam, R. Yosef Karo) clearly do not accept it. But we respect this view, which does find some support in the Rishonim,[157] and we will say more about how to address it later on.[158]

However we address the concerns of obligation (or lack thereof), the heart of our conversation will also always return to the issue of *kevod tzibbur*; just as communal honor limits the pool of appropriate Torah readers, so too it will shape who is fit to assume communal leadership of other prayers. We surveyed that question above and it has been dealt with at length elsewhere.[159]

Beyond that, the question is one of custom and stability. What seemed reasonable (or at least not worthy of controversy) to the rabbis of Amsterdam seemed radical and destabilizing to the Ḥavvot Yair. The same disputes abound today; many contemporary communities that address these questions worry that a greater degree of egalitarianism in the synagogue does—and will—correlate with general laxity with regard to *mitzvot*. Others argue precisely the opposite: Against a broader social backdrop of gender equality, any service that is **not** egalitarian will risk driving people away from committed Jewish practice. The real argument, therefore, is over the extent to which women assuming the role of *sha"tz* destabilizes widespread custom. One must weigh the risks of such destabilization against the religious risks of excluding women living in a social environment that grants them access to even the highest corridors of power.

---

157 See n. 154.

158 Below, Part Two, nn. 76–81.

159 Even when the concerns are not described with the technical term of *kevod tzibbur*, issues of honor, dignity, and propriety continue to surface in various forms. Another halakhic discussion of this sort is articulated in the terms of זילא מילתא, the notion that a certain protocol is beneath one's dignity. The language of זילא מילתא is used by Tosafot Sukkah 38a s.v. *be-emet* to describe Halakhot Gedolot's objection to women reading *megillah* for men in public. This concern functions independently of obligation; even when a woman is as equally obligated to a man, such considerations can apply. For the application of such considerations to Kiddush on Shabbat, see Berkovits, "Women's Obligation," and the sources cited there. These issues, like *kevod tzibbur*, must be addressed based on the social context that they are designed to respond to. Cf. the Ra'avad's discussion of the reasons why a minor cannot lead prayers for an adult even when they share an equal obligation. See above nn. 103, 121, and 129.

Precisely such an argument led R. Ahron Soloveichik to cite the Ḥavvot Yair as support for his ruling permitting (and requiring permission for) women to say Kaddish in the synagogue. While the threat in the time of the Ḥavvot Yair was, in his view, the dissolution of the unified Jewish community, R. Soloveichik felt the greater risk in his own day to be the temptations of heterodoxy, such that contemporary Orthodoxy's mission was to permit participation by women to the extent possible while retaining maximal allegiance to tradition among the Jewish population:

> **עוד ישראל יוסף בני חי סימן לב**
> ועיין בתשובות חוות יאיר...שכתב שאם אין למת בן רק בת...מצד עיקר הדין הבת יכולה לומר קדיש אלא שלא תעשה כן שעל ידי זה יתחלשו מנהגי ישראל וכיון דאיכא פרסום יש למחות.
>
> ונראה עכשיו שכמה אנשים ונשים מישראל לוחמים בעד שווי הנשים לעומת האנשים ביחס עם עליות בשביל הנשים א"כ אם הרבנים החרדים ימנעו אשה מלומר קדיש במקום שישנה אפשרות שע"י זה תתרבה ההשפעה של הרבנים השמרנים והריפורמים אז אסור למנוע בת מלומר קדיש.
>
> **Od Yisrael Yosef Beni Ḥai #32**
> See Responsa Ḥavvot Yair…where he wrote that if the deceased has no son, but only a daughter…according to the essence of the law, the daughter may say Kaddish. However, she should not do so because this will lead to the weakening of Jewish practice and since the case was public, one should object.
>
> It seems that today, when there are many Jewish men and women fighting for gender equality with respect to *aliyot* for women, if Orthodox rabbis prevent a woman from saying Kaddish in a context where it is possible that this will lead to increased influence of Conservative and Reform rabbis, it is forbidden to prevent a daughter from saying Kaddish.[160]

---

160 The denominational assumptions in this passage remain a matter of lively dispute today. We cite R. Soloveichik here not as an endorsement of his specific concern but for his sensitivity to the ways in which the Ḥavvot Yair's concerns may play out very differently in different times and places.

In addition to these considerations of stability and custom, contemporary opposition to women's inclusion in communal prayer roles may reflect political concerns regarding broader social boundary issues. Indeed, in a 2004 responsum, R. Yehudah Herzl Henkin opined that nowadays the reason to restrict women from having *aliyot* to the Torah is not communal honor, but as a bulwark against assimilation:

> **שו"ת בני בנים ד:ג**
> היום שרק הבעל-קורא קורא בתורה ואילו העולים לתורה מברכים אבל אינם קוראים אם כן בטל ענין כבוד הצבור...וכתבתי כמה פעמים שלדעתי עיקר איסור עליות נשים היום אינו משום כבוד צבור אלא משום שהן פתח למתבוללים.
>
> **Responsa Benei Banim IV:3**
> Today, when the reader reads Torah, whereas those with *aliyot* to the Torah say the blessings but do not read, the whole matter of communal honor is irrelevant.... I have written several times that in my opinion the essence of the prohibition on giving aliyot to women today is not on account of communal honor, but because they are an opening to assimilationists.

Similarly, in his response to R. Mendel Shapiro's aforementioned article, R. Henkin concludes his opposing argument as follows:[161]

> Where does all this leave us? Regardless of the arguments that can be proffered to permit women's *aliyot* today—that *kevod ha-tzibbur* can be waived, that it does not apply today when everyone is literate, that it does not apply when the *olim* rely on the (male) *ba'al keri'ah* and do not themselves read—women's *aliyot* remain outside the consensus, and a congregation that institutes them is not Orthodox in name and will not long remain Orthodox in practice. In my judgment, this is an accurate statement now and for the foreseeable future, and I see no point in arguing about it.

---

161 See R. Henkin's comments in his responses to R. Shapiro's article, Shapiro, "Keri'at ha-Torah."

In these two passages, R. Henkin is discussing only the issue of *aliyot* for women; nevertheless, similar considerations animate discussions of other issues of gender in synagogue life, even if they are not explicitly acknowledged. Of course, these assessments are subjective and often controversial: R. Henkin's concern with certain practices being outside of the Orthodox consensus is less of a concern for R. Daniel Sperber, who has emerged as a forceful advocate for women's *aliyot* in the context of Orthodox communities. Some communities may well evaluate that maintaining difference from non-Jews or from self-defined heterodox Jewish groups trumps many local, internal issues. In their estimation, blurring those boundaries may lead to other more serious problems than those caused by unnecessary exclusion of women. Our own sense is that, in many communities, the exclusion of women from public roles poses a great risk to the ongoing stability and vitality of Torah in an increasingly egalitarian world. We approach our own leanings on these questions of communal honor, dignity, and stability with a sense of humility and hope others will have similar honesty and transparency to do the same.

PART TWO
Counting in a *Minyan*

I. Biblical and Classical Rabbinic Sources

The number ten has ancient significance as a figure signifying a quorum. For example, in Rut 4:2, ten elders are assembled for the legal procedure of enacting a kinsman's redemption or relinquishing an inheritance claim: "ויקח עשרה אנשים מזקני העיר ויאמר שבו פה וישבו — And he took ten men from the elders of the city and said, 'Sit here,' and they sat." Non-rabbinic sources also prominently feature ten as the minimum needed for a quorum in various communal settings.[1] The Sages found ways to connect this number back to verses in the Torah itself. In Mishnah Sanhedrin 1:6, we see that the term עדה (community), which is used by the Torah to describe a judging body, is understood to be represented by a panel of ten:

משנה סנהדרין א:ו
ומנין לעדה שהיא עשרה, שנאמר "עד מתי לעדה הרעה הזאת" (במדבר יד:כז), יצאו יהושע וכלב.

1 For two examples, see the Damascus Document, col. X, and the Community Rule, col. VI. See Metso, "The Term Yaḥad."

Mishnah Sanhedrin 1:6

How do we know that an *eidah* [a term evoked in Bemidbar 35:24–25 as a judicial unit] is ten? As it says, "Until when will I have to bear this evil *eidah*?" (Bemidbar 14:27) [referring to the spies, who were twelve in number], and Yehoshua and Kalev do not count [because they brought back a good report, leaving ten].

This *mishnah* identifies the traditional number of ten as the minimum number that could plausibly be called an *eidah*. It grounds this in the use of the term *eidah* to refer to the ten spies (of the twelve total) who brought back a negative report of the Land of Israel to Moshe (as told in Bemidbar 13–14). This wicked group is (the smallest group) called an *eidah* in the Torah, thus establishing other uses of the term *eidah*—as in the context of the judging court mentioned in Bemidbar 35—as referring to a minimum of ten people.

Mishnah Megillah 4:3, without any recourse to supporting verses or justification, requires ten for a variety of functions, including the repetition of the Amidah and reading the Torah:[2]

משנה מגילה ד:ג

אין פורסין את שמע, ואין עוברין לפני התיבה, ואין נושאין את כפיהם, ואין קורין בתורה, ואין מפטירין בנביא, ואין עושין מעמד ומושב, ואין אומרים ברכת אבלים ותנחומי אבלים וברכת חתנים, ואין מזמנין בשם, פחות מעשרה. ובקרקעות, תשעה וכהן. ואדם, כיוצא בהן.

Mishnah Megillah 4:3

We do not responsively recite the Shema, nor have a communal prayer leader, nor offer the Priestly Blessing, nor read Torah, nor read from the Prophets, nor perform the standing/sitting [ritual for the dead], nor say the blessing of the mourners, nor the formal comforting the mourners, nor recite the wedding blessings, nor say *zimmun* with the Name in a group of fewer

2 We explored this *mishnah* in greater depth above and saw how later sources clarify that Kedushah, Kaddish, and Barekhu are also among the rituals that require a group of ten.

than ten. And when redeeming land we require nine and a *kohen*; and so too with [redeeming] people.

Strikingly, this text does not specify who is eligible to count as one of the ten. All we can infer is that, except for the evaluation of land, there is no need for one of the ten to be a priest.[3] But what other limits are there on the constitution of this group? The Mishnah's silence on this point only reinforces the idea that we are dealing with a preexisting notion of a quorum that has certain assumed protocols that are not fully spelled out here.

Later texts attempt to ground the quorum of ten required for these rituals in verses, by trying to extract meaning from the verse "ונקדשתי בתוך בני ישראל — I shall be sanctified in the midst of the children of Israel." This verse (Vayikra 22:32) is understood to be the scriptural anchor for the sacred rituals requiring a *minyan* listed in Mishnah Megillah. The term *devarim shebikdushah,* applied to many of the rituals in this list, is understood to be a manifestation of the broader *mitzvah* to sanctify God's name in public. Texts in the Talmud Yerushalmi and the Talmud Bavli attempt to cross-reference the language of this verse with other verses in order to justify the necessity of a quorum often. The Talmud Yerushalmi has the following:

תלמוד ירושלמי מגילה ד:א, דף עד טור ג
אמ' ר' סימון: נאמר כאן "**תוך**" ונאמר להלן "ויבאו בני ישראל **בתוך** הבאים" (בראשית מב:ה). מה "תוך" שנאמר להלן עשרה אף כאן עשרה. אמר ליה רבי יוסה בי רבי בון: אם מ"תוך" את למד סגין אינון! אלא נאמר כאן "בני ישראל" ונאמר להלן "בני ישראל", מה להלן עשר' אף כאן עשרה.

Talmud Yerushalmi Megillah 4:1 (74c)
Said R. Simon: It says here, "**in the midst**" (*tokh*) and it says there, "And *benei yisrael* came to get grain **in the midst** (*tokh*) of those coming" (Bereishit 42:5); just as *tokh* there signifies ten, so here too it is ten. Said to him R. Yose b. R. Bun: If you

3 The requirement for a priest has echoes in non-rabbinic literature as well. See above, n. 1.

derive it from *tokh*, there will be too many![4] Rather, it says here "*benei yisrael*" and it says there "*benei yisrael*"; just as there [i.e., in Bereishit 42:5] it refers to ten, so too here [i.e., Vayikra 22:32] it refers to ten.

This passage in the Talmud Yerushalmi picks up on linguistic affinities between the verse in Vayikra and another verse in Bereishit that describes the descent of the **ten** children of Israel (the man, i.e., Ya'akov) to Egypt in the midst of all the others seeking food during the famine.[5] Whether through use of the common word *tokh* or the use of *benei yisrael* in a verse speaking about only ten people, these scriptural arguments aim to prove that the verse ונקדשתי בתוך בני ישראל applies to groups of at least ten.

The Talmud Bavli features a slightly different and more complex derivation:

תלמוד בבלי מגילה כג:
מנא הני מילי? אמר רבי חייא בר אבא אמר רבי יוחנן: דאמר קרא "ונקדשתי בתוך בני ישראל" (ויקרא כב:לב) – כל דבר שבקדושה לא יהא פחות מעשרה. מאי משמע? דתני רבי חייא: אתיא תוך, תוך: כתיב הכא "ונקדשתי **בתוך** בני ישראל", וכתיב התם "הבדלו **מתוך העדה**" (במדבר טז:כא). ואתיא עדה, עדה: דכתיב התם "עד מתי **לעדה** הרעה הזאת" (במדבר יד:כז), מה להלן עשרה אף כאן עשרה.

Talmud Bavli Megillah 23b
How do we know this [that we need a quorum of ten]? Said R. Ḥiyya b. Abba said R. Yoḥanan: The verse says: "And I will be sanctified in the midst of the children of Israel"—any *davar shebikdushah* shall not be said with fewer than ten. What suggests this? R. Ḥiyya taught in a *baraita*: We derive it from the double usage of *tokh*: It says here, "And I will be sanctified **in the midst** of the children of Israel" (Vayikra 22:32) and it says there, "Separate yourselves out **from the midst** of this **congregation** (*eidah*)" (Bemidbar 16:21); and then we derive

4 Meaning, "those coming" (to Egypt) were many more than ten. A term more clearly referring to only ten people is required.

5 Binyamin was left back in Canaan (Bereishit 42:4); Yosef was in Egypt.

> it from the double usage of "congregation": it says there, "How long must I suffer this evil **congregation**" (Bemidbar 14:27): Just as there it refers to ten, so here too it refers to ten.

Here we have an unusual double association that produces the expected outcome. Like the Talmud Yerushalmi, this text begins with the double appearance of *tokh*. But here, the association points us not to the Ya'akov and Yosef narratives, but to a verse taken from Bemidbar's telling of Koraḥ's rebellion. That verse on its own has no context of ten, but it features **both** the term *tokh* **and** the term *eidah*, allowing us to return to the text about the ten spies who return with an evil report. Through these two steps, we once again have an anchor for the number ten being the minimum required to trigger the relevance of Vayikra 22:32.[6]

Neither text gives us much further insight into who qualifies to make up this group of ten. That discussion is anchored around Mishnah Berakhot 7:2, which more broadly also engages the question of *zimmun*, the invitation to a joint blessing after eating a meal. The Mishnah states: "נשים ועבדים וקטנים אין מזמנין עליהם — One does not make a *zimmun* with women, slaves, and minors." The interpretation of this text has a complex history; we will not go into it here.[7] A quorum of three is assumed

---

6 This sort of doubled *gezeirah shavah* is so unusual that it seems plausible that something like the following happened: A tradition regarding the double usage of תוך came to Babylonia from Eretz Yisrael. Perhaps it arrived without specifying what other verse was referred to, or perhaps it arrived with the challenge we see lodged against the use of תוך in the Yerushalmi itself, or perhaps the Babylonian sages who received it could not imagine grounding a ritual practice in a verse describing events prior to the giving of *mitzvot* at Sinai. One way or another, it is easy to imagine how a prior *midrash* involving the word תוך would inspire a search to connect it to the rock-solid association of ten with the word עדה, as found in the Mishnah. With these two building blocks in place, the structure was completed by locating a verse containing both the word תוך and עדה to serve as the bridge. The doubled *gezeirah shavah* may thus make more sense when understood as connecting two prior traditions, rather than as an original quest to wend such a complex path through the Torah's language.

7 For one summary and analysis, see Gershon, "Tzirufan shel Nashim le-Zimmun." See also Koren, "Tziruf Nashim le-Zimmun." Koren argues there that this text only precludes a *zimmun* that includes a **combination** of women, slaves, and/or minors. As Koren herself points out, Talmud Bavli Berakhot 47b clearly understood the ban on counting minors to be absolute, not only operative in the context of counting women and slaves at the same time. Nonetheless, Koren advances her reading in part

here, with a likely extension as well to the quorum of ten referred to in Mishnah Megillah 4:3 for the *zimmun* that incorporates God's name. This text is obviously situated in the context of a shared meal and may well present concerns that are not relevant to the context of prayer. Specifically, concerns regarding joint meals between men and women in general may well be behind the Mishnah's rule with respect to a mixed-gender *zimmun*.[8] In any event, this *mishnah* is the anchor for Talmud Bavli Berakhot 47b–48a's broader discussion of various traditions that attempt to define our quorum of ten more precisely:

תלמוד בבלי ברכות מז:–מח.

אמר רבי יוסי: קטן המוטל בעריסה מזמנין עליו. והא תנן: נשים ועבדים וקטנים אין מזמנין עליהם! הוא דאמר רבי יהושע בן לוי, דאמר רבי יהושע בן לוי: אף על פי שאמרו קטן המוטל בעריסה אין מזמנין עליו, אבל עושין אותו סניף לעשרה.

ואמר רבי יהושע בן לוי: תשעה ועבד מצטרפין. מיתיבי: מעשה ברבי אליעזר שנכנס לבית הכנסת ולא מצא עשרה, ושחרר עבדו והשלימו לעשרה; שחרר אין, לא שחרר לא! תרי אצטריכו, שחרר חד ונפיק חד...

אמר רב הונא: תשעה וארון מצטרפין. אמר ליה רב נחמן: וארון גברא הוא? אלא אמר רב הונא: תשעה נראין כעשרה מצטרפין...

אמר רבי אמי: שנים ושבת מצטרפין. אמר ליה רב נחמן: ושבת גברא הוא? אלא אמר רבי אמי: שני תלמידי חכמים המחדדין זה את זה בהלכה מצטרפין...

אמר רבי יוחנן: קטן פורח מזמנין עליו. תניא נמי הכי: קטן שהביא שתי שערות מזמנין עליו, ושלא הביא שתי שערות – אין מזמנין עליו.

---

to explain the otherwise puzzling view of the medieval sage R. Yehudah ha-Kohen, who permitted a joint *zimmun* between men and women.

8 Other *zimmun*-specific issues may be at work as well, including a potential gender obligation gap in the blessing after a meal. See Gershon, "Tzirufan shel Nashim le-Zimmun," 9–19.

Talmud Bavli Berakhot 47b–48a

Said R. Yose: One makes a *zimmun* with a child resting in a cradle. But doesn't the Mishnah say, "One does not make a *zimmun* with women, slaves, and minors?" [R. Yose] follows the view of R. Yehoshua b. Levi, for R. Yehoshua b. Levi said: Even though they said one does not make a *zimmun* with a child resting in a cradle, we do make him an adjunct to the ten.

And said R. Yehoshua b. Levi: Nine and a slave combine. They challenged this from a *baraita*: "Once R. Eliezer came to the synagogue and did not find ten; he freed his slave and completed the quorum of ten." He was only able to do so because he freed him, but an unfreed slave would not [have counted]! They must have needed two; he freed one and counted one....

Said Rav Huna: Nine and an ark combine. Rav Naḥman said to him: Is an ark a person? Rather, Rav Huna said: Nine, when they look like ten, combine....

Said R. Ami: Two and Shabbat combine. Rav Naḥman said to him: Is Shabbat a person? Rather, R. Ami said: Two scholars who sharpen one another with [words of] *halakhah* combine....

Said R. Yoḥanan: One makes a *zimmun* with a "flowering" minor. This is also taught in a *baraita:* One makes a *zimmun* with a minor with two hairs [that indicate the onset of puberty], but not with one who has not.

This text jumps back and forth freely between discussions of quorums of three and ten, among the categories of people, objects, and times, as well as between the contexts of *zimmun* and prayer. Our passage begins with R. Yose allowing one to count an infant toward a *zimmun*. The Gemara notes that this seemingly stands in direct contradiction to the Mishnah, which excludes minors (and certainly infants) from those who are counted toward a *zimmun*. The Gemara deflects the challenge by citing a view of R. Yehoshua b. Levi and molding R. Yose's statement to fit it: While an infant is not counted toward a *zimmun* of three (per the Mishnah), a baby may serve as an adjunct[9] to the quorum needed for a *zimmun* of ten, the ritual referred to in Mishnah Megillah 4:3.

The passage continues with a statement by R. Yehoshua b. Levi that permits nine free people to join with a slave to form a quorum of ten. On its own, this might be a statement about *zimmun*, with no consequences one way or the other for prayer.[10] But once the *sugya* challenges it from the story about R. Eliezer in the synagogue, it is clear that we are meant to understand it as applying to prayer (as well). The *sugya* construes R. Eliezer's actions such that they do not conflict with R. Yehoshua b. Levi (i.e., positing that there were two slaves in the story), leaving us with a viable position that counts a single slave toward the quorum of ten required for saying *zimmun* with God's name and for prayer. Rav Huna continues this section on prayer, allowing the ark in the synagogue to complete the quorum along with nine people. When this is dismissed as outrageous, Rav Huna is cited for another proposal: When nine people look like ten, they can form a quorum.[11]

The *sugya* then returns[12] to play with the boundaries of the quorum for the *zimmun* of three. R. Ami allows a *zimmun* of two on Shabbat, counting

---

9 It is not clear what is meant by סניף ("adjunct") here. Most commentators understood this to refer to counting a single infant along with nine adults. This approach is strengthened by assuming congruency with R. Yehoshua b. Levi's statement permitting a slave to join with nine free people. R. Tam argued for this reading, as we will see below. This reading seems to have been the original historical meaning of R. Yehoshua b. Levi; see Bereishit Rabbah 91:3. Others read the term סניף more broadly. See R. Ya'akov of Marvege in Responsa Min ha-Shamayim #53, who holds that two minors can be counted according to this view. R. Zeraḥiah ha-Levi pushes the logic even further in the Ma'or ha-Katon on Rif Berakhot 35b, allowing for counting up to four minors, since they are still a minority of the ten and can therefore be classified as adjuncts to the group. See Bereishit Rabbah 91:3 for an analogue to this sort of ruling. The Ma'or clarifies that this is only true for minors, but that R. Yehoshua b. Levi clearly would not have counted more than one slave.

10 As we noted, we cannot tell from Mishnah Berakhot 7:2 alone whether its concerns about women, slaves, and minors in the context of *zimmun* transfer entirely, partially, or not at all to the realm of *tefillah*.

11 The Gemara reports views that this may be when they are standing especially close together, or especially spread out.

12 In fact, the prior statement may already begin to return the conversation to *zimmun*. In Bereishit Rabbah 91:3, R. Asi is quoted as permitting a group of nine that looks like

the sacred day itself as the third. When this is dismissed as outrageous, R. Ami is cited for another proposal: Two scholars who are learning *halakhah* intensely during their meal are sufficient to form a quorum on their own. R. Yoḥanan then adds that the exclusion of minors from a *zimmun* only applies to those not displaying the physical signs of puberty, and a *baraita* is cited to confirm this point.

What does this text tell us about the quorum of ten and who can count toward it? The story involving R. Eliezer assumes that slaves do not count equally in a *minyan* for prayer, as does R. Yehoshua b. Levi's second tradition, even as the latter allows for counting a single slave toward the quorum of ten. His language of סניף, "adjunct," also indicates that minors are not counted as equals toward the quorum of ten in *zimmun*. There is little reason to think he would include them any more broadly for a quorum for prayer.

The Gemara does not here or elsewhere spell out why minors and slaves are normally excluded nor why they might be included in these liminal situations. It is possible that the latter section of this passage suggests that there was a tendency to "cheat" on the last member of the *minyan*, effectively considering nine to be like ten. In any event, these various lenient rulings were controversial, and our printed text of the Gemara here ends with a rejection of these various statements: "ולית הילכתא ככל הני שמעתתא — The *halakhah* does not follow any of these traditions." While this legal rejection is in fact a later geonic gloss that was added to the text,[13] it reveals that even toying with the margins of the definition of *minyan* was controversial.

An additional relevant passage engages another facet of the commandment to sanctify God's name: the obligation to martyr oneself when forced to violate certain *mitzvot* under the duress of a Gentile aggressor. The Talmud reports a number of traditions on the topic, including one that obligates Jews to give up their lives if coerced to engage in idolatry, sexual prohibitions, or murder. The Talmud reports a further series of decisions that held that one must martyr oneself before violating **any** sort of *mitzvah* if the violation will occur in public. It then defines

---

ten to form a *zimmun*, suggesting that this tradition might be about both contexts.

13 For confirmation of this point, see Otzar ha-Geonim Berakhot Teshuvot #314–316.

the quorum for this more expanded obligation in "public" martyrdom as being a group of ten:

> **תלמוד בבלי סנהדרין עד.–עד:**
> וכמה פרהסיא? אמר רבי יעקב אמר רבי יוחנן: אין פרהסיא פחותה מעשרה בני אדם. פשיטא, ישראלים בעינן, דכתיב "ונקדשתי בתוך בני ישראל". בעי רבי ירמיה: תשעה ישראל ונכרי אחד מהו? תא שמע, דתני רב ינאי אחוה דרבי חייא בר אבא: אתיא תוך תוך, כתיב הכא "ונקדשתי **בתוך** בני ישראל" וכתיב התם ב"הבדלו **מתוך** העדה הזאת" (במדבר ט"ז). מה להלן עשרה וכולהו ישראל, אף כאן עשרה וכולהו ישראל.

> **Talmud Bavli Sanhedrin 74a–b**
> And how many [people] form a "public" (*parhesiya*) [such that a person is obligated in martyrdom to avoid even a comparatively minor transgression]? Said R. Ya'akov said R. Yoḥanan: "A *parhesiya* cannot be fewer than ten people." Obviously, we require Jews [for this number], as it says, "And I will be sanctified in the midst of *benei yisrael*." R. Yirmiyah asked: "Nine Jews and one Gentile—what is the law?" Come and learn what R. Yannai the brother of R. Ḥiyya bar Abba taught: We derive it from the double usage of *tokh*: It says here, "And I will be sanctified in **the midst** of the children of Israel," and it says there, "Separate yourselves out from **the midst** of this congregation" (Bemidbar 16:21)—just as there all ten are Jews, also here all ten must be Jews.

The Gemara here explores the parameters of the quorum of ten for public martyrdom, taking it as obvious that non-Jews are not primary members of this group. Nonetheless, R. Yirmiyah asks whether a Gentile could be the tenth member of a group triggering the obligation of public martyrdom. The Gemara then rejects this possibility and insists that all ten members of the group must be Jews, invoking the Jewish identity of all ten of the wicked spies.

Neither of these passages weighs in on the question of whether women count toward the quorum of ten. It is hard to know whether the passage in Talmud Bavli Berakhot (quoted above) would take it for granted that women are included in the concept of *minyan* and therefore it explores only the cases of slaves and minors, or whether the total exclusion of women from *minyan* is so obvious that the liminal roles explored for these other groups are not even entertained for them. Though the Talmud's citation of Mishnah Berakhot 7:2 shows that a *zimmun* of three is not gender-blind,[14] we cannot tell from this passage what ramifications, if any, that has for the quorum of ten mentioned in Mishnah Megillah 4:3.[15] The passage in Bavli Sanhedrin would seem to push us in the former direction: A plausible reading of that passage would claim that if the Gemara is

---

14 When the Talmud on Berakhot 47b uses Mishnah Berakhot 7:2 to eliminate the possibility of counting a single minor toward a *zimmun* of three, it clearly reads the Mishnah as forbidding even a single member of the three classes mentioned to join in with free adult males to make that *zimmun*. Almost all Rishonim, with the exception of R. Yehudah ha-Kohen and a few others, read the Mishnah in this way as well. See above, n. 7, for Koren's argument that the original meaning of the Mishnah is that women and men may in fact make a *zimmun*; only groups of women, slaves, and minors are precluded from forming. We are less sure. Her evidence from Talmud Bavli Arakhin 3a presumes that all individuals fully obligated in *zimmun* can join to form a *zimmun* with all other similarly obligated individuals. This may not be the case; men and women might be fully equal in their obligations and nonetheless be forbidden from forming the core quorum of *zimmun* with one another. Nonetheless, R. Yehudah ha-Kohen's position must indeed be explained, and perhaps he felt that the dismissal of the legally binding nature of much of the material on Berakhot 47b–48a also rendered some of the assumptions of its literary give-and-take to be legally non-binding as well. Obviously, were one to accept Koren's arguments, there would then be no evidence at all for excluding women and men from forming any sort of joint quorum, whether of three or ten.

15 R. Ephraim Halivni has suggested that Bavli Berakhot 47b **does** provide explicit evidence that women do not count in a *minyan*. His reasoning is as follows: R. Yehoshua b. Levi's second statement is about forming a *zimmun* of ten, but the Gemara nonetheless challenges its validity from a text that speaks about the quorum of ten for *tefillah*. That should lead us to the conclusion that the quorums of *zimmun* and *tefillah* are interchangeable and knowing that a person is excluded from one teaches us that they are excluded from the other as well. Accordingly, a text that excludes slaves from the quorum for prayer (R. Eliezer) would be in conflict with a text that includes slaves in the quorum for *zimmun* (R. Yehoshua b. Levi). In this, Halivni follows an argument laid out in Tosafot Berakhot 48a s.v. *ve-leit*, which proposes that including a minor in a *zimmun* of ten would lead us to include him in the ten of prayer as well, seemingly equating the two. Following this logic, Halivni argues that the Gemara would thus derive from the Mishnah's exclusion of women from *zimmun* their exclusion from the quorum of ten for prayer. See Halivni, *Bein ha-Ish la-Ishah*, 80. While Halivni's reading of the Gemara is certainly possible, our goal here is merely to argue that it is by no means **necessary**, and therefore the text in the

willing to entertain the liminal status of a Gentile in such a quorum, then

---

Bavli does not definitively help later commentators resolve the question of gender and *minyan*. There are several problems with his line of analysis:

1. Perhaps R. Yehoshua b. Levi's second statement was **also** about prayer, as suggested by R. Tam in Tosafot Berakhot 48a s.v. *ve-leit*. Note the shift from מזמנין עליו to מצטרפין (although see the use of מצטרפין later in the *sugya* in the context of a *zimmun* of three). If so, then that section is an internal dialogue between dueling sources on prayer and nothing can be learned from the model of *zimmun*. Perhaps the rules of quorums for *zimmun* and prayer do not cross their respective legal boundaries. Admittedly, this deflection is not strong, as Mishnah Megillah 4:3 itself suggests that the quorums for a *zimmun* of ten and other prayer rituals are most likely identical. But if we are asking whether the Talmud provides any conclusive evidence on the question of counting women toward the quorum of ten, these distinctions (even if unlikely) are important.

2. Even if R. Yehoshua b. Levi's second statement is **only** about *zimmun*, the Gemara, strictly speaking, only concludes that being excluded from the ten for prayer implies an exclusion from the ten for *zimmun*. It does not make the converse claim. One could be excluded from the ten for *zimmun* and still potentially count for the ten required for prayer. True, Bereishit Rabbah 91:3 **does** make the converse claim, suggesting it is harder to count for the ten of prayer than the ten of *zimmun*. But R. Tam points out that the Bavli's use of R. Eliezer to challenge R. Yehoshua b. Levi must indicate a different way of thinking than Bereishit Rabbah. If the Bavli thought like Bereishit Rabbah, it could not possibly challenge a lenient ruling on *zimmun* from a stringent ruling on *tefillah*. And if R. Yehoshua b. Levi's statement is indeed about *tefillah*, then we do have a case of someone (a slave) who is excluded from *zimmun* (by the Mishnah) and yet included in *tefillah*, which also contradicts Bereishit Rabbah's way of thinking. Thus, even if Mishnah Berakhot 7:2 is properly read as ruling that women do not count toward the ten of *zimmun*, it does not logically follow from this *sugya* that they do not count toward the ten of prayer.

3. Mishnah Berakhot 7:2 does not necessarily say anything about a *zimmun* of ten. Indeed, it is noteworthy that the Gemara does not challenge R. Yehoshua b. Levi's inclusion of a slave from the Mishnah's ban on including him in a *zimmun*. The Gemara's choice here might have been more literary than substantive, motivated by a desire to link two pre-existing sources (R. Yehoshua b. Levi and R. Eliezer) through a challenge. Nonetheless, the Gemara's failure to set up a conflict between R. Yehoshua b. Levi and Mishnah Berakhot 7:2 makes it possible, if not plausible, that the Mishnah only excludes the slave from the quorum of three, but not from the quorum of ten. Again, Bereishit Rabbah 91:3 thinks differently and does seem to think that it is a bigger deal to count someone for the quorum of ten than for the quorum of three. But there is nothing to force a later reader to see that in the Bavli *sugya*. Indeed, Rosh Berakhot 7:20 assumes the exact opposite: "דכולה שמעתתא מוכחא דזימון חמור מסניף עשרה — Counting toward the quorum of ten is less weighty than counting toward the quorum of three." Absent a specific

it clearly considers women to be included in those that the verse terms בני ישראל, and thus women would be included in *minyan*.[16] Furthermore, all other factors being equal, one might well assume that women count toward the *minyan*, given their equal obligation in prayer (in the context of which many of the situations requiring a *minyan* are clustered), and their explicit inclusion in the similar *mitzvah* of martyrdom.[17] But women's participation in the *minyan* is nowhere directly addressed in classical rabbinic sources, leaving us simply to say that it impossible to prove from

---

text excluding a woman from the quorum of ten, we would then have no dispositive evidence on that score from Mishnah Berakhot 7:2.

4. Whatever the evidence may be with respect to minors, we do not know that the concerns barring women from *zimmun* are identical, and there is good reason to think they are not. Bavli Berakhot 45b already seems clear that women make a *zimmun* on their own in a way that minors do not. Even if one concludes that exclusion from *zimmun* leads to exclusion from *tefillah*, we simply do not know whether that equation is only true for minors, or for minors and slaves, or for minors, slaves, and women. See the direct statement to this effect in Sefer ha-Me'orot Berakhot 45a: "וליכא משום פריצות הגדול עם הנשים דדוקא עבדים שהם פרוצים בעריות... אבל בבני חורין לא אמרינן הכי — It is not because of great lack of restraint with women, because it is specifically slaves that are unrestrained with sex...but we do not say this for freemen."

5. Mishnah Berakhot 7:2 says nothing about an all-female *zimmun*. Even if one follows Halivni's reading of the *sugya*—which is not necessary, given all the above—it maximally proves that men and women should not join to form a group. It says nothing about whether ten women are valid as a *minyan* on their own. Here the broader evidence of the Talmud is clear, as Berakhot 45b cites a *baraita* saying that women do form groups for *zimmun* on their own, and Bavli Arakhin 3a cites a *baraita* that mandates them to do so. Of course, following this line of analysis might lead one to require single-gender *minyanim* of ten. See below at nn. 82–87.

6. Perhaps the most significant point: Many later sources search for a basis for the claim that women do not count in a minyan for *tefillah*. None cite this *sugya*, and several are explicit that there is no talmudic evidence for the claim, despite it being reasonable in their eyes. See n. 23.

We reiterate our basic claim: There is nothing in the *sugya* on Bavli Berakhot 47b–48a that would force a later *posek*'s hand to exclude women from the quorum of ten required by Mishnah Megillah 4:3.

16 Similar reasoning is used by the Urah Shaḥar, cited below nn. 61–63.

17 The latter point is made clear by the Talmud's initial assumption on Sanhedrin 74b that Esther ought to have been required to martyr herself rather than allow herself to be taken as Aḥashveirosh's wife.

those sources either their normative exclusion or inclusion. In short, there is no dispositive evidence one way or the other.[18]

---

18 Claiming that women are obligated in *tefillah* and martyrdom does not automatically positively dispose of the question of their inclusion in the *minyan* associated with those practices. Note that the Shulḥan Arukh at one and the same time holds that women are obligated in prayer but that only men could constitute the *minyan*. Despite much argument to the contrary, by both proponents and opponents of counting women in a *minyan*, there is simply no good evidence for the notion that one counts in *a minyan* if and only if one is obligated in the respective *mitzvot* associated with that *minyan*. All of the rituals we have been discussing are in one way or another associated with the *mitzvah* of sanctifying God's name in public. While anyone (including women) may be eligible/obligated to engage in the relevant practice, it could well be that the requisite quorum to give these acts meaning must be made up of those with some sort of principal group identity that extends beyond obligation in these *mitzvot*. In other words, if the quorum is intended to assure that some microcosm of the Jewish community is present, it could be that women are sufficiently a part of that community to be obligated in the performance of the practice, but insufficiently **representative** of the community to create the quorum. Naturally, one could argue in the other direction as well. Because the contrary argument has been advanced by so many, it is worth briefly engaging with one passage in the Rishonim that is claimed to support the notion that obligation in a *mitzvah* and counting toward its quorum go hand in hand. The Ran on Rif Megillah 6b s.v. *matnitin*, after positing that women can fulfill the obligation of men in the reading of the *megillah*, says the following:

> וי"א שאע"פ שהן מוציאות אין מצטרפות...וא"א...היאך אפשר שמוציאות אנשים ידי קריאה ואין מצטרפות עמהם למנין אלא ודאי מצטרפות.

> Some say that even though they [can] discharge [others] they do not join.... But this is impossible...How is it possible that they [could] discharge men of [their obligation of] reading but not join with them for the *minyan*? Rather, certainly they join.

Some have taken this as a general principle that once one is obligated in a *mitzvah* one is eligible to count for all associated quorums. This is an overreading of the Ran. More likely the Ran is making a point local to the reading of the *megillah*. Whereas other quorums may be wrapped up in representing the community in microcosm, the ten for *megillah* (itself a disputed requirement in the Talmud) is required only in order to publicize the miracle of Purim and thus serves a different function from the quorum of ten required for *devarim shebikdushah*. The Ran is making the claim that, **with respect to** *megillah*, there is absolutely no reason to think that there are any requirements beyond obligation for counting in the *minyan* for that *mitzvah*, since the only point of that quorum of ten is to get ten *megillah*-obligated people together to do this *mitzvah* more publicly. The voices he is arguing with apparently do not limit the quorum for *megillah* in this way and understand it to entail the same sorts of requirements as for other quorums. See the debate between the Ma'or and Ramban

II. Medieval Rulings, Interpretations, and Additions

Just as the question of a woman counting toward the *minyan* for public prayer and *devarim shebikdushah* does not arise in classical rabbinic sources, so too most Rishonim do not discuss it. They simply cite the language of the Mishnah, "ten," and add in the exclusions of minors and slaves that are explicit in talmudic material.[19] However, several medieval authorities do say that a woman does not count for various functions. Some give no reason, such as R. Sa'adiah Gaon (with reference to *devarim shebikdushah*), the Rambam (with reference to Torah reading), the Tosafot (public prayer and application to all requirements of ten),[20] R. Meir b. Shimon ha-Me'ili

---

on precisely this point. This reading of the Ran is supported by the following passage from his teacher, the Ritva, on Megillah 4a s.v. *ve-kheivan*, which is likely his source:

> הילכך הכא דעשרה אינם אלא לפרסומי ניסא בעלמא ולא חשיב צירוף כולי האי כיון דחייבות במקרא מגילה מצטרפות.
>
> Therefore here, since ten are only needed to publicize the miracle, and it is not considered so much of a joining since they (the women) are obligated in reading the *megillah*, they can join.

There is therefore no solid support for the claim that anyone, including the Ran, thinks that being obligated in a *mitzvah* automatically and generally validates one as counting toward the quorums associated with it.

19 One typical example of this sort can be found in the language of Tur OḤ 55:

> אומר קדיש וא"א אותו בפחות מעשרה דכל דבר שבקדושה כגון קדיש וברכו וקדושה א"א אותו בפחות מעשרה...ואלו היו"ד צריך שיהו כולם בני חורין וגדולים שהביאו ב' שערות.
>
> He says Kaddish, and it is impossible with less than ten, because every *davar shebikdushah*—like Kaddish, Barekhu, Kedushah—cannot be with fewer than ten...And these ten need to be all free adults who have signs of puberty.

20 Note that the Tosafot claim that their interpretation is grounded in the claim on Berakhot 45b that "והא מאה נשי כתרי גברי דמיין — A hundred women are like two men." This line is part of a discussion exploring whether two men can exercise the option to form a *zimmun*, even though they are not obligated. A *baraita* authorizing an all-female *zimmun* is cited as proof, along with this tag line about a hundred women being like two men. The Tosafot read this as indicating the exclusion of women from all quorums, including those of ten. In other words, the Tosafot assert that women have no capacity for group identity in halakhic discourse. The *sugya* would then be arguing that if women, with no group identity, can nonetheless form a *zimmun*, there should be no barrier to two men forming a *zimmun*, even if they lack the proper group identity. Rashi there, however, does not take this interpretation,

(the reading of Megillat Esther and application to all requirements of ten), R. Menaḥem ha-Meiri (with reference to *devarim shebikdushah*), and R. Tzidkiyah b. Avraham ha-Rofei (stated generally):

סידור רב סעדיה גאון פירושו על תפילת שחרית, אחר ישתבח
ואם צבור מתפלל את שלש התפלות האלה, ושיעור הציבור הוא עשרה זכרים שהגיעו לפרקם.

Siddur R. Sa'adiah Gaon, commentary following weekday Yishtabaḥ
If the community prays these three *tefillot*—the measure of a community for this being ten males who have reached puberty.

רמב"ם הלכות תפילה יב:ג
אין קורין בתורה בציבור בפחות מעשרה אנשים גדולים בני חורין.

Rambam, Hilkhot Tefillah 12:3
We do not read from the Torah in public with fewer than ten adult free males.[21]

---

and most other Rishonim follow Rashi, seeing this line as specifically discussing *zimmun* and asserting that even the largest group of women is not obligated to form a *zimmun*. He reads "a hundred women are like **two** men" to indicate that they are short of the obligatory characteristics of a group of **three** men. Others, like the Ritva, understand this line to mean that even the largest group of women is not more socially significant than two men; therefore, if women are allowed to form their own *zimmun*, two men should have the right to do so as well if they wish. Also note that the *baraita* coupled with this line is deflected by the *sugya* as ultimately irrelevant to the discussion. Given the broad interpretational dispute with the Tosafot, it is best to assess their position as a halakhic statement in its own right rather than engage Bavli Berakhot 45b directly as a relevant text for our topic. Because Bavli Berakhot 45b is plausibly only about a *zimmun* of three, we did not include it in our discussion of potentially dispositive talmudic evidence above. See also above, n. 15.

21 This follows our printed text of the Mishneh Torah. A number of commentators on this passage seem not to have had the word אנשים in their text, in which case there would be no explicit source from Rambam's writing excluding women from the *minyan* required for *devarim shebikdushah*. These include Sefer ha-Menuḥah and the Kesef Mishneh (but cf. Beit Yosef OḤ 199). But note that R. Avraham b. ha-Rambam's Sefer ha-Maspik le-Ovdei Hashem, 190, indeed includes men as a

תוספות ברכות מה:
"והא מאה נשי כתרי גברי דמיין" – לענין קבוץ תפלה ולענין כל דבר שבעשרה.

Tosafot on Berakhot 45b
"But a hundred women are like two men"—for the matter of a prayer quorum and all other matters that require ten.

ספר המאורות מגילה ה.
ונראה לומר שאף על פי שאשה כשירה להוציא את האיש ממקרא מגלה, שאין ראוי להשלים בה עשרה, דהיכא דבעינן עשרה, אנשים דוקא בעינן.

Sefer ha-Me'orot Megillah 5a
It seems that though a woman may fulfill a man's obligation in reading the *megillah*, it is not proper to count her toward the ten for the reading, because wherever we require ten, we specifically need men.

בית הבחירה להמאירי ברכות מז:
ואין דבר שבקדושה מסור לנשים...אינה עולה למנין י' של מעמד ותפלה.

Beit ha-Beḥirah Berakhot 47b
Devarim shebikdushah are not the domain of women...she may not count [even as a tenth] for the necessary quorum for Torah reading and prayer.[22]

---

criterion for who is eligible to count in a *minyan*. Regarding Rambam's approach to women and the ten required for *zimmun* with God's name, see Appendix D.

22 The first part of this passage in the Meiri is in the context of a discussion of whether ten women can perform *zimmun bashem*, adding God's name into the introductory invitation to Birkat ha-Mazon. The immediate surrounding text reads as follows:

> אבל אם היו עשר אע"פ שמזומנות מכל מקום אין מזומנות בשם, שהזכרת השם דבר שבקדושה הוא, ואין דבר שבקדושה מסור לנשים. ויש חולקים בכך.

> But if they were ten, even though they [can be] invited, nevertheless they do not do *zimmun* with [God's] Name, because mentioning the Name is a *davar*

שבלי הלקט הלכות תפלה ט
ונשים ועבדים אינן משלימין לעשרה.

Shibbolei ha-Leket, Hilkhot Tefillah 9
Women and slaves may not complete the quorum.

Other Rishonim, especially several from Provence, also specify men, but provide textual or logical support for this position. In each example of textual evidence, a particular Rishon focuses on one of the verses the Talmud cites to explain why some ritual requires ten, and explains that this verse must refer only to men. A summary of these various explanations

---

shebikdushah, and *devarim shebikdushah* are not handed over to women. But some disagree about this.

It is syntactically possible to read this line in the Meiri as claiming that there are some who disagree that *devarim shebikdushah* are not the domain of women and they would thus permit ten women to perform rituals that require a *minyan*. In fact, there is a possibility, albeit unprovable, that Rabbeinu Simḥah of Speyer subscribed to such a view, a point we will note below at n. 41. Nonetheless, given that there is no explicit evidence for such a view anywhere in the Rishonim, it seems safer to read the view cited in the Meiri here as agreeing with the basic claim that *devarim shebikdushah* are not the domain of women. Rather, it rules that ten women doing a *zimmun* may mention God's name because adding God's name there is not a *davar shebikdushah*, and therefore the agreed-upon fact that women are not included in such rituals is irrelevant. This conservative reading is also supported by: (1) the fact that the next line in the Meiri cites a proof specific to the question of *zimmun bashem*, which seems to be arbitrating a dispute over ten women and *zimmun bashem*, as opposed to a broader debate over quorums of ten more generally, and (2) the second part of the passage we have quoted here, where the Meiri takes for granted, even against the backdrop of the possibility that ten women might sometimes form a group, that ten women **never** add up to a quorum for *devarim shebikdushah*. This approach also comports with explicit evidence for views in the Rishonim that *zimmun bashem* is **not** in fact a *davar shebikdushah*. See Ra'avan, Even ha-Ezer #185 and Rashba Megillah 23b s.v. *ve-ein nos'in*. Note also that all manuscript witnesses to the text of Bavli Megillah 23b explain the reason for the quorum of ten required to mention the Name in *zimmun* as לאו אורח ארעא, which might be taken as a claim that this ritual, unlike the first group of rituals in the Mishnah, is not a *davar shebikdushah*. For more, see Benei Tziyyon 199:6. On the other hand, it might be that the Gemara here is explaining that the whole notion of a quorum of ten for a *davar shebikdushah* (including *zimmun*) is that it is לאו אורח ארעא to engage in such a serious ritual without significant numbers. We will return to the latter reading below, n. 61 and onward. For more on questions of *zimmun bashem* and the passage in Sefer ha-Mikhtam on which the Meiri referred to here is largely based, see Appendix D.

is found in Rabbeinu Manoaḥ's Sefer ha-Menuḥah. After noting that the Rambam's ruling in Hilkhot Berakhot 5:7 that ten women may not mention God's name in their *zimmun* has no explicit basis in the Talmud,[23] R. Manoaḥ offers three readings of biblical verses to strengthen both the Rambam's point and his assumption that women are generally excluded from the *minyan* for *devarim shebikdushah* as well:

ספר המנוחה על משנה תורה, הלכות ברכות ה:ז
וצ"ע...ועניין זה אינו בגמרא בפירוש, מיהו דינא הכי הוא...דהא כתיב "במקהלות ברכו" (תהלים סח:כז), והני לא איקרו קהל כלל. והכי נמי אמרינן בתפלה דאחייבי בה ואפילו הכי לא מצטרפי לעשרה, והן עצמן נמי אמרי' לא קדיש ולא קדושה, דכל דבר שבקדושה אינו בפחות מעשרה, דכתיב "ונקדשתי בתוך בני ישראל", ולא בנות ישראל. ו"עדה" נמי בזכרים היא ולא בנקבות, דהא מרגלים אנשי הוו. וכיון דדבר שבקדושה ליתי' בפחות מעשרה אנשים, והזכרת השם בברכת זמון ליתא אלא בעשרה משום דהוי דבר שבקדושה, ממילא אימעיטו להו נשים...ואף הסברא נותנת שלא יזמנו בשם, שהרי אין בהם דעת לגדל ורומם שמו של הקב"ה כאנשים, וכתיב "גדלו לה' אתי".

Sefer ha-Menuḥah, Commentary to Hilkhot Berakhot 5:7
This requires consideration...This matter is not explicit in the Gemara, but nonetheless it is the law...for it is written, "bless in *mak'heilot*" (Tehillim 68:27), and they [i.e., women] are not at all called a *kahal*. And we hold similarly with regard to prayer, in which women are obligated, but nonetheless they do not

23 This is a point also noted by Sefer ha-Me'orot 45a. He adds that, because this is the case, one should not protest against those who violate the Rambam's ruling. This is an important text for helping to reframe an issue that often suffers from hot tempers and intolerance for divergent views, given that women's exclusion from the quorum of ten is nowhere explicated in classical rabbinic literature. R. Manoaḥ and Sefer ha-Me'orot are important support for our final point in n. 15 above. See also the Rashbatz on Berakhot 10b, who argues that the Rambam drew this ruling from the Talmud's comment: "והא מאה נשי כתרי גברי דמיין — a hundred women are like two men." This comment of the Rashbatz is already heavily influenced by Tosafot Berakhot 45b s.v. *ve-ha* and is unlikely historically to have been the source of the Rambam's ruling. See above, n. 20.

> form the quorum of ten,[24] and they as a group on their own do not say Kaddish or Kedushah, for any *davar shebikdushah* may not be said in a group of fewer than ten, since it is written, "And I will be sanctified in the midst of *benei yisrael*"—and not *benot yisrael*. And "*eidah*" also applies only to males, because the spies were men. And since a *davar shebikdushah* may not be said in a group of fewer than ten men, and the restriction on mentioning the Name in *zimmun* in a group of fewer than ten is because this act is a *davar shebikdushah*, women are thus excluded... and further, common sense tells us that they should not conduct *zimmun* with the Name, because they do not have the intellectual capacity to magnify and exalt the name of the Holy One as men do, and it is written: "Magnify God with me" (Tehillim 34:4).

R. Manoaḥ begins by quoting Tehillim 68:27 ("**במקהלות** ברכו א-להים — Bless God **in assemblies**"), which appears in Mishnah Berakhot 7:3 as the prooftext for using increasingly elaborate language in praising God, as the size of the gathering for *zimmun* increases. He then proceeds to state that women are not considered a *kahal*, and since *zimmun* with God's name is associated with the term *kahal*,[25] ten women may not perform it. This notion that women are not a *kahal* finds earlier roots in an exegetical tradition in Sifrei Bemidbar #109, which assumes that the term *kahal*

---

24 Note that R. Manoaḥ here makes explicit what we showed earlier, namely that obligation in prayer is irrelevant to—or at least, insufficient to answer—the question of counting toward the *minyan*.

25 While R. Manoaḥ here only seems to invoke קהל in the context of *zimmun*, others engage it more broadly. Sefer ha-Eshkol, Hilkhot Keri'at Shema 6a associates במקהלות ברכו א-להים with the ten required for Barekhu more generally, influenced by the word ברכו in the verse. The Ramban on Bavli Pesaḥim 85a associates it with all cases of *devarim shebikdushah*, likely influenced by R. Abahu's statement on Bavli Ketubot 7b that this verse is the basis for requiring ten for Birkat Ḥatanim. Since Birkat Ḥatanim is one of the rituals listed in Mishnah Megillah 4:3, it is a small step to suggest that במקהלות is a relevant associated text for all of them. R. Manoaḥ seems to have been the first to take this well-known association and use it to derive a point about gender in order to support the Rambam. The Ritva, a slightly later contemporary, follows this gendered approach to קהל in his comments on Ketubot 7b, where he asserts that the ten for Birkat Ḥatanim must be all male.

only includes men. He then cites " ונקדשתי בתוך בני ישראל — And I shall be sanctified among the people [literally: 'sons'] of Israel" (Vayikra 22:32), the core verse adduced in the Talmud to justify requiring ten for *devarim shebikdushah* (Megillah 23b). He explains here that the Torah intentionally specifies the "sons" of Israel, and not the daughters.[26] R. Manoaḥ is presumably basing himself on a tannaitic *midrash*, recorded in a number of places, that when the Torah commands *benei yisrael* with regard to certain procedures in Temple sacrifices, it means males specifically: "בני ישראל סומכין ואין בנות ישראל סומכות — male Jews lay the hands [on their sacrifices], but female Jews do not lay the lands."[27] R. Manoaḥ's innovation is to apply that reading to the context of *devarim shebikdushah* as well. His final scriptural evidence is the word *eidah*: When the Gemara demonstrates the necessity of ten for *devarim shebikdushah* from the story of the spies, it must mean men specifically, since all ten spies were men. He then concludes that common sense alone justifies a gendered practice around a *zimmun* of ten (and presumably other quorums of ten as well): Women, he states, do not have the same intellectual disposition as men and cannot therefore serve as their equals and peers in these rituals.

As we noted above, R. Manoaḥ conveniently collects these scriptural associations and derivations, which are also found in other Rishonim. Do these actually reflect claims about objective biblical interpretations of our topic, which generate law like any other classical *midrash*? Or do they function as *asmakhta'ot*—*post facto* supports for a law already assumed, perhaps grounded primarily in intuitions and well-worn patterns of behavior? These *midrashim* all have analogues in classical rabbinic literature and the use of the spies' identity to derive law simply continues the legacy of the Gemara on Bavli Sanhedrin 74b, which used the Jewish identity of the spies to exclude Gentiles from the *minyan*. Indeed, there is

---

26 A century later, Orḥot Ḥayyim also cited this verse for the same point. A similar appeal to gendered language is made by the Ritva on Ketubot 7b in the context of the ten required for Birkat Ḥatanim. In addition to his gendered reading of קהל, he suggests that the word אנשים in Rut 4:2 specifies males and not females.

27 Sifra Dibbura de-Nedava Parashah 2:2; Bavli Eruvin 96b and parallels. See also Sifrei Bemidbar #39 and Sifrei Zuta 15:25, where בני ישראל is understood to exclude converts, women, and slaves.

a significant tradition of sources that views various qualities of the spies as paradigmatic of various points of law about inclusion in *minyan*.[28]

Nonetheless, there is an equally strong and compelling tradition that insists that such *midrashim*—**on a matter of rabbinic prayer**—must be understood as rich and authoritative language ("*asmakhta'ot*") for deeply held religious convictions, and not as generative prooftexts.[29]

A number of reasons recommend that approach in this instance:

1. First, despite Sifrei Bemidbar's prior reading of *kahal* as a gendered term, several *mitzvot* in the Torah that equally apply to women and men also use that word. Examples are the *pesaḥ* sacrifice ("ושחטו אתו כל קהל עדת ישראל בין הערבים — The whole assembly of the congregation of Israel shall slaughter it at dusk," Shemot 12:6); the prohibition of a *mamzer* (child of an incestuous or adulterous relationship) entering God's "assembly" (לא יבא ממזר בקהל ה', Devarim 23:3); and, most strikingly, the commandment of "Assembly (*hak'hel*)" ("הקהל את העם האנשים והנשים והטף — Assemble the nation: the men, the women, and the children," Devarim 31:12). Why favor the Sifrei Bemidbar's gendered interpretation of *kahal* as the plain sense of that word to the exclusion of these other possibilities? Moreover, if we view the use of *kahal* as generative of the laws surrounding the identity of the *minyan* members, we might take the claim on Bavli Horayot

---

28 Ra'avan, in Even ha-Ezer #185, uses the fact that the spies were adults to exclude minors. Shulḥan Arukh ha-Rav 55:2 uses R. Manoaḥ's logic here as a basis for excluding women. R. Moshe Feinstein in Iggerot Moshe OḤ 2:19 argues that since the spies were wicked, it must be permissible to count one who violates Shabbat in a *minyan*.

29 See Rosh Berakhot 7:20:

ואפילו הוי מלתא דרבנן כגון לשמוע קדושה וברכו **שלא מצינו לו עיקר מן התורה.**

Even if it were something rabbinic, like to hear the Kedushah or Barekhu, **for which we do not find a source in the Torah.**

See also the Ran's statement about Mishnah Megillah 4:3 (found on Rif Megillah 13b):

ומיהו הני מילי כולהו אסמכתא דרבנן נינהו דסדר תפלה גופה דרבנן.

All of these derivations are *post facto* supports for rabbinic laws, since the whole order of prayer is itself rabbinic.

6b that *levi'im* are not called *kahal* to exclude them from the *minyan* as well. No one would ever have suggested that. However, if we understand the use of this *asmakhta* as an expression of an assumption that women do not participate in corporate entities nor create communities, these Rishonim make quite a bit more sense—what could be a more appropriate verse to cite to this effect than one that invokes the notion of community?

2. Second, the appeal to *benei yisrael* as a gendered term in this context runs up against its use in other contexts that are gender blind, such as the *mitzvot* regarding evaluative oaths, *arakhin* (Vayikra 27). Moreover, Sifrei Bemidbar #115 states:

   ויאמר ה׳ אל משה לאמר דבר אל בני ישראל ואמרת אליהם ועשו להם ציצית, אף הנשים במשמע.

   "Tell *benei yisrael* and speak to them that they shall make themselves *tzitzit*," this suggests that women are included as well.[30]

   As we noted above, there is a clear tradition that explicitly excludes women from *benei yisrael* that cuts the other way as well.[31] But when asking what the Rishonim are doing, it remains unclear why they would favor one midrashic bias over another, given that no gendered conclusion on *minyan* is ever spelled out in classical rabbinic literature. If, instead, we understand this use of the verse not as a formal proof but as an allusive expression of a deeply held belief—that the Jewish "community" is not properly represented by its female members—then the use of a phrase about the Jewish people is a perfectly reasonable support.

3. Third, though the use of the spies' identity to derive law is well attested, it should also be clear how slippery and unreliable that usage can be. For instance, why not demand that the *minyan* be

30 This view is then followed by the dissenting view of R. Shimon, who exempts women from *tzitzit*, but not through an appeal to the terminology of בני ישראל.

31 See n. 27.

formed only by males over the age of thirty (as were Yosef's older brothers when they went down to Egypt)? Why not demand some tribal diversity among the participants, as was the case with the spies? Why not exclude male converts from the *minyan*? It seems more reasonable to see the use of these biblical verses in the Rishonim, like many other exegeses found in rabbinic literature, as *post facto* support for an accepted practice. These scriptural citations, while weak as formal proofs, express the religious sensibilities of their authors and their communities.

4. Fourth, R. Manoaḥ also ends this passage with an appeal to reason. That suggests that he does not feel (nor does he intend others to feel) that the prior proofs are meant to be uncontested legal derivations that settle the matter. Indeed, this final sentiment, which grounds women's exclusion from *minyan* in common sense and the *posek*'s reality, may shed light on the deeper motivations behind the scriptural anchors. The fact is that R. Manoaḥ did **not** consider the exclusion of women from *minyan* to be an oddity imposed on him by ancient texts. Rather, that exclusion rang true to him given his experiences with women, as a class, being insufficiently educated to form a community for the purposes of publicly praising God.[32] He considered this reality to be a relevant and, apparently, decisive factor in the question of their participation.

---

32 These words burn in the ears of many contemporary readers and we in no way intend to minimize or dismiss that pain. At the same time, well-founded modern critiques of R. Manoaḥ's social setting as well as R. Manoaḥ's own troubling formulation should not lead us to a facile dismissal of his core point. If we consider a world in which education for women was minimal (even in comparison to the relatively spartan education of many Jewish men), then it should not surprise us that women would have been viewed as intellectually inferior to men. In R. Manoaḥ's time, a group of women lacked the social capital that a comparable group of men would have had. In the context of a reality very different from our own, R. Manoaḥ is emphasizing the weightiness of the sanctification of God's name—and the way in which this is played out through *devarim shebikdushah*. Perhaps his words can thus contribute something to our appreciation of the gravity of *devarim shebikdushah*, even if they do so in the context of a different social reality that might be disturbing to us, and even if R. Manoaḥ's seeming complicity with this reality might be disappointing.

All of this supports the general idea that those Rishonim who see *minyan* as gendered—whether without justification, by recourse to scriptural anchors, or by invoking common sense—all intuit and assume the exclusion of women as something obvious, rather than something counterintuitive imposed on them by a text. Indeed, given the absence of any dispositive source material in the Talmud, this would almost seem to be the only reasonable conclusion to draw. That women do not count is intuitive to these Rishonim, just as the exclusion of slaves and minors was intuitive to R. Yehoshua b. Levi. Their citation of verses is not meant to **prove** these religious intuitions, but rather to provide some allusive Scriptural context for them.

But however we read the gendering of *minyan* in these Rishonim, a core substantive question remains: Why? What is behind the exclusion of women that emerges clearly in the medieval period? How might we more precisely define the considerations at work in medieval discussions of this topic? And based on those considerations, how would we answer questions relating to gender and *minyan* in our own day?

III. What is *Minyan* and What Are the Implications for Gender Inclusion?

We turn now to the question of understanding the essence of *minyan* and the criteria that stand behind some of the practical rulings we have seen so far.

A. MODEL I: COVENANTAL BELONGING, CONNECTION TO *MITZVOT*, AND "HONOR OF HEAVEN"—R. TAM

The earliest (and only) thorough attempt in the Rishonim to define what *minyan* is all about was proffered by R. Tam. Following R. Yehoshua b. Levi's ruling on Bavli Berakhot 47b that one baby—even an infant in a cradle—could be counted in a *minyan*,[33] R. Tam comments as follows:

---

33 It seems that R. Tam arrives at this view by arguing that the statement ולית הלכתא ככל הני שמעתתא—already an integral part of his text—only applied to the

תוספות ר״י שירליאון ברכות מז:
ואני מוסיף אפי׳ מוטל בעריסה, דאכל בני י׳ שכינתא שריא, דכי גמירי קדושה בעשרה מ״ונקדשתי״, ל״ש גדולים ול״ש קטני׳, ובלבד שיהיו תשע גדולים, דטפי מחד לא, כדאמרי׳ גבי עבד, **דליכא יקרא דשמיא כולי האי**, ועבד נמי אייתי בכלל ונקדשתי, דשכינה שריא אכל מחוייבי מצות ובני ברית.

Tosafot R. Yehudah Sirleon on Berakhot 47b
And I add even an infant in his cradle, for the Divine Presence dwells among all groups of ten, for when we learn that matters of sanctity are done in a quorum of ten from the verse, "I will be sanctified," no distinction is made between minors and adults. But there must be nine adults, because more than one [minor] may not be counted, as it is taught with respect to a slave, for [with more than one] **there is insufficient honor for heaven**. And a slave also comes under the principle "I will be sanctified," for the Divine Presence dwells among all who are obligated in commandments and who are members of the covenant.

Recall that the Talmud's source for the numerical makeup of *minyan* is Vayikra 22:32 (ונקדשתי בתוך בני ישראל). R. Tam explains that this "sanctity" inheres in all who are obligated in *mitzvot* or are members of the covenant. His point is to argue that slaves (who are obligated in *mitzvot*—to the same extent as Jewish women—despite not being Jews) and children (who are Jews but not yet obligated in *mitzvot*) are essentially eligible to count in the *minyan*,[34] as evidenced in his eyes by the talmudic phrase "כל בי עשרה שכיתנא שריא — the Divine Presence dwells among

immediately prior statements, and not to R. Yehoshua b. Levi's rulings on counting a slave and a minor. See Tosafot Berakhot 48a s.v. *ve-leit*. This, of course, is just a return to possibilities of the original text of the Gemara prior to the incorporation of the geonic gloss.

34 This assumes the *vav* of ובני ברית is disjunctive. If one, however, reads the *vav* as conjunctive—which seems to be the reading of Rosh Berakhot 7:20—one would have to say that infants are obligated in *mitzvot* because they will be obligated in *mitzvot* as adults. Slaves would be considered בני ברית in the sense that they are circumcised (an interpretation advanced by R. Yom Tov Lippman Heller's commentary on the Rosh, Ma'adanei Yom Tov on Rosh Berakhot 7:20, likely influenced by Bavli Bava Kama 15a

all groups of ten" (Talmud Bavli Sanhedrin 39a). However, even the most inclusive opinion in the Talmud allows counting only one slave, and not many.[35] Therefore, R. Tam explains that the reason a *minyan* should not include more than one child or slave is because more than that would be "insufficient honor for heaven." R. Tam does not appeal here to precedent or a formal definition; he is expressing that it is inappropriate to form a *minyan*—the representative microcosm of the community for the task of exalting God's name—with such peripheral, undignified members. He argues that this is the case even though, from a theological perspective, the Shekhinah does descend on any group of ten individuals who are connected to the Jewish people, either through obligation (slaves) or birth (minors). For R. Tam, *minyan* is nothing less and nothing more than a convocation of ten people anchored to the Jewish people through ancestry or obligation and any such group is theoretically an appropriate manifestation of *benei yisrael*, the group in which God's name is sanctified. Beyond that, a *minyan* must not violate the standard of יקרא דשמיא, "the honor of heaven," which captures the notion of a gathering that is objectively dignified and worthy of God's serious attention.

Now, we have no record of R. Tam discussing the question of women and *minyan*, but his conceptual framework can further our understanding. His description of what *minyan* is about would include women, who were obligated in all the same *mitzvot* as slaves in his context, and were also considered part of the covenant.[36] Purely following R. Tam's logic, we might well conclude that ten women can constitute a *minyan*. There is no rabbinic source that limits the participation of women, as there is regarding slaves and minors, and no indication that counting more than one woman

---

and driven by the Rosh's reading of R. Tam's two criteria as jointly necessary rather than individually sufficient). The first reading seems stronger to us.

35 It is plausible that R. Yehoshua b. Levi's statement about making an infant a סניף also only imagined counting one, and this is clearly how R. Tam understood him. Others, however, understood him to be more liberal on infants, possibly permitting counting up to four toward the *minyan*. See n. 9.

36 If the term "covenant" is meant generally to refer to Jews, then women are obviously included (for a usage of בת ברית to refer to a woman in this sense, see Sifrei Zuta 35:12), and if it refers to circumcision, the Talmud considers women to be already circumcised (Avodah Zarah 27a).

would violate the honor of heaven.[37] At that point, we could revert to R. Tam's original definition of where the Divine Presence dwells, about which he says, "no distinction is made between minors and adults"—i.e., ten minors (or ten women) could theoretically make up a *minyan*.

Indeed, this basic conceptual extrapolation was made by Rabbeinu Simḥah of Speyer, who ruled that a woman could count toward the ten. From the context in which his ruling is cited, however, it seems that he limited the extrapolation to a more conservative extension from R. Tam's actual ruling regarding one slave or one minor and only allowed one woman to count toward the *minyan*:[38]

מרדכי ברכות קעג
מצאתי בשם רבינו שמחה: עבד ואשה מצטרפין בין לתפלה בין לברוך א-להינו, ומעשה דר׳ אליעזר ששחרר עבדו והשלימו לי׳ דמשמע דוקא בשחררו אבל אי לא שיחררו לא, והוא הדין לאשה, יש לומר תרי הוו ושחרר חד ומילא בחד.

Mordekhai Berakhot #173
I found in the name of R. Simḥah: A slave or a woman can join toward the ten required for prayer and for *barukh eloheinu* [the formula mentioning God's name in *zimmun*]. And regarding the case where R. Eliezer freed his slave in order to complete the quorum, which makes it sound as if an unfreed slave may not count toward the ten—and the same restriction would apply to a woman—we can say that there were two slaves present; one he freed [in order to count as the ninth] and one he counted as the tenth [while still a slave].

According to a different tradition, R. Simḥah acted upon this ruling:[39]

---

37 R. Tam never applies the concern of יקרא דשמיא to women, which just reflects the fact that there is no talmudic statement that limits counting women in a *minyan*—in contrast to slaves and minors, who are so limited.

38 This conservative reading of R. Simḥah is maintained by Beit Yosef OḤ 55 and many others. See n. 41.

39 It should not be surprising to find this kind of leniency specifically in the writings of R. Tam and the Tosafists, who, by and large, lived in tiny Jewish communities in northern France and Germany. Making a *minyan* is much more difficult when the

מרדכי ברכות קנח (= מרדכי גטין תא)

גם רבינו שמחה היה עושה מעשה לצרף אשה [לי'] לזימון, ואפילו אם תמצא לומר דאשה לא מיחייבא האשה אלא מדרבנן...ה"מ לאפוקי אחרים י"ח, אבל לצרוף בעלמא להזכרת שם שמים, שפיר מצטרפת.

Mordekhai Berakhot #158 = Mordekhai Gittin #401

R. Simḥah used to count a woman toward the [ten required for][40] *zimmun*. Even if you say that a woman is only rabbinically obligated [in Birkat ha-Mazon]...that is only a concern for her fulfilling the obligation of others, but there is no problem with her counting toward the ten needed to mention the Name.[41]

---

pool of potential participants is so small. Perhaps of additional significance is the greater financial independence enjoyed by women in these communities, as opposed to those in southern Europe and the Mediterranean. For the broader religious context, see Grossman, *Pious and Rebellious.*

40 The notation לי' (standing for לעשרה), which is added here by a later hand to clarify that the context is a *zimmun* of ten, is no doubt influenced by the final words in this passage, which speak of הזכרת שם שמים, "mentioning God's name." That suggests that R. Simḥah was only dealing with a quorum of ten, and not a quorum of three. However, Agur #289 quotes R. Simḥah, in the name of the Mordekhai, as counting a woman toward the quorums of both three and ten: "וכן רבינו שמחה בין לעשרה בין בין לג' — And so too R. Simḥah, whether for ten or for three." R. Simḥah's positions seem to have been filtered through various later editorial layers that interpreted him differently. Indeed, the whole final clause here—beginning with ואפילו—may be a later addition. Traditions allowing a woman to count toward the quorum of three were attacked by the Maharam of Rothenberg in his Responsa IV:227. The language here in our version of the Mordekhai seems to account for the Maharam's attack while still defending a more modest version of R. Simḥah, applied to the less radical case of counting women toward the quorum of ten. See n. 15 for more on the relative hierarchy of the quorums of three and ten and see n. 41 for further reflections on the processing of R. Simḥah's positions in these sources.

41 R. Simḥah's position on counting women toward the *minyan* is reported here secondhand, filtered and repackaged along with other sources. The language in this latter source actually sounds as if R. Simḥah allowed women to count as equals toward the ten of *zimmun*. This opens the possibility that R. Simḥah permitted women to count as equals toward the quorum of ten, even as he limited slaves and minors to one of the ten slots, in keeping with R. Tam's rulings on the matter. Indeed, R. Moshe Blau seems to understand R. Simḥah—and R. Tam—similarly in his edition of Sefer ha-Me'orot (135, n. 9), as does R. Shmuel Dikman in his

Even if R. Simḥah restricted his practice of counting women in the *minyan* to a single woman, the basic claim is clear: R. Tam's definition of *minyan* includes them in principle, with the only remaining question being whether, and to what degree, the honor of heaven limits this being carried out in practice.

B. MODEL II: ONLY MAXIMALLY OBLIGATED MEMBERS OF THE COMMUNITY CAN REPRESENT IT IN MICROCOSM—THE LEVUSH

While R. Tam's theory of *minyan* is the only such explicit articulation in the medieval period, there are possible hints of another approach that eventually flowers more fully in the modern era. As we noted above, a geonic-era gloss on Talmud Bavli Berakhot 48a dismissed R. Yehoshua b. Levi's rulings that were inclusive of slaves and minors. Another definition of *minyan* built on this tradition and suggested that minors and slaves were excluded from counting toward a *minyan* not on account of honor alone, but on account of a more fundamental deficiency: insufficient obligation in *mitzvot.*

In discussing *minyan,* a number of authorities use the term *mitzvah* to get at the essence of what it means to count toward a *minyan.* For instance, Rabbeinu Yonah of Gerona explains why one might count minors toward the *zimmun* but not toward the ten required for aspects of public prayer:

רבינו יונה על הרי"ף ברכות לה:

ודוקא לענין בהמ"ז עושין אותן סניפין מפני שכל אחד בפני עצמו יכול לפטור עצמו מחיוב ברכת המזון. אבל לקדיש ולקדושה ולברכו שכל

edition of Beit ha-Beḥirah (179, n. 152). It might be that only a later hand bringing his positions on women and slaves together in the first passage in the Mordekhai cited above assumed that the rulings were identical and that R. Simḥah permitted only one woman to count in a *minyan.* This reading of R. Simḥah is unprovable, but it is important to establish its historical possibility given the later views that we will see that in fact establish the theoretical plausibility of counting ten women toward a *minyan.* In the discussion here, however, we will assume, so as to be as cautious as possible, that R. Simḥah **practically** permitted counting only one woman toward the *minyan,* even as we will maintain that he **theoretically** permitted ten women to count, following R. Tam's criteria.

אחד ואחד לא היה יכול לפטור עצמו מחויב בשום ענין צריך שיהו כולם בני מצוה.

R. Yonah on Rif Berakhot 35b
Specifically with regard to the Birkat ha-Mazon, we can add minors as adjuncts, because each person that makes up the *zimmun* can fulfill their own obligation Birkat ha-Mazon. But with respect to Kaddish, Kedushah, and Barekhu, where each person cannot in any way fulfill his own obligation, the group must be entirely *benei mitzvah.*

R. Yonah here appeals to the minor's lack of obligation in *mitzvot* to justify his exclusion from the *minyan* required for *devarim shebikdushah.*[42] This may hint at a broader theory that, contrary to R. Tam, minors are not even theoretically eligible for *minyan* on account of this lack of obligation.[43] While the precise meaning and intent of R. Yonah on this front is far from

---

42 Note that R. Yonah thinks there is some sort of individual obligation in *devarim shebikdushah*, though the exact nature of his view is unclear. See our discussion above, Part One, nn. 122–142.

43 Use of the term בני מצוה to exclude children from being the tenth can also be found in Sefer ha-Orah II:156 (= Maḥzor Vitry #81). The term is also used to define the normal group required for a *minyan* in Or Zarua II:370:

> מיהו הא מספקא לי [מגילה] שלא בזמנה שצריכה עשרה אם צריכ׳ עשרה שיהו בני מצוה כמו כל הטעונים עשרה.
>
> But this is doubtful to me: *megillah* that is not at its time that needs ten—if it needs ten who are *benei mitzvah* like all [others] that require ten?

See also R. Ya'akov Moellin in Responsa Maharil #106:

> וחרש שמדבר ואינו שומע אם יש לצרפו לעשרה, לא ידענא מאי קא [מבעי] ליה למר... אי משום דבור הוא, מאי נפקא מינה הואיל ובר דיעה ובר מצוה הוא, אכל בני עשרה שכינתא שריא.
>
> With respect to the question of whether a deaf person who can speak can count toward a *minyan* of ten, I am not sure what you are asking. . . If you are concerned that he is unlearned, why would that matter? Given that he has intelligence and is a *bar mitzvah*, the Divine Presence dwells on all groups of ten.

But this source may simply be saying that this deaf person, once obligated in *mitzvot* on account of having the power of speech, has no other basis for being disqualified.

clear, an explicit articulation of a *mitzvah*-centered approach to *minyan* is delivered by R. Mordekhai Jaffe:

> **לבוש או"ח נה:ד**
> ועבד ואשה וקטן אין מצטרפין שאינם חייבים במצות. ויש מתירין בט' וצירוף כיון שיכול להגיע לכלל חיוב מצות.
>
> **Levush OḤ 55:4**
> Neither a slave nor a woman nor a minor may count toward the *minyan*, because they are not obligated in *mitzvot*. And some permit joining nine adults with one minor, since the minor will eventually become obligated.

The Levush is clearly operating with a different definition of *minyan* from that of R. Tam, despite some of the linguistic similarities. Though both authorities talk about obligation in *mitzvot* as a criterion for counting in a *minyan*, they mean very different things. R. Tam thought this criterion **included** slaves (and, by extension, women), since they are obligated in many *mitzvot*. The Levush, by contrast, uses this criterion to **exclude** slaves and women. For him, "obligation in *mitzvot*" clearly means **maximal** obligation and excludes those, like women and slaves, who, though obligated in many *mitzvot*, are exempt from a range of others (those of the positive, time-caused variety explored above).[44] This paints a significantly different picture of *minyan*. R. Tam is able to conceive of a "community" that comprises free adult males as well as more marginal types, such as slaves, minors, and, most likely, women, but he feels that most such convocations are not so respectful to the honor of heaven. However dishonorable, such a group nonetheless does constitute the *eidah/kahal/benei yisrael* grouping that is the essence of *minyan*. The Levush cannot even conceive of such a convocation being considered a representation of the larger community. By his logic, how can someone who is exempt from a whole category of *mitzvot* possibly help constitute a microcosm of the Jewish people? Justifying a gender-blind *minyan* according to the Levush would require claiming that contemporary women **are** obligated in (all)

---

44 The Levush is here borrowing language of the sort used in Tosefta Berakhot 6:18, שאין הנשים חייבות במצות. That formulation clearly refers to an absence of **maximal** obligation, not to an absence of any obligation whatsoever.

mitzvot and are thus—unlike slaves, minors, and women of the past—indeed fitting representatives of the community. Pursuing gender equality in *minyan* through this model would require addressing not only issues of honor, but more fundamental inequalities of obligation.

C. WEIGHING THE TWO MODELS

As we noted earlier, most of the Rishonim who exclude women from the *minyan* do so without articulating any support for that view, and even those who cite verses and *midrashim* to support their positions do not offer a theory of *minyan* different from those we find either in R. Tam or in the Levush. Many authorities, in both the medieval and the modern period, reject R. Tam's ruling on minors and slaves, but the theoretical implications are unclear. Those who exclude minors and slaves even as the tenth might be doing one of two things:

1. Perhaps they accept R. Tam's theoretical model but reject implementing it for even a single minor or slave. In other words, even if minors are the theoretical equals of adults in constituting a *minyan* and count toward *benei yisraei*, it might offend the honor of heaven to count **even one** toward the quorum of ten. Whereas R. Tam agreed to a modest infraction on the dignity of heaven (relying upon one minor or slave), these authorities would not allow even that level of infraction. Under this reading of the silence in the Rishonim, even those who ban minors and slaves entirely agree with R. Tam that the only criteria to count in a *minyan* are:
   (a) evincing sanctity through some basic connection to the Jewish people, and
   (b) not creating a situation that offends the dignity of heaven.
2. The disagreement regards only criterion (b) and whether some degree of adjunct participation is tolerated.
3. Perhaps their rejection of R. Tam's practical ruling is bound up with a rejection of the theory that undergirds it. In this reading, any authority who refuses to count a minor or a slave even as a tenth has also made a claim that *minyan* has more robust requirements than posited by R. Tam. Since it is silly to speculate about theories of *minyan* that no one ever bothered to articulate, the most

straightforward reading would be that such positions are proto-versions of the Levush. In other words, the wholesale exclusion of minors and slaves from *minyan* in practice would thus indicate a definition of *minyan* that excludes them in essence as well.

An honest analysis will concede that there is no way to tell which of these two interpretations is correct when dealing with a source that simply excludes minors and slaves without explicating that decision. The exclusion might be minor and local, focused on the proper boundaries of the honor of heaven. Alternatively, it might be over the very notion of whether minors and slaves can even theoretically represent the community in microcosm—a rejection of R. Tam's more fundamental principle of "no distinction is made between adults and minors," i.e., that the essence of *minyan* does not depend on the presence of ten free adult males. On the one hand, R. Yosef Karo in Beit Yosef OḤ 55 takes no issue with R. Tam's model in theory; he simply explains the opposition to using that model to count women as an issue of ingrained practice: "וכיון דר"ת בעצמו לא רצה לעשות מעשה מי יקל בדבר — But since R. Tam himself did not want to do such a thing, who can be lenient regarding it?" This suggests a more modest, practical dispute between R. Tam and his opponents. On the other hand, R. Shneur Zalman of Liady, among others, reads the Levush's model back into these Rishonim, setting up a more fundamental divide:

שולחן ערוך הרב או"ח נה:ה

יש מתירין לומר דבר שבקדושה בט' וצירוף עבד או אשה או קטן לפי שעל כל עשרה בני ברית השכינה שורה, אלא שאינו כבוד שמים לומר דבר שבקדושה בפחות מט' בני מצות, שט' נראים כי'...וי"א שאין אשה ועבד או קטן מצטרפים בשום ענין אלא צריך שיהו כל עשרה זכרים בני חורין גדולים שהביאו שתי שערות ובפחות מכן אין השכינה שורה ואין אומרים דבר שבקדושה.

Shulḥan Arukh ha-Rav OḤ 55:5

Some permit saying a *davar shebikdushah* with nine joined together with a slave, a woman, or a minor, because the Shekhinah dwells on any ten members of the covenant—nonetheless it would not be honoring heaven to say a *davar*

> *shebikdushah* with fewer than nine *benei mitzvot*,[45] because nine look like ten...but some say that a woman, slave, or minor may not count at all and all ten must be free male adults who have reached puberty, and with fewer than that, the Shekhinah does not dwell and one may not say a *davar shebikdushah.*

Note that Shulḥan Arukh ha-Rav's formulation here considers slaves, minors, and women to be בני ברית, "members of the covenant," but **not** בני מצות, which here must mean "fully obligated adults." Minors are exempt by dint of their age, whereas women and slaves are exempt from a whole class of *mitzvot* (those positive *mitzvot* caused by time, which we explored above). This is a different usage from that of R. Tam, who explicitly puts slaves in the category of "those obligated in *mitzvot.*" In any event, Shulḥan Arukh ha-Rav's characterization of R. Tam's position is clear: Ten women are theoretically valid for a *minyan*, but in deference to the honor of heaven, we must reserve nine slots for free adult males.[46] This lays bare the contrast between R. Tam and the Levush. The core dispute is whether in fact the

---

45 Note that Shulḥan Arukh ha-Rav's reading of R. Simḥah fits the more conservative reading we offered above: Only one woman can count toward the ten and any additional women would present a problem of יקרא דשמיא/כבוד שמים. But we noted that R. Simḥah himself is less clear on this matter and there is nothing in R. Tam himself to suggest that כבוד שמים applies to gender as well, even though this would be a reasonable claim, as we will explore further below.

46 Note that Shulḥan Arukh ha-Rav was so influenced by the Levush's model of *minyan* that he reads it back into R. Tam's position as well. R. Tam himself thought that a basic level of obligation and membership in the covenant make one a fitting vehicle for the Divine Presence but that the factor of יקרא דשמיא—seemingly unrelated to issues of obligation—prevents allowing more than one such undignified member from counting toward the quorum. Shulḥan Arukh ha-Rav sees membership in the covenant (an attribute he assigns to women, slaves, **and** minors) as the criterion for being a theoretically fitting vehicle for the Divine Presence and mentions nothing about *mitzvah* obligation. But he then assumes that the concern of יקרא דשמיא is **itself** about obligation: It is the lack of maximal obligation that makes someone an undignified candidate for more than one *minyan* slot. Thus, according to Shulḥan Arukh ha-Rav's reading of R. Tam, even the latter's model would require a wholesale reevaluation of contemporary women's obligations in order to have a gender-equal *minyan*. This does not seem like a very plausible reading of R. Tam. The latter only engages one level of obligation, which is the level of obligation that makes one theoretically eligible for the *minyan*. As we will see, most other interpreters of R. Tam did not read him as Shulḥan Arukh ha-Rav does here. Nonetheless, this passage

Divine Presence can dwell amidst anything other than a group of ten free adult males, on account of the issues of maximal obligation raised in the Levush. R. Tam says yes; the Levush says no.

We will return to this "debate within a debate," the question of whether to see the practical disagreement between R. Tam and his opponents in theoretical terms as well, as we turn to the considerations of practical *halakhah*. For now, we note that the difference between the models of R. Tam and of the Levush is stark as it relates to assessing the role of gender in contemporary *minyanim*. If one understands the dignity of heaven to be the only possible obstacle to counting women as equals in the *minyan*, then a determination that claims such a concern does not apply closes the issue. If, however, one understands the question of gender and *minyan* to be a subset of the question of gender and *mitzvot*, women's inclusion in the *minyan* would hinge on a broader reformulation of the role of gender in halakhic discourse.

D. AFTERMATH OF R. SIMḤAH AND GENDER INCLUSIVITY IN *MINYAN* IN PRACTICE

If we follow R. Tam's definition of *minyan*, then its application to women becomes a live halakhic question, beginning with R. Simḥah's ruling above. The subsequent history of this ruling—at least in practice—is somewhat checkered. R. Ya'akov Landau in Agur #240 does not formally reject R. Simḥah's practice on *zimmun*, but he states: "ואני המחבר לא ראיתי מעולם נוהגים כך ולא שמעתי מקום שנוהגין כן — I have never seen anyone practice this way nor have I heard about a place that practices this way."

R. Yosef Karo curiously does not cite any of the authorities who explicitly exclude female participation, but he does mention R. Simḥah's position to count one woman in the context of *tefillah* and rejects it, arguing that it would be unseemly to practice that way since R. Tam himself never did so, nor did common custom include even one woman:

---

is a good example of the conceptual power of the Levush's model, as demonstrated by the tendency of some to read it back into earlier positions.

בית יוסף או״ח נה

וכתוב במרדכי בשם רבינו שמחה דעבד ואשה מצטרפין לתפלה ולברכת המזון בעשרה ופשוט הוא שזהו לפירוש ר״ת דפסק כרבי יהושע בן לוי בעבד אחד מצטרף. וסובר רבינו שמחה דהוא הדין לאשה דבכל דוכתא אשה שוה לעבד. וכיון דר״ת בעצמו לא רצה לעשות מעשה מי יקל בדבר. וכן נהגו העולם שלא לצרף אשה כלל.

Beit Yosef OḤ 55

And it is written in the Mordekhai in the name of R. Simḥah that a slave or a woman may be included for *tefillah* and for Birkat ha-Mazon in the ten; and clearly, this is according to the explanation of R. Tam, who ruled like R. Yehoshua b. Levi that one slave may be included, and R. Simḥah opined that this is also the law for a woman, for in every situation, a woman is equal to a slave [with respect to ritual roles]. But since R. Tam himself did not want to do such a thing, who can be lenient regarding it? And it is also the universal practice not to include a woman at all.

Based on this reasoning,[47] he states summarily in the Shulḥan Arukh that the *minyan* consists of ten free adult males.

שולחן ערוך נה:א

אומרים קדיש. וא״א אותו בפחות מי׳ זכרים בני חורין גדולים שהביאו ב׳ שערות, וה״ה לקדושה וברכו שאין נאמרין בפחות מעשרה.

47 It is also possible that R. Karo was influenced to reject R. Simḥah in light of what he understands to be behind the Rambam's ruling in Hilkhot Berakhot 5:7, that ten women may not mention God's name in *zimmun*. In Beit Yosef OḤ 199:7, R. Karo explains the Rambam as rejecting the possibility of ten women forming this quorum because *zimmun* with God's name is a *davar shebikdushah*, and a *davar shebikdushah* can only be done in the presence of ten free adult males. But see Sefer ha-Me'orot Berakhot 45a, who understands the Rambam differently, as well as yet another analysis of the Rambam in Benei Tziyyon 199:6, based on differing manuscript traditions of Bavli Megillah 23b. See above n. 22 and Appendix D, especially n. 16 there.

Shulḥan Arukh OḤ 55:1

Kaddish is said. And it is said only in the presence of ten free adult males who have reached puberty, and the same is true of Kedushah and Barekhu, which are not said with fewer than ten.

Not all rejected R. Simḥah, however. R. Yoel Sirkes rules like R. Simḥah on *zimmun* and permits counting one woman toward a *zimmun* of ten.[48] The Maharshal , R. Ḥayyim Benveniste, and R. Aharon Shmuel Kaidonover, all cite R. Simḥah on *zimmun*, suggesting that they endorse his ruling as valid as well.[49]

In principle, R. Simḥah's ruling applied to *zimmun* and *tefillah* equally, and we find various authorities who discuss the ramifications of his position for public prayer as well. R. Ya'akov Emden, while affirming the Shulḥan Arukh's exclusion of women, asserts that the only barrier to their exclusion pertains to the honor of heaven, following R. Tam and R. Simḥah:

מור וקציעה או״ח סימן נה

כתוב במרדכי דעבד ואשה מצטרפין לתפלה ולברכת המזון בעשרה. עכ״ל. נראה דבודאי יש יסוד גדול לדברי רבינו שמחה גם בדרך הסוד, מלבד דרך הנגלה, שבלי ספק האשה מצטרפת בין למנין עשרה בין למנין שבעה המבין יבין. ולכן אמרו חז״ל בפירוש שהיא עולה למנין שבעה הקורין בתורה. **אלא שמכל מקום אמרו שלא תקרא בצבור מפני כבוד צבור, והוא הדין לדברים הצריכים עשרה, בודאי שכן הלכה, שאין מצרפין אותה מפני הכבוד בלבד**, ואין אחר הסכמת הפוסקים כלום. אף על פי שהיה מקום לומר לפי מה שכתבתי שיש

48 Baḥ OḤ 199. He quotes the Rambam's view that ten women must not make a *zimmun* with God's name and explains the Rambam's objection as grounded in a requirement that *devarim shebikdushah can* only be done with ten free men. The Baḥ does not seem to reject this core point about *devarim shebikdushah* in general, but he does not accept it in the context of a *zimmun* of ten, preferring R. Simḥah's position: מיהו להצטרף בעלמא להזכרת שם שמים כתב רבינו שמחה דשרי באשה ומשמע ודאי שהוא הדין בעבד דשרי להצטרף לעשרה להזכיר שם שמים והכי נקטינן. The Baḥ's ruling is even more remarkable given that he rejects counting a child as a tenth later on in his commentary on Tur OḤ 199.

49 The Maharshal's notes on Tur OḤ 199 and testimony that he ruled this way in Ateret Zekeinim 199:1; Shiyarei Kenesset ha-Gedolah on OḤ 199, citing the Baḥ; Tiferet Shmuel on Rosh Berakhot 7:5.

להקל לענין צרוף עשרה יותר מקריאת התורה, דלא אפשר אלא עם הצבור במקום אחד ובמעמד אחד בתוכם ממש, מה שאין כן בצירוף לעשרה, דאפשר לאשה לעמוד מן הצד או בחדר, ובחצר קטן הפרוץ במלואו לגדול, שבאופן זה כבר תוכל להצטרף עם שמירת כבוד הצבור במקומו עומד, אף על פי כן אין לזוז מהכרעת הרב"י עדותו נאמנה, שפשט המנהג שלא לצרפה כלל.

Mor u-Ketziah OḤ 55

It is written in the Mordekhai that a slave and a woman can count toward the ten required for the Amidah and Birkat ha-Mazon. R. Simḥah's position clearly has solid kabbalistic—as well as halakhic—grounding, because a woman clearly counts toward the quorum of ten and toward the total of seven.[50] Therefore, Ḥazal explicitly said that a woman counts toward the seven who read from the Torah. **But they nonetheless said that she may not read in public because of the honor of the community, and that is also the problem with counting women toward the quorum of ten. It is clearly the law that the only obstacle toward counting her is the issue of honor,** but no more can be said now that all the authorities agree [to exclude women entirely]. Even though we might have said, according to what I have written, that one could be lenient in counting her toward the quorum of ten, more than in the case of reading from the Torah, which is possible only in one [clearly visible and central] location, because in the case of counting toward the ten, she could stand on the side or in an adjoining room such that she could join without impinging on the community's honor. Nonetheless, one should not depart from

50 The point here about Kabbalah seems to be that Malkhut is the *sefirah* that corresponds to the female qualities of the Godhead and it is both one of the ten *sefirot* as well as part of the seven lower *sefirot* that are often grouped separately. Women therefore have an appropriate part to play in the quorums of ten and seven, which correspond to these groupings.

> the decision of the Beit Yosef, whose testimony is faithful, that custom has become widespread not to count her at all.[51]

R. Emden forcefully argues that we accept R. Tam and R. Simḥah's definition of *minyan* in theory, even as he does not allow for any practical deviation from the Shulḥan Arukh's decision. A similar analysis was offered by an anonymous rabbi, in the context of the question of whether it is permissible to count an *androgynos* (someone with both male and female sex organs) toward the *minyan* for public prayer. The anonymous *posek* advances the claim that ten people in the category of *androgynos* can indeed make a *minyan*, basing himself on R. Tam. The *androgynos*, he says, is obligated in both *tefillah* and *mitzvot* in general and is also a member of the Jewish people. Regarding his potential exclusion on account of "the honor of heaven," he argues that there is no reason to think this applies to the *androgynos*. At that point in the argument, he says the following:

> **שו"ת אורח לצדיק סימן ב**
> ואם תאמר, אי הכי מהאי טעמא נמי נצטרף לאשה דהא היא גם כן בת ברית כעבד, והא לא קיימא לן הכי, ובהדיה מצאנו דאינה מצטרפת. יש לומר שאין הכי נמי הדין מצטרפת...ובהדיא כתב המרדכי בשם הרב שמחה הביאו הבית יוסף בסימן נ"ה דאשה מצטרפת לתפלה. **אבל אין לנו לצרפה מפני כבוד הציבור**...וכן נראה

---

51 Frimer, "Nashim u-Minyan," argues that R. Emden here was only suggesting that *kevod ha-tzibbur* prevented counting one woman toward the *minyan*; the exclusion of women from the other nine slots is due to other, unspecified reasons. In our estimation, this is an unsustainable reading: (1) There is no indication of another factor at work here excluding women, and the entire conversation is built around R. Simḥah's extension of R. Tam, which aims to give a fundamental definition of who counts toward a *minyan* in theory and in practice. (2) The kabbalistic argument that kicks off this paragraph appeals to the numbers seven and ten as a way of justifying women's inclusion in Torah reading and the *minyan* for prayer. R. Emden, in his glosses on Bavli Megillah 23a s.v. *aval amru* and in Mor u-Ketziah #282, rules clearly that women may read all *aliyot* under certain circumstances. His logic thus intends to support the notion that once the feminine aspect of the Godhead is included in the count of either seven or ten, femininity has been admitted to the quorum, and there is no basis for arguing that the theoretical inclusion of women in a *minyan* does not extend to all ten slots, just as it allows for all seven Torah readers to be women. Also, as we will demonstrate, other Aḥaronim also state that the only barrier to counting women as equals in a *minyan* is that of honor and dignity. There is thus no reason to resist reading R. Emden in this straightforward way as well.

דברי הבית יוסף על ההיא דהרב שמחה שכתב "וכן נהגו העולם שלא לצרף אשה כלל", ע"כ **מנהג בעלמא**...ואם באשה מצאנו בהדיא שמצטרפת אי לאו משום כבוד הציבור, כל שכן בנדון דידן שעדיף טפי דלא שייך האי טעמא...והאנדרוגינוס פשיטא שמחוייב בתפלה כשאר בני ישראל דמינה שאין להוציאו מכללם אלא לצרפו לכל דבר שבקדושה **או אחד או יותר** בכל מקום ובכל זמן.

Responsa Oraḥ la-Tzaddik #2[52]

You might object: According to my logic we would have to count a woman toward the quorum of ten, because she also is a member of the covenant[53] just like a slave, and yet we explicitly hold that a woman does not count! I would respond that, in fact, a woman should by all rights count...and the Mordekhai wrote in the name of R. Simḥah (cited in Beit Yosef 55) that a woman counts toward the ten needed for *tefillah.* **But we may not actually count her because of the honor of the community**...and this seems to be the point of the Beit Yosef when he writes in reaction to R. Simḥah that "the custom everywhere is not to count a woman at all"—**on account of**

---

52 This collection of responsa belongs to R. Avraham Ḥayyim Rodrigues, though this specific responsum is the work of an anonymous sage. R. Rodrigues cites this opinion in order to attack it. We will turn to his attacks below; for now we seek to understand this view on its own terms.

53 The author here refers to both slaves and women as "members of the covenant." There are a few possibilities for understanding this locution: (1) This is an imprecise way of referring to both criteria of מחוייבי מצות **and** בני ברית laid out in R. Tam, but he simply only mentions one of them. Slaves are considered "members of the covenant" via circumcision, as are women, as they are considered already circumcised (i.e., born without a foreskin). (2) This is an imprecise way to sum up R. Tam's approach of requiring **either** being part of the Jewish people **or** being obligated in *mitzvot.* The author here would then be saying that what truly matters is a connection to the Jewish people—being a member of the covenant—which can be attained either through birth or as an acquired obligation in the commandments. These two readings correspond to the conjunctive and disjunctive readings of R. Tam we explored above in n. 34. It is not viable to read the author here as claiming that slaves and women are in through circumcision **alone** (a version of the disjunctive reading), since babies would qualify under this criterion as well and there would then be no place for the מחוייבי מצות terminology we find in R. Tam.

> **custom alone**...and if it is the case that a woman can clearly count were it not for the problem of *kevod ha-tzibbur,* we can obviously count an *androgynos,* where that concern does not exist.... It is obvious that an *androgynos* is obligated in *tefillah* like all other Jews, and from this we can deduce that there is no reason to distinguish them from other Jews, rather, we should count such a person toward all *devarim shebikdushah,* **whether one or many,** anywhere, anytime.[54]

In other words, women meet the theoretical definition for being full members of the *minyan,* but it would violate standards of honor and dignity to count them in practice, even as a tenth.

Others maintained the legitimacy of practically following a narrow reading of R. Simḥah at times, defending the legitimacy of counting a woman as a tenth in pressing circumstances. Indeed, the continued viability of applying R. Tam's inclusive model even in the context of *tefillah* is attested to by R. Shneur Zalman of Liady. Though he prefers the Shulḥan Arukh's ruling insisting on a *minyan* of ten men, he says not to protest against those who are lenient in dire situations, since they have authorities on whom to rely:

> **שולחן ערוך הרב או"ח נה:ה**
> יש מתירין לומר דבר שבקדושה בט' וצירוף עבד או אשה או קטן... וי"א שאין אשה ועבד או קטן מצטרפים בשום ענין אלא צריך שיהו כל עשרה זכרים בני חורין גדולים שהביאו ב' שערות...וכן עיקר. ואעפ"כ אין למחות באותן שנוהגין להקל בשעת הדחק...כיון שיש להם על מי שיסמכו.

> **Shulḥan Arukh ha-Rav OḤ 55:5**
> Some permit saying a *davar shebikdushah* with nine joined together with a slave, a woman, or a minor... And some say that a woman, slave, or minor may not count at all and all ten must be free male adults who have reached puberty...the latter opinion is correct. Nonetheless, one should not protest against

54 Note that the argumentation here fundamentally assumes that R. Simḥah—at least in theory—would have counted ten women toward a *minyan,* in keeping with the broader reading we offered above at n. 41.

> those who are lenient in pressing circumstances...they have authority on which to rely.[55]

Later authorities, even when not authorizing counting women in a *minyan,* continue to affirm R. Tam's and R. Simḥah's model as a viable way of thinking about the issue. R. Ya'akov Ze'ev Kahana struggles to find a basis for **not** counting women in a *minyan* and concludes that issues of honor and shame are ultimately at the root of the matter:[56]

> **תולדות יעקב, אורח חיים סימן ה**
> נסתפקתי אם נשים מצטרפות לעשרה לתפילה יען דמחויבות המה בתפילה כמו אנשים...ולכאורה משמע דאינן מצטרפות ליו"ד מדהוצרך רבי אליעזר לשחרר עבדו להשלים ליו"ד...טפי היה לו להצטרף לאשתו או לבתו ולא לעבור על עשה דלעולם בהם תעבודו. ודוחק לומר שלא היה לו אשה אז...הגם שיש לדחות ולומר דאין הכי נמי דהצטרף לאשתו אך בכל זה לא היו יו"ד ונצטרך גם לשחרר עבד. אבל האמת יורה דרכו דלא רצה להצטרף לאשה. ואפשר דנהי דאשה מצטרפת ליו"ד אבל זילא בהם מלתא להצטרף לאשה דומיא דאין אשה מוציאה את הרבים במגילה משום דזילא בהו מילתא טובא.
>
> **Toledot Ya'akov OḤ 5**
> I am unsure as to whether women count toward the ten for prayer, since they are obligated in prayer just like men.[57]... It seems that they do not count toward the ten, since R. Eliezer

55 For Shulḥan Arukh ha-Rav, this latitude is clearly limited to counting a single woman; see n. 41. However, note that while he tolerates R. Simḥah's position on counting a single woman in the context of prayers in the synagogue, he seems to take a harder line in forbidding it in the context of a meal, since sexual impropriety is a greater threat there, though perhaps he would not object strongly there either and is only giving his preferred position. See Shulḥan Arukh ha-Rav OḤ 199:7.

56 We do not know why R. Kahana does not engage with the Shulḥan Arukh's explicit ruling on this front. One could potentially suggest that the Shulḥan Arukh only **explicitly** excludes women from the *minyan* required for Kedushah, Kaddish, and Barekhu, whereas R. Kahana is asking about the ten for the Amidah alone. That seems forced, especially given that the public Amidah includes Kedushah. It instead seems that he is examining the essence of the law here, trying to understand the essential principles that might lie behind the restrictive rulings he is well aware of.

57 Here is further evidence for our analysis in Part I above.

> had to free his slave in order to get a tenth... [If it had been an option to count a woman as the tenth] he should have counted his wife or his daughter rather than violate the commandment to work slaves forever [and not to emancipate them.][58] It is difficult to say that he had no wife at that time. Nonetheless, we might deflect that objection by saying that he **did** count his wife, but he was still one short and he needed to free his slave as well. It seems more honest to admit that he did not want to count a woman. Then again, perhaps women do indeed count toward the quorum of ten, but it would have been shameful for them to count a woman, just as a woman cannot fulfill men's obligations in *megillah* because it would be extremely shameful.[59]

Even though it would be a shameful departure from normal practice to count women toward the *minyan,* argues R. Kahana, there is nothing essentially gendered about the quorum of ten. It is not surprising, then, that he tentatively suggests counting women toward the quorum of ten needed for Birkat Ḥatanim (that is, the Sheva Berakhot) when there are insufficient men available.[60]

R. Natan Nata Landau also affirms R. Tam and R. Simḥah's basic theoretical analysis of *minyan* and explains that women do not count toward the *minyan* in practice because "לאו אורח ארעא — it is not the

58 This refers to Bavli Berakhot 47b's discussion, which wonders how R. Eliezer could have violated this law that is articulated elsewhere.

59 The back-and-forth here is a striking example of how the Talmud's silence on the matter of gender and *minyan* leaves it open to such different interpretations. The language of זילא בהו מילתא ("it would be shameful for them") used here is taken from Tosafot Sukkah 38a, where it is used to describe why it might be inappropriate and shameful for women to fulfill the obligations of men even when they share equal obligations. This clearly has to do with the social shame of men being led by women, in contrast to an earlier suggestion in the Tosafot that has to do with gaps in religious obligation. See Tosafot ha-Rosh there for a clearer parallel. The Tosafot themselves seem to take the term זילא בהו מילתא from Bavli Kiddushin 32a, where the term מאירה, local to Bavli Sukkah 38a, appears in conjunction with it. The Ritva and R. Avraham min ha-Har express the Tosafot's idea of זילא בה מילתא through the tannaitic language of מאירה itself; see Part One, nn. 85–97.

60 Toledot Ya'akov Even ha-Ezer 5.

way of the world," not because they lack any essential religious quality necessary for *minyan*. In fact, he argues that the Talmud's implicit inclusion of women in the quorum of ten that triggers an obligation in martyrdom leads us to this conclusion. He even entertains the notion that ten women might form a *minyan* for *devarim shebikdushah*:

עורה שחר, קדושה (אות ק, ו)
ובב"י...מביא דעת רש"י [צ"ל: ר' שמחה] דאשה או עבד מצטרף לעשר', וכתב הב"י דזהו לפיר"ת...ובסנהדרין ס"פ בן סורר מבעיא לן לענין מצות קידוש השם תשעה ונכרי אחד מהו, משמע דאשה ועבד ודאי מצטרפין. ולא עוד אלא דמשמע בתוך עשרה נשים שייך "ונקדשתי בתוך בני ישראל"...**ואפשר הא דאשה אינה מצטרפת לתפילה משום דלאו אורח ארעא**...אבל בקידוש השם ודאי מצטרפת...ועיין בר"פ ג' שאכלו גבי והא מאה נשי כתרי גברי דמיא, לשיטת רש"י שם אפשר דעשרה נשים יכולות להצטרף לומר דבר שבקדושה.

Urah Shaḥar s.v. *kedushah* (letter *kof*, #6)
And in the Beit Yosef...he cites the opinion of [R. Simḥah] that a woman or a slave can be included in the ten, and the Beit Yosef wrote that this is according to the explanation of R. Tam...And on Sanhedrin 75a, we ask regarding the *mitzvah* of *kiddush hashem*: "Nine [Jews] and one non-Jew, what is the law?"—which implies that a woman or a slave certainly are included. And not only this, but it also implies that amidst ten women, [the principle derived from the verse] "And I will be sanctified" applies.[61]...**And it is possible that this situation that a woman is not included for the purpose of *tefillah* is because it is not the way of the world**...but regarding *kiddush hashem*, they certainly are included....And see the beginning of Berakhot chapter 7 regarding [the statement]: "And a hundred women are like two men." And according to the opinion of

61 This obviously stands in tension with the tradition that excludes women from the term בני ישראל and supports our claim above that that derivation should be seen as *post facto* support for an already assumed practice, rather than an obvious interpretation of the language of the verse.

> Rashi there,[62] it is possible that ten women can be included to say a *davar shebikdushah*.[63]

R. Landau's main contribution here is to engage the broader context of *kiddush hashem*, the sanctification of God's name, as reflected not only through rules surrounding *tefillah*, but martyrdom as well. As we saw earlier, a persecuted Jew, forced to choose between violating a law in public and death, is expected to choose martyrdom. Women share this obligation as well,[64] and several other Aḥaronim are also explicit that they count toward the quorum of ten required to trigger the broader obligations of public martyrdom—the requirement to give up one's life even for the smallest of violations when a group of ten is present.[65] However, some authorities who count women toward the quorum of public martyrdom reject their participation in the quorum for *tefillah*, even though the two are derived from the same verses and fall under the same religious obligation to sanctify God's name in public.[66] Why?

Though the verses used by the Talmud to anchor the obligation of *kiddush hashem* (martyrdom) are the same as those used by at least some sages to define *minyan*, R. Landau accepts that we might not, in practice,

---

62 Because Rashi interprets this line differently, this phrase is irrelevant to *minyan*, thus eliminating any possible talmudic hook for the exclusion of women from *minyan*, as we noted above.

63 The rest of this passage notes the various sources that argue against allowing this in practice, but it ends with ועדיין צ"ע, unsatisfied with articulating a blanket ban and seeming to hold minimally that any *minyan* that did count women would be valid after the fact.

64 See n. 16 above.

65 R. Shmuel Aboab was in doubt about this possibility in Responsa Devar Shemuel #63, but see R. Yosef Ḥayyim Al-Ḥakham in his Responsa Rav Pe'alim II OḤ #62 and R. Reuven Margaliyot in Margaliyot ha-Yam on Bavli Sanhedrin 74b for clear rulings that women count toward this quorum. Those who oppose counting women toward the ten of martyrdom either think that concerns about insufficient social and religious capital apply to these situations as well or are working with something like the Levush's model of *minyan*: One is not considered to have engaged in a public violation unless the Jewish community—defined by its fully obligated members—is out in full force.

66 For one contemporary example, see Yabia Omer IV OḤ #9.

simply equate these two categories.[67] Thinking that it is religiously destabilizing and desecrating of God's Name to violate *mitzvot* in front of a given group of people certainly does not imply that said group represents the community in microcosm when calling down God's presence in the synagogue. Though there is not an iron wall dividing these two issues, they are easily enough separated. We can surely understand the many Aḥaronim who consider women part of the quorum for public martyrdom while unequivocally excluding them from the quorum required for prayer: Conventional hierarchies and perceptions of dignity dissolve in times of communal stress, as marginal members of a community get persecuted along with the more central citizens. Furthermore, communal destabilization and desecration of God's name—which the demand for public martyrdom is intended to avoid—is potentially much more gender-blind than a society's definition of a sufficiently august group whose presence is fitting for an active, public sanctification of God.

Nonetheless, R. Landau notes that the shared verses and themes that these two categories hold in common do reveal significant overlap, if not congruity. Though public martyrdom and public prayer invoke different concerns and priorities, they are by no means unrelated; they fall under the same rubric of *kiddush hashem*. This controlling idea permeates both categories and influences the rulings of numerous authorities, as they borrow principles and details from one topic to elucidate the other.[68] Indeed, those who include women not only in the obligation of public martyrdom but also in the quorum required to trigger this obligation effectively think about *minyan* as did R. Simḥah. It cannot be that women are **ontologically** excluded from the *minyan* of prayer even as they count for the *minyan* of martyrdom, seeing as these are two aspects of the same

---

67 We disagree here with R. David Golinkin's responsum on this matter (Golinkin, "Nashim be-Minyan"); the inclusion of a set of people in one quorum does not necessarily lead to their practical inclusion in the other, given their different social functions and resonances. R. Golinkin is certainly correct that the logic employed by R. Moshe Feinstein in Iggerot Moshe OḤ 2:19 does presume the equation of the two quorums. Nonetheless, we feel it is important to account for views, such as that of R. Ovadiah Yosef in Yabia Omer IV OḤ #9, that apply different standards for the quorum of martyrdom than for the quorum for prayer.

68 See Iggerot Moshe OḤ 2:19. While R. Feinstein's practical conclusion is not accepted by R. Ovadiah Yosef, his analysis is important evidence for how closely linked these two areas of *halakhah* are for many *poskim*.

mitzvah. If women are fitting vehicles for the sanctification of God's name anywhere, they must, at least in theory, be fitting for its sanctification everywhere.

One can embrace the coherence of a position that excludes women from the *minyan* for prayers without endowing this exclusion with metaphysical power. The inclusion of women in the rubric of *kiddush hashem* in the context of public martyrdom does not automatically resolve the question of whether they count in the synagogue, but it does limit their exclusion in the synagogue to a secondary factor, as opposed to writing them out of what falls under the verse, "I shall be sanctified in the midst of the children of Israel." Or, in other words, the obstacle to counting women as equals in a *minyan*, according to this view, is nothing more and nothing less than יקרא דשמיא (honor of heaven) / כבוד ציבור (honor of a community) / וילא בהו מילתא (the matter would disgrace them) / אורח ארעא (the way of the world)—a sense that the community is doing a disservice to the honor of heaven, to its own dignity, and to common-sense standards that define "the way of the world."[69] Indeed, more recently, R. Ahron Soloveichik has been cited[70] as explicitly saying that the only reason women do not count in a *minyan* is because of *kevod ha-tzibbur*.

Even after all this, though, we must note that aside from the few exceptions we noted above, very few *poskim*—even among those who embrace R. Tam's analysis—allow for gender-blind *minyanim* in practice.[71]

---

69 Sperber, "Congregational Dignity," 5, offers yet another translation of this concept: "As the Yiddish expression has it, *es passt nicht*. [It is unseemly.]"

70 Frimer and Frimer, "Women's Prayer Services," write (in n. 85): "Interestingly, R. Ahron Soloveichik, in conversation with Dov I. Frimer, July 8, 1997, maintains that men and women share the same obligation (or lack thereof) in both *tefilla betzibbur* and *keriat haTorah*. However, even were women personally obligated, R. Ahron Soloveichik posits that they are, nonetheless, specifically excluded by Ḥazal from counting toward a *minyan* or serving as a hazzan or *ba'alat keri'a* because of *kevod hatzibbur*. Further discussion of this position is beyond the scope of this paper." In fact, R. Soloveichik's points seem to be central to any discussion of this topic and run counter to what the Frimers argue throughout their paper. Our analysis both of prayer leadership and *minyan* accords entirely with R. Soloveichik's position and shows the rich set of halakhic sources that help us understand it.

71 We will mention one other interesting train of thought here that has led to some interesting practical rulings. Tashbetz Katan 201 reads Tosafot Berakhot 48a s.v. *ve-leit* as holding that since a minor can read from the Torah, a minor can surely count

Can the concerns of "יקרא דשמיא / כבוד הציבור / אורח ארעא — honor of heaven / *kevod tzibbur* / way of the world" that bar the practical implementation of R. Tam's theory be addressed, such that women could count as equals in a contemporary *minyan*?

Here we return to our conversation of *kevod tzibbur* in our analysis of Torah reading above.[72] There, we saw that some authorities defined *kevod tzibbur* as a protection for the community's honor, a communal prerogative subject to the community's waiver. This understanding of *kevod tzibbur* cannot be the meaning of "honor of heaven" as that term is used in R. Tam's analysis of *minyan*. Even those authorities who equate *yekara di-shmaya* with the terms *kevod tzibbur* and *oraḥ ar'a*, such as the anonymous *posek* cited in Oraḥ la-Tzaddik #2 and R. Landau in Urah Shaḥar, cannot

---

as a tenth for the required quorum for Torah reading. (This interpretation of the Tosafot is disputed, so we do not cite this view in their name. See Yabia Omer IV OḤ #9, sec. 9.) Magen Avraham 55:4 cites this view, though he suggests it is problematic. R. Tzvi Hirsch Grodzinski, in Mikra'ei Kodesh, Sha'arei Kedushah 4:1, argues that the Magen Avraham's resistance to this view (and what ought to be our rejection of it) is grounded in the fact that minors have no obligation to hear Torah reading. (We engaged the question of obligation in Torah reading above at length; see Part One, nn. 59–81.) Women, he argues—citing Magen Avraham 282:6—have an equal obligation to men in public Torah reading, and this obligation is fundamental, different even from their obligation in *megillah* reading, which is grounded in the more derivative formulation of אף הן היו באותו הנס. He also notes that the Shulḥan Arukh mentions the requirement for males in OḤ 55, where Torah reading is not mentioned, and does not mention males when discussing the requirement for Torah reading in OḤ 143. R. Grodzinski uses this inconsistency in the text and Massekhet Soferim's claim that women and men are equally obligated to hear Torah reading to conclude that women count toward the ten of Torah reading, but not toward the ten for other *devarim shebikdushah*! R. Hillel Posek, in Responsa Hillel Omer #187, put this theory into practice, recommending that a small community that would otherwise not read Torah ought to count women for Torah reading rather than cancel it. But he does not permit counting women toward the other quorums of ten spelled out in Shulḥan Arukh OḤ 55, since that would contradict the Shulḥan Arukh. These are highly technical arguments that are not of great practical use to a discussion about a more comprehensive egalitarian practice. They are nonetheless significant in complicating the history of gender and *minyan*, demonstrating further that there have been some *poskim* who have been willing to take a practical stance on some of the theory explored here. They are also important indicators of the absence of any clear talmudic exclusion of women that would have shut this sort of conversation down immediately.

72 See above, Part One, nn. 99–113.

have thought that *yekara di-shmaya* is subject to communal waiver. First, the language of "the honor of heaven" itself indicates a factor that is not subject to communal discretion. Second, there is no record of anyone—including those who embrace R. Tam's definition of *minyan*—suggesting that an individual community is entitled to waive its honor and thereby allow counting minors for half of the *minyan*. The only practical rulings to emerge from R. Tam's school are those that did not tamper with *yekara di-shmaya* by suggesting it was some kind of relative concern. Rather, *yekara di-shmaya* is an objective claim about honor and dignity, which is apparent to anyone willing to honestly assess the situation. A *minyan* made up mostly of children is something everyone would agree we do not—and ought not to—take seriously.

When later Aḥaronim, such as those we cited above, understand *yekara di-shmaya* as *kevod tzibbur,* they are therefore using the latter term in the sense we saw it used by the Baḥ. *Kevod tzibbur* here means an objective assessment of communal action when viewed from afar. Is the act in question something one would do when presenting oneself to an earthly sovereign? Would it meet our standards for seriousness in other realms of life? If not, then it is inappropriate to settle for anything less in a communal, ritual context. *Yekara di-shmaya* is not a force subject to communal discretion; it is a demand that communities live up to the standards of dignity and seriousness that they are capable of. The same is true of Urah Shaḥar's rendition of *yekara di-shmaya* as "אורח ארעא — the way of the world." The honor of heaven demands that we not serve God in a manner that would be recognized as mediocre, unseemly, and falling short of broadly recognized standards.

The honor of heaven can only be appeased when the quorum in question quite obviously and objectively presents no indignity whatsoever. We would suggest an even more conservative standard: The inclusion as equals in the *minyan* of previously marginal members is consistent with the value of *yekara di-shmaya* when the **exclusion** of these members would offend this value. Groups consisting mostly of minors were not taken seriously in the ancient world, nor in the medieval world, nor today—in all kinds of contexts. The same was true of groups made up mostly of women, until very recently in modern times. In this sense, a highly gendered definition of *minyan* exactly matched the standards for seriousness in the broader society in pre-modern times. But the times have now changed so dramatically that, for many of us, groups that are defined as not including women as equals cannot meaningfully represent society writ large. In our contemporary society, communal bodies that do not include women and men as equals are themselves seen as marginal, or at best are nostalgic places of gathering that are denied any serious power or influence over society as a whole. Such gatherings may serve a valuable purpose, but they are not designed to evoke "the honor of heaven."

If one follows R. Tam's definition of *minyan* but maintains its all-male nature in practice on the basis of *yekara di-shmaya,* one may in fact be undermining the very value one intends to uphold. *Yekara di-shmaya* certainly cannot be waived, but society's changing standards can affect how we do and do not experience it. R. Tam's analysis shows that women count in theory. The question has only been whether the realities of Jewish life could and should support the theory's practical implementation. It has never—and likely will never—support the practical implementation of the theory with respect to minors (nor would it extend to slaves if they still existed in our contexts), and there may be communities where that reality will persist for women as well. The question before the communities that grapple with this issue today is what the consequences are of perpetuating that reality. The very existence of this moral dilemma for certain communities, and the intensity with which it is engaged in those spheres, demonstrates a conviction that the message that says women compromise the honor of heaven is today palpably false and distorting, perhaps even threatening to the vitality of the Jewish community. Communities who count women as equals in the *minyan* based on R. Tam's theoretical approach to *minyan* and a contemporary, gender-neutral assessment of *yekara di-shmaya* in practice have strong halakhic grounds on which to base themselves.

E. THOSE WHO REJECT R. TAM, AND THE CONSEQUENCES FOR GENDER AND *MINYAN*

Our entire analysis in this last section was predicated on R. Tam's definition of *minyan* as theoretically including all those obligated in *mitzvot* and those who are members of the covenant. As we noted, the Levush demurred from this definition and excluded women (and slaves and minors) from *minyan* in a more fundamental way, based on their lack of maximal obligation in *mitzvot.* We thus also find practical discussions surrounding gender and *minyan* that draw much more restrictive lines when it comes to gender equality.

We already saw the words of R. Shneur Zalman of Liady above, who acknowledged R. Tam's theory of *minyan* and granted it some legitimacy under certain circumstances, while nonetheless arguing that the Levush's approach was superior and correct. Other Aḥaronim similarly considered R. Tam's approach and rejected it, some with great force. Recall the position we cited above of one anonymous rabbi who argued that the exclusion of women from *minyan* was about one factor and one factor alone: *kevod tzibbur*. That *posek* used this claim to argue for counting hermaphrodites as equals in a *minyan*, based on the theory that *kevod tzibbur* would not apply as a concern to these otherwise qualified members of the *minyan*. As we saw above, R. Avraham Ḥayyim Rodrigues[73] cites this anonymous view in his collection of responsa, Oraḥ la-Tzaddik. He then proceeds to rebut it in strident fashion:

שו"ת אורח לצדיק סימן ג

דאטו משום שחייב בתפלה משום דרחמי נינהו יתחייב להתפלל בעשרה? הא אשה חייבת בתפלה מהאי טעמא ואינה חייבת להתפלל בעשרה, ומינה דאינה מצטרפת!... אחר כך יגע ולא מצא שהביא ראיה מהא דכתב הבית יוסף בשם המרדכי דטעמא דמאן דשרי לאיצרופי קטן נראה דהיינו משום דכל בי עשרה שכיתנא שריא ואמאי נוציא האנדרוגינוס מכלל זה כיון דהוי זרע קדש וכו'. כל דבריו אינם אלא דברי תימא, דהא הודה ולא בוש שכל ראיותיו שהביא מקטן ואשה לאו הלכתא נינהו, ואם כן טעמא דבית שמאי אתא לאשמועינן וההיא טעמא לאו בר סמכא הוא כיון דלא קיימא לן הכי...ולפי דבריו בואו ונצרף לנשים לעשרה לתפלה, בין אחת או יותר, כיון שחייבות בתפלה וגם הן זרע קדש, ולכל דבר שבקדושה. חי נפשי שמתבושש אני ונכלם להשיב על דברים אלו.

Responsa Oraḥ la-Tzaddik #3

Do you mean to say that because one is obligated to pray the Amidah, on account of its being a personal request for mercy, one is obligated to pray with a *minyan* of ten? A woman is obligated to pray the Amidah but is not obligated to pray with a *minyan* of ten, and we can deduce from this that she may not

73 R. Rodrigues taught, among others, R. Malakhi ha-Kohen, author of the great methodological work Yad Malakhi.

> count toward that *minyan*!...Then you tried, without success, to cite proof from the Beit Yosef's citation of the Mordekhai that those who permit counting a minor do so because the Shekhinah dwells in any group of ten; why would we exclude the hermaphrodite, who is also of holy stock? Everything you say is surprising; you yourself admit without shame that your proofs are drawn from rejected positions regarding minors and women! If so, are you coming to teach me the reasons for Beit Shammai's opinion? Those reasons have no authority given that we do not follow their practical implementation...According to your logic, we should count women toward the quorum of ten for *tefillah*, whether one or many, based on the fact that they are obligated to pray the Amidah and are of holy stock, and toward the quorum needed for every *davar shebikdushah*. By my life, I am ashamed and embarrassed even to have to respond to such an argument.

R. Rodrigues makes a number of arguments here. First, while conceding that women have a full obligation in prayer, he claims that they do not have an obligation to pray in a *minyan*, and if one is not obligated to pray in a *minyan* then one certainly does not count in that *minyan*.[74] But then he proceeds with a more direct attack. He argues that the entire argument for theoretically including women and minors in the *minyan* stems from a theory (R. Tam's) that is not followed in practice. Since it is common practice not to count a minor or a woman even as a tenth, this indicates,

---

74 This claim is unsourced here and has no precedent in the Rishonim. While there are views in the Rishonim that think that individuals have an obligation to pray in a *minyan*, there is no ancient or medieval source that suggests that such an obligation to pray with a *minyan* would be gendered. See Appendix C for more on the topic of the obligation to pray with a *minyan*. In particular, see the Shevut Ya'akov there, who seems to assume that we learn that women are not obligated to pray with a *minyan* from the fact that they do not count toward it! That claim is unprecedented in the medieval period as well. Nonetheless, it is of course not an unreasonable position to see linkage between one's ability to constitute a quorum and the expectation that one be present to help make it a reality. R. Rodrigues seems to be making that sort of claim here: Of course anyone who would count in a *minyan* would be obligated to help constitute one; from the fact that we do not expect women to come, it must be that they do not count.

argues R. Rodrigues, that this theory is rejected as well. R. Rodrigues refers to R. Tam's theory as "Beit Shammai's opinion" in that our refusal to implement it in practice is reflective of our rejection of it in theory as well, just as we treat the many views of Beit Shammai that are largely discarded as legally inoperative. *Minyan* is not, for R. Rodrigues, simply a collection of individuals with some basic connection to *mitzvot* and the covenant, as it is for R. Tam. As a result, he ends with his shock that a person would ever entertain the possibility that ten women could count for a *minyan,* since this would be based on a rejected theory of what *minyan* is all about.

In truth, R. Rodrigues's attack on his interlocutor here is not entirely fair. The anonymous *posek* did **not** argue that women could be counted for a *minyan* in practice. Indeed, he would have strongly opposed counting even one. He only argued that this exclusion was due to *kevod tzibbur* as opposed to more fundamental issues of identity, responsibility, and belonging. He would have agreed with R. Rodrigues that counting a woman toward the *minyan* would be unthinkable **in practice in his time and place**. But he would likely advocate for resisting the notion that just because something is wildly inappropriate in a **given** social context, it is therefore theoretically unimaginable in **any** possible context. This approach flows directly from R. Tam's model. The real gulf here is that the anonymous *posek*—like R. Ya'akov Emden—feels that R. Tam's theory remains live even when not implemented in practice. By contrast, R. Rodrigues rejects R. Tam entirely and works with a different definition of *minyan,* almost certainly that of the Levush. Hermaphrodites would then not be included as equals in the *minyan* because they are not unambiguously maximally obligated like free adult men.[75]

Anyone following the approach of the Levush and others who define *minyan* as a group of ten bearing maximal Jewish obligation would have to make a different argument in order to justify a gender-equal *minyan.* Since, for the Levush, only a Jew obligated in the full range of *mitzvot* can count as a member of the *minyan,* one would have to claim that contemporary

---

75 Tosefta Bikkurim 2:4 states that hermaphrodites indeed have all the same obligations in positive *mitzvot* as men. But the larger context there indicates that this may well be because they are treated with the dual stringencies of both men and women, such that their maximal obligation in practice is in fact derivative of a more doubtful claim about their maximal obligation in theory. This matches rulings elsewhere that do not allow a man to fulfill his obligations through the agency of a hermaphrodite. See Tosefta Rosh Hashanah 2:5.

women (at least in some communities) are no longer exempt from the category of positive commandments caused by time.

F. ARE CONTEMPORARY WOMEN MAXIMALLY OBLIGATED?

Throughout our analysis, we have reached various points in the discussion where fully gender-equal practice in a given ritual context has been linked to the broader obligation gaps between men and women in classical sources. We saw this most clearly in the Ran's analysis of Torah reading and the Levush's definition of *minyan*. We noted that in order to make an argument for gender equality that would address the concerns of these authorities, one would have to claim that contemporary women, unlike their female predecessors, are indeed maximally obligated in *mitzvot* no different from men.

Is it possible to make such a claim? We can only briefly outline the contours of such an argument here. As is the case with any legal term, one must carefully examine its original context before assuming what it means in a different context. While it is possible to read Ḥazal's term נשים ("women") as applying across history to all those who are biologically female, it is also possible—particularly when נשים is juxtaposed with the categories of slaves and minors—that this term is intended to refer to adjunct members of society who are dependent on and subservient to their husbands and a larger patriarchal structure for support. Indeed, R. Yoel Bin-Nun has recently been advancing precisely this argument, suggesting that those women in our day and age who understand themselves to be בנות חורין, freed from earlier patriarchal structures, are thus subject to all the traditional ritual obligations of men:[76]

> רוב הנשים של ימינו בנות חורין הן...ואינן דומות לעבדים בשום פנים, שהרי אין רשות אחרים עליהן. לפיכך, כל מי שמצטט פסקי חכמים, שהתבססו על כך ש"אישה דומה לעבד" בכל מקום, איננו מבין שהוא מעביר הלכה ממציאות אחת למציאות אחרת, בלי יסוד. "נשים שלנו", לא רק שכולן חשובות, כדברי הרמ"א, אלא שהן "בנות חורין"...פשוט לא מדובר באותו סוג של נשים.

76 Bin-Nun, "Birkat Ḥatanim."

> Most women in our day are independent/liberated [*benot horin*]...and they bear no resemblance to slaves, because there is no power of others over them. Therefore, anyone who cites the rulings of the Sages, which are based on the notion that "a woman is similar to a slave" in all arenas, fails to understand that they are transferring a *halakhah* from one reality to another without any basis whatsoever. "Our women" are not only all important—as the Rema already said—but they are independent/liberated...It is obvious that we are not speaking about the same category of *nashim*.

For R. Bin-Nun, the entire terminology of אשה must be revisited, particularly when the term is used in conjunction with terms like עבד, "slave." This juxtaposition suggests the legal categories share some fundamental characteristics and that the term אשה **may** in such contexts map better onto sociology (i.e., being a social adjunct) as opposed to biology (i.e., having a certain chromosomal makeup). If the terms of the local *halakhah* are driven by sociology, then contemporary females—at least those in societies that afford them full rights and equality—in fact have no exemption from positive commandments caused by time.[77] In this reading, "נשים עבדים וקטנים — women, slaves, and minors" is best translated as "social adjuncts" or "not full citizens," and may map onto biology differently in a society where the correlation between biology and power has undergone transformation or revolution. For instance, telling a contemporary neurosurgeon who happens to be biologically female that she is exempt from reciting the Shema might be a **violation** of the Torah's

77 In a personal communication, R. Bin-Nun confirmed that he would extend this logic to the realm of vicarious fulfillment; i.e., a woman in this category could blow *shofar* for a man. Interestingly, in discussing the concept of *minyan*, R. Bin-Nun says: "לכן, לכאורה, היה אפשר בימינו להיאחז בשיטת רבנו תם — Therefore, it would seem that one can, in our day, follow the position of R. Tam." R. Bin-Nun means this in the practical sense that R. Tam's position theoretically allows for ten women to constitute the *minyan*. But the essence of R. Bin-Nun's argument is in fact that contemporary women often have a different status than the women spoken of by Ḥazal, such that, according to R. Bin-Nun's analysis, ten women can constitute a *minyan* even under the Levush's theory.

values, which would expect all of those who wield power to be subject to the command to accept the yoke of heaven twice a day.[78]

In order to count women as equals in the Levush's *minyan*, one would have to take this broader step, arguing that women not only have the social capital they would need for R. Tam, but also the broader religious equality that would enable them to constitute the community in microcosm.[79] Indeed, there are already many communities where men and women are functionally equal in this regard: where women do not make room for men when a *sukkah* is too small, where women are no more lenient about the *mitzvot* of *lulav* and *shofar* than are men, and where Sefirat ha-Omer reveals no trace of any gendering. Such communities may already be implicitly adopting R. Bin-Nun's model and could, with integrity, make explicit the implicit theory behind their practice. R. Bin-Nun's model supports allowing women to count as equals in the *minyan* even according to the Levush's definition of a quorum of ten as being comprised of ten maximally obligated Jews.[80] We find this model to be honest and plausible as a halakhic pathway and are drawn to its emphasis on ritual gender equality as a stringency rather than a leniency. But we also acknowledge

---

78 This sort of linguistic redefinition is well-attested in halakhic literature. See Appendix A.

79 R. Joel Roth, in the context of the conversation regarding the ordination of women as rabbis in the Conservative movement, also attempted to square the desire for a gender-equal *minyan* with the Levush's standard of ten maximally obligated individuals. He suggested that women could electively obligate themselves in all *mitzvot* and thereby be eligible to be treated identically to men, even according to the Levush. See Roth, "Ordination of Women." Engaging this approach of self-obligation and its effectiveness is beyond the scope of our discussion. Note that R. Bin-Nun's argument is different, arguing that women are **automatically** obligated in the *mitzvot* from which they were traditionally exempt, as a result of their changed social status. Therefore, for R. Bin-Nun, women's actual record of performing those *mitzvot* or their theoretical commitment to them is not relevant to their ritual status as citizens and leaders. This, of course, was always the case with Jewish men, whose actual record of *mitzvah*-observance was never relevant to their status. Nonetheless, a community that adopts R. Bin-Nun's theory without having gender-equal *mitzvah* observance in practice will not have as much self-evident religious integrity.

80 Note that adopting an approach like R. Bin-Nun would make women eligible to perform other rituals that we are not addressing in our current analysis, such as fulfilling men's obligations in *shofar* blowing and in the recitation of the full Hallel. See Introduction, n. 7.

that this mode of halakhic thinking remains novel and is still being considered and digested in many quarters. For those who are not yet prepared to accept it, gender-equal *minyanim* would depend on R. Tam's approach and a reassessment of the honor of heaven in contemporary settings.[81]

IV. The Propriety of Mixed-Gender Quorums

Whether following the approach of R. Tam or of the Levush, one might still engage the question of the propriety of having men and women join together to create a public ritual space.

The Ra'ah, cited in Ritva Megillah 4a, advances the argument that women, as an extension of their obligation in *megillah* reading, ought to be able to count toward the quorum of ten that is ideally required for reading it. He contrasts the case of the quorum of ten needed for *megillah* reading with Mishnah Berakhot 7:2's apparent ban on women joining with men to form a *zimmun*, which the Ra'ah understands to be motivated by concerns about sexual impropriety.[82] Why wouldn't such sexual impropriety be a concern in the context of the *minyan* for *megillah* reading? The Ra'ah proposes that we are only concerned about sexual impropriety when the dual-gender nature of the quorum is obvious from the form of the ritual itself: צירוף כולי האי or צריכי גברי לצירוף דידהו לגמרי. Specifically, when two men and one woman join for a *zimmun*, an entire introductory section is added to the blessings after food. All are thus aware that the *zimmun* ritual is happening only because the men and women present have been melded into a group and are dependent on one another's presence. By contrast, *megillah* reading looks the same when done for one person or for ten. Since the quorum of ten in that case is a requirement with no effect

81 The same would be true for a fully gender-equal Torah reading, which, absent R. Bin-Nun's sort of analysis, requires following R. Tam's approach, which largely sidelines the relevance of the identity of the leader.

82 This interpretation of Mishnah Berakhot 7:2 is not universal. See Koren, "Kullam Baki'im ba-Hallel," and Appendix D.

on the form of the liturgy,[83] it is not as obvious that men and women are forming a group and thus is not inappropriate.[84]

The Ra'ah's logic would obviously extend to mixed quorums of men and women for *devarim shebikdushah*, which are only done in a group of ten, such that the interdependence of the members of the *minyan* is obvious. The Ra'ah's opinion was far from universal.[85] R. Simḥah and those who followed in his wake clearly reject it. Others, like R. Ya'akov Emden, did not consider this to be a factor in the ban on counting women as equals. Yet others, such as Sefer ha-Me'orot, dispute the notion that concerns about sexual impropriety are the issue with a mixed-gender *zimmun* in the first place.[86] And even for those, like the Ra'ah, concerned about potential

---

83 Either the Ra'ah does not subscribe to the view taken by some Rishonim that the final *berakhah* after the *megillah* is only done in a group of ten, or he does not consider this sort of addition to be significant enough to trigger a *peritzut* problem. Depending on how one answers this question, one would reach a different conclusion as to whether, for the Ra'ah, a mixed group of ten men and women could perform *zimmun* with God's name, given that the fundamental structure of the *zimmun* is already in place via the presence of three men and/or three women.

84 This line of thought is then also cited in the Ran on Rif Megillah 6b. This is a novel articulation of the nature of the concern of *peritzut*. All sources earlier than the Ra'ah assume that *peritzut* is a problem of interaction in the context of the ritual, such that it would theoretically apply to any case of either a man or a woman performing rituals for someone of the other gender. Indeed, based on such an assumption, Sefer ha-Me'orot on Berakhot 45a argues that *peritzut* cannot be an area of concern when dealing with a mixed-gender group of free adults, since men perform rituals for women all the time and women, were it not for *kevod ha-tzibbur*, are eligible to read Torah for a community that includes men. The Ra'ah is the first to advance the notion that though leading a ritual for someone else is devoid of *peritzut*, being **dependent on the presence** of the other person in order to do so is, and said concern applies to mixed-gender groups of free adults as well. In part because earlier sources implicitly reject this notion and in part because it does not necessarily translate easily into intuitive notions of how *peritzut* would actually work in a human context, it seems best to understand the Ra'ah here as coming up with a *post facto* defense of his ruling that women count as equals for the ten of *megillah* in order to defend it from any challenges from the realm of *zimmun*.

85 Note the tacit disagreement of all authorities prior to the Ra'ah on his novel definition of *peritzut*.

86 The Ra'ah also does not address Sefer ha-Me'orot's evidence from women's principled inclusion in Torah reading. For more on the view of Sefer ha-Me'orot and the question of *zimmun*, see Appendix D.

sexual improprieties in mixed-gender quorums, that concern is anchored in a broader social reality in which male-female interactions in public spaces are obviously inappropriate. That assessment would need to be evaluated in each time and place according to its character. As we noted, we are not exploring those issues in depth in the context of this analysis.

Nonetheless, the Ra'ah's concerns may continue to be compelling for many contemporary communities. Those communities, even if following the pathways to a gender-equal *minyan* that we outlined above, might choose to avoid mixed quorums and allow for *minyanim* composed of ten men **or** ten women.[87]

---

87 A number of Aḥaronim resist mixed-gender quorums even when it can be demonstrated that women have identical obligation to men. For one example, see R. Simḥah Bamberger, in Responsa Zekher Simḥah #75, who argues that women and men can never form a group because of R. Yonah's reason for the problem of mixed-gender *zimmun*: "אין חברתן נאה — Their group is not appropriate." While not an issue of sexuality, this is a claim that there is simply never a proper sense of group when men and women are both involved.

Indeed, a similar approach is taken by R. Yoel Bin-Nun, who draws a sharp distinction between contemporary women's equality to men and the permissibility of women and men collaborating to create a shared ritual space:

> אבל יש דבר שלא נשתנה כל עיקר, והוא "יצר לב האדם". ולכן, כל צירוף של גברים ונשים יחד בדברים שבקדושה אין לו מקום, מעצם העובדה שהוא מכנים מתח מיני אל הקודש, חס ושלום, וכל הטענות, הנכונות כשלעצמן, של שינוי במעמד הנשים בזמננו, אינו קשור כלל ליצרי מעללי איש. אפשר אף להפך: השינוי הדרמטי מחייב זהירות מיוחדת בדברים בשקדושה. תפילת נשים – כן, על פי רצונן והלחטותיהן. צירוף גברים ונשים יחד בתפילה או בזימון – לא ולא.

> But there is one thing that has not changed at all, which is the human sexual drive. Therefore, there is no place for men and women to join together [for the *minyan*] for *devarim shebikdushah*, on account of the fact that this would introduce sexual tension into sacred space—God forbid. All the claims about the change in the status of women in our time, which are correct, have no connection to the sexual desires of human beings. Indeed, it might be that just the opposite is true: The dramatic shift [in the social status of women] necessitates heightened vigilance around sacred rituals (*devarim shebikdushah*). Women's prayer—yes, subject to their desire and decision. Joining men and women together in *tefillah* or in *zimmun*—absolutely not.

V. Are Gender-Equal *Minyanim* Wise?

Beyond our analysis here, some may argue that counting women in the *minyan*, though theoretically appropriate today, is too destabilizing to countenance, while others will argue that counting women does not entail any more risks than the benefits it would bring. This argument echoes the dispute we saw above between the rabbis of Amsterdam, who had no objection to women saying Kaddish, and the Ḥavvot Yair, who thought such a practice would be disruptive of norms,[88] and the contemporary dispute between R. Mendel Shapiro and R. Daniel Sperber, who see women reading Torah and having *aliyot* as appropriate, and R. Yehudah Henkin, who thinks that such a practice will inevitably correlate with a more lax standard of observance and is therefore unwise. We of course have precedent in the halakhic tradition for recognizing that these concerns, as well, are contextual. As we noted previously, R. Ahron Soloveichik permitted women to say Kaddish, precisely because, in his community, to refuse to do so would lead to the weakening of Jewish observance via the abandonment of Orthodox communities by Jewish women searching for synagogues that would allow such a practice. Any assessment of risk and benefit will ultimately be made by each community based on what it experiences on the ground. In communities where distinctions between men and women remain strong generally, tampering with an all-male definition of *minyan* may weaken the status of communal prayer and the seriousness with which it is approached. But as we have noted repeatedly, maintaining all-male *minyanim* in an increasingly gender-equal society has its own risks, including the relegating of communal prayer to a nostalgic activity decoupled from the real data of life. And as R. Bin-Nun points out, such a standard may not only be unwise, but might even be a distortion of the *halakhah* as it is meant to be applied to a contemporary community that treats men and women in the public realms with equal seriousness and respect.

---

88 See above, Part One, n. 160.

VI. Summary

A *minyan* is the manifestation of the Jewish community in microcosm. The earliest sources demand ten members for this purpose, though they minimally define who is eligible to constitute this group. Talmudic sources clarify that slaves and minors are clearly marginal members at best, but they are silent on the question of counting women. The Middle Ages brought a mix of views: some continued silence, some unsourced exclusion of women from *minyan*, some attempts to ground the exclusion of women in verses and terms that evoke microcosmic Jewish community, and some appeals to common sense for the obviousness of the female exclusion. In addition, at least one medieval source advocated including women at least partially in the *minyan*.

Peering behind the data to discover the theory underlying them, we discovered two main conceptions of *minyan*:

1. R. Tam argued that all those attached to the Jewish community through *mitzvah*-obligation and covenantal membership are theoretically eligible to count toward the *minyan*. The only bar to doing so in practice is "the honor of heaven."
2. The Levush argued that the essence of the *minyan* is ten maximally obligated Jews. As such, women, slaves, and minors, with their varying exemptions from many or all *mitzvot*, cannot ever constitute a *minyan*.

These two theories present two distinct pathways for assessing the validity and legitimacy of gender-equal *minyanim*. R. Tam's theory—which is followed by a range of medieval and modern authorities, even if they reject implementing it in practice—allows for the counting of women as equals provided that no offense results to the honor of heaven. Jewish communities of today still share this instinctive feeling about counting children as equals in the *minyan*. For a significant communal act such as public prayer, the community should bring out its finest: its full citizens, not its peripheral members. We discussed this concept of "the honor of heaven," demonstrating that it is not a communal prerogative to be waived. Rather, it demands an honest assessment: Will the de-gendering of *minyan* be experienced as a cheapening of communal prayer in order to lower standards and increasing the participation of marginal members? Or will it be experienced as raising the dignity of communal prayer to keep it in line with the standards of gender equality that reflect the dignity and seriousness found elsewhere in society? If the honor of heaven will honestly be advanced—rather than compromised—by embracing a gender-equal standard for *minyan,* then R. Tam's theory is a strong basis for egalitarian practice in this area.

The Levush's theory can only countenance counting women as equals if accompanied by the claim that contemporary women have a broader set of obligations than those described in classical rabbinic sources. One would need to argue that the term אשה, "woman," in classical literature is sometimes used as a placeholder for a sociological status that women shared with slaves and minors in most times and places in human history. Under that reading, contemporary changes in the status of women have resulted in corollary shifts in women's religious obligations such that they now are, through proper application of *halakhah,* maximally obligated Jews and thus self-evidently included in a *minyan* just like men. Pursuing this approach with integrity would demand educational and religious messages that communicate equal expectations of men and women, treating gender equality not just as an excuse for greater flexibility but also as a source of redoubled religious commitment. Communities that manifest that application of *halakhah* to their contemporary lives can reasonably claim not only R. Tam but also the Levush as support for their egalitarian practice.

According to either model, the delicate questions of whether equality should be played out through mixed-gender practices as opposed to separate-gender ones can—and must—be assessed community by community, with great sensitivity to the social context.

At the end of the day, we and others grapple with these questions because much of human society has recently experienced seismic shifts in the role of gender in our lives. It was crystal clear to so many of our ancestors that women do not represent a microcosm of the body politic, on account of their adjunct status, whether in the social sphere or regarding their less central role in certain areas of Jewish ritual practice. And yet for many of us, almost the opposite of that is true. When we confront structures that place limits on female citizenship, we are uncomfortable and become concerned that the community is not fully represented when half of its members are excluded.

Human society sometimes has a more difficult time with gender equality than does God. God may tolerate—and even, in certain cultural settings, endorse—social arrangements that discriminate based on gender. But our tradition also tells us that many such distinctions are contextual and contingent. They are not necessarily, in their essence, divinely ordained. Our Sages of blessed memory expressed this point in their midrashic expansion on the story of the daughters of Tzelofeḥad:

ספרי במדבר קלג
ותקרבנה בנות צלפחד (במדבר כז:א): כיון ששמעו בנות צלפחד שהארץ מתחלקת לשבטים, לזכרים ולא לנקבות, נתקבצו כולן זו על זו ליטול עצה. אמרו: לא כרחמי בשר ודם רחמי המקום – בשר ודם רחמיו על הזכרים יותר מן הנקבות אבל מי שאמר והיה העולם אינו כן אלא רחמיו על הזכרים ועל הנקבות רחמיו על הכל, שנאמר...טוב ה׳ לכל ורחמיו על כל מעשיו (שם קמה:ט).

Sifrei Bemidbar #133
"And Tzelofeḥad's daughters drew near" (Bemidbar 27:1): When Tzelofeḥad's daughters heard that the land would be divided according to the tribes to males and not to females, they all gathered to take counsel with one another. They said, "The goodness of God is not like the goodness of flesh and blood. Flesh and blood show greater goodness to males than to females, but the One-Who-Spoke-the-World-into-Being is not so, but is good to all, as it is said…'God is good to all and shows kindness to all creatures'" (Tehillim 145:9).

We pray that our investigation of this topic can lead Jewish communities to a deeper understanding of their own practices, a sense of the underlying values that have guided these conversations throughout the centuries, and a profound desire to properly apply God's eternal *mitzvot* to our personal and communal lives.

APPENDIX A:
Category Shifts in Jewish Law and Practice

I. Introduction

Halakhah is, and always has been, about applying an eternal divine will to the shifting facts of life. The details of halakhic discourse focus not on philosophy, nor even primarily on state of mind, but on specific actions taken in response to our experience in the world. The goal of Jewish law is to filter and direct our lived experience. Some of the most interesting material in *halakhah* relates to the tensions that emerge between the halakhic language of an earlier generation and the emerging halakhic facts of a subsequent one. How do legal authorities and communities respond to the changing significance of certain objects and actions over time and place, such that the performance of a given act in one context may achieve a specific goal, while it may fail to do so—or even act contrary to that goal—in another context?

We think it is fair to say that much of the energy in contemporary halakhic discussions is around precisely these sorts of questions. Our world is vastly different from that of Ḥazal both due to dramatic technological change and the often corollary social upheavals that go with it. (It has been quipped that Julius Caesar would have been more comfortable at Thomas Jefferson's inauguration than Jefferson would have been at Ronald Reagan's.) Questions surrounding identity, and gender in particular, are among the most bewildering and destabilizing in this regard. Risks are high all around. Maintaining legal forms from an earlier age can distort the underlying meaning and purpose of a law. On the other hand, jumping to adjust eternal values to contemporary trends can sap the Torah of its often intentional countercultural purpose.

In this appendix, our goal is to explore a series of examples that demonstrate these challenges and to explore one solution for dealing with them. We call this solution a "category shift": a claim that a certain object or action that was once properly classified under one rabbinic category has now shifted categories and the applied law should look different. Rather than arguing for a change in the law in light of new circumstances, this approach claims that the new facts lead to a different application of the old, inherited categories. While exploring these examples, we will consider differences between various types of category shifts and analyze why some are more controversial than others. In the context of this book, the most important application of such a category shift is of the rabbinic concept of אשה.

II. An Early Precedent: Laundry and Mourning

Let's begin with an example found in the Talmud itself. Bavli Ta'anit discusses various laws related to Tisha B'Av, the national day of mourning that marks the destruction of the two Temples, among other tragedies. Mishnah Ta'anit 4:7 discusses a penumbra of prohibitions that extend beyond the fast day itself. Specifically, it forbids doing laundry (כיבוס) during the week in which Tisha B'Av falls. The relatively straightforward text would seem to produce a relatively straightforward rule: When your clothes are dirty in the week prior to Tisha B'Av, you may not use water in order to clean them.

But then a Babylonian *baraita*[1] on Bavli Ta'anit 29b glosses the Mishnah's rule with the following phrase: "וגיהוץ שלנו ככיבוס שלהן —

1 By "Babylonian" *baraita*, we mean that this text has no parallel anywhere in the literature of Eretz Yisrael and thus its ideas may well reflect later, Babylonian assumptions and teaching, as opposed to a historically accurate picture of the teachings of Eretz Yisrael. Nonetheless, it is a *baraita* in the sense that it is preserved and presented as a tannaitic teaching and thus was understood by those who taught

Our ironing (or pressing) is like their laundering." This text, which speaks about the application of the Mishnah to "our" (Babylonian) setting, produces two legal consequences. First, it quite plainly forbids ironing clothing in the days leading up to Tisha B'Av. But this text does not simply forbid ironing. If so, it should have read "ואף גיהוץ שלנו אסור — And so too our ironing is forbidden." By mapping ironing onto laundry (גיהוץ שלנו כביבוס שלהן) the text points to a second consequence: In Babylonia, laundry is permitted during the days leading up to Tisha B'Av! Rashi makes this explicit:

> **רש"י תענית כט:**
> וגיהוץ שלנו אינו יפה אלא כביבוס שלהן, ואסור לגהץ לפני תשעה באב...אבל כיבוס שלנו מותר.
>
> **Rashi Ta'anit 29b**
> "Our ironing" is not any better than their laundering and it is forbidden to iron before Tisha B'Av...but our laundry is permitted.

This is a classic example of what we refer to as a "category shift." There is a legal category of כיבוס; all other activities that do not rise to the level of this category are permitted (such as folding clothing or hanging it up). There is then a physical activity (laundering) that consists of taking dirty clothing and placing it in water in order to clean it. In the Mishnah, the mapping is simple: Laundering is כיבוס and is forbidden. The Babylonian *baraita* claims that the prohibition on כיבוס was never about laundry *per se*, but rather כיבוס is a legal category intended to capture the significance of a type of physical activity. Therefore, it is possible that the act of laundering might, in another time and space, fall outside of the Mishnah's prohibitive legal category and a different type of activity might take its place. In the world of the Talmud Bavli, laundering no longer fits into the Mishnah's category and is therefore permitted. Ironing or pressing, however, now defines the category of prohibited care for clothing in the week of Tisha B'Av. Laundering, in other words, has undergone a legal category shift.

---

it to be a faithful transmission of the intentions of tannaitic teachings. In this case, the Babylonian provenance of the text is blatantly obvious from its very syntax, as we shall see.

Once falling into the Mishnah's forbidden category, it is no longer in that category, but is now permitted. And the forbidden category is now filled by a different activity, which becomes the focus of the prohibition.

What is the basis for this shift? The Talmud does not explicate it, but the reason seems fairly obvious and is already hinted at by Rashi above. The quality of laundering—and therefore the perceived social significance of laundering a garment and wearing laundered garments—was different in Eretz Yisrael and Babylonia. In Eretz Yisrael, the water sources ran faster and were full of more abrasive minerals. Both of these factors led to a superior laundering process. In Babylonia, the waters of the Tigris and the Euphrates—and especially the irrigation canals that branched off of them—were slow-moving and brackish. Laundering in Babylonia was simply not as effective as in Eretz Yisrael, and there was thus no reason to forbid this activity in the days surrounding Tisha B'Av. However, there was a Babylonian cultural equivalent of laundering: pressing or ironing clothing. This then becomes forbidden as an expression of the underlying value the Mishnah seems to be getting at here: In the week leading up to Tisha B'Av, do not clean and care for your clothes in a way that makes them look new and fresh again.

Let us note two significant things about the dynamics here, one of them stabilizing and the other destabilizing. The stabilizing dynamic is that Jews from both Eretz Yisrael and Babylonia would recognize one another's practices surrounding Tisha B'Av as focusing on a key provision of caring for clothing and improving its appearance. While the details might differ, a core value or principle would unite both sets of practice. They might even have translated their differing details of practice into a shared statement: "In the days surrounding Tisha B'Av, we do not make our clothing look like it is brand-new." In Eretz Yisrael laundering would have accomplished this, whereas in Babylonia only pressing or ironing would do the trick. Without the Babylonian remapping, pre-Tisha B'Av practice in Eretz Yisrael and Babylonia would start to **mean** two very different things. Maintaining a ban on laundry in Babylonia would threaten to turn a practice geared to avoid new-looking clothing into an odd, overly strict ban on more basic forms of cleaning that were never forbidden in Eretz Yisrael.

The destabilizing dynamic, of course, inheres in the *baraita*'s claim that "laundering" does not mean "laundering," or more precisely, that כיבוס does not mean laundering. Note that Babylonians also have the word כיבוס as part of their lexicon, and it means the same act of cleaning clothing in water. It is not as if the *sugya* says: "מאי כיבוס? גיהוץ — What is the meaning of כיבוס? [It is] ironing." That sort of formulation would have indicated that the word כיבוס was no longer a common term in the Babylonian context. In other words, despite the consistency of the language and the **action** it describes, a physical and cultural shift changes the **legal** significance dramatically. This claim, that consistency of language may mask inconsistent meaning—think of it as a version of "it depends on what the meaning of the word 'is' is"—is subject to charges of hyper-legalism and antinomianism.

Ironically, these dueling dynamics here produce a situation where what we have called a category shift is simultaneously (1) the most honest and direct path to understanding the true purpose of the law, and (2) a great threat to the law's perceived stability, particularly across time and space. It should be no surprise, therefore, that such category shifts are often quite controversial. While Rashi simply accepts the notion that laundering, in the wake of the Talmud's *baraita*, has become permitted during the week of Tisha B'Av, the Tosafot report greater reticence among medieval French Jews to adopt this understanding. The Tosafot note that the common practice was still to refrain from laundering מתוך המנהג, which we would render here as "in order to preserve continuity of practice." In other words, Jews carried with them a literary and physical practice of not washing dirty clothing in water during the week of Tisha B'Av. Even if the physical and cultural significance of that action had changed over time, the language describing it and the basic parameters of the action had not. Many Jews thus apparently resisted permitting what had previously been forbidden, even if this meant shifting the essential meaning of the category of כיבוס to include levels of cleaning far below what concerned the Mishnah.

This example also brings to light another important dynamic of category shifts. Once one engages in a category shift, one must be vigilant to assure that the action in question has not shifted categories again. This point is hammered home by the Ran:

ר"ן על רי"ף תענית ט:

ולכבסן בארץ ישראל אסור מפני שהם מתלבנין אבל בבבל מותר מפני שאין מתלבנין שם יפה לפי שמימיהן עכורין שאינה ארץ הרים וגבעות כארץ ישראל. הלכך כיבוס שבארצות הללו אפשר שהוא ככבוס ארץ ישראל.

Ran on Rif Ta'anit 9b

To do laundry in Eretz Yisrael is forbidden, because their clothes are truly whitened, but in Babylonia it is permitted, because they do not get truly whitened since their waters are cloudy, for it is not a land of mountains and valleys like Eretz Yisrael. Therefore, laundering in these lands might well be considered like the laundry of Eretz Yisrael.

The Ran begins by articulating the underlying facts motivating the category shift—the move from abrasive, spring-fed water in Eretz Yisrael to the brackish waters of the Fertile Crescent. And he explains that the underlying value of the ban on laundry is not to clean clothing to a certain standard during this intensive period of mourning, a value that may translate differently to different contexts. However, despite the general Diasporic medieval trend to follow the Babylonian Talmud over Eretz Yisraeli traditions, the Ran argues that the rivers used for laundering in Europe seem more similar to those of Eretz Yisrael. In other words, the very same substantive considerations that led the Talmud to redefine laundering for Babylonia might—and indeed should—lead future generations to redefine it once again, this time for Europe.

The Shulḥan Arukh gives a good summary of the various dynamics here:

שולחן ערוך או"ח תקנא:ג

שבוע שחל בו ט׳ באב אסורים...לכבס...וכיבוס שלנו מותר אבל גיהוץ...שלנו אסור...

ונהגו לאסור אפי׳...בכיבוס שלנו... ואין להקל בדבר כיון שנהגו.

וכ"ש דאפשר דמדינא נמי אסור שהרי יש מי שכתב דכיבוס שלנו קרוי (גיהוץ) לשל בני בבל שאין מתלבנים יפה לפי שמימיהם הם עכורים שאינה ארץ הרים וגבעות כארץ ישראל וכיבוס של שאר ארצות אפשר שהוא ככיבוס של ארץ ישראל ואסור.

Shulḥan Arukh OḤ 551:3

The week in which falls Tisha B'Av they are forbidden…to launder…but our laundering is permitted, although…our ironing is forbidden…

> But they practice to forbid...even our laundering...and one should not be lenient about this because they practice [this way].
>
> And all the more so since it is possible that, by strict law, it is forbidden [to launder even outside Eretz Yisrael]. For there is one who wrote that our laundering is called Babylonian ironing, since the people of Babylonia could not clean properly because their waters are murky since it is not a land of hills and valleys like Eretz Yisrael, and [therefore regarding] the laundry of other lands it is possible that it is like the laundering of Eretz Yisrael and [thus] forbidden.

R. Karo begins by codifying the Babylonian *baraita* and its claim that laundering is no longer forbidden during the week of Tisha B'Av, while pressing or ironing is. He then cites the Tosafot's report of popular resistance to this shift and an ongoing practice of forbidding laundering. The Shulḥan Arukh then gives legal imprimatur to this resistance on two counts: First, this restrictive practice has its own legal weight and should not be destabilized; and second, the Ran may be right that contemporary laundering in Diasporic lands outside of Babylonia is indeed more similar to the laundering of the Land of Israel and therefore forbidden by the Talmud's own criteria.

The example of laundry during the week of Tisha B'Av lays out the basic contours of category shifts: their necessity for any honest application of the substance of a law, the threat they pose to constancy of practice, and the need for constant vigilance to make sure that laws are correctly applied over time and space.

With this model in place, we can examine a range of other category shifts, with the following questions in mind: Why do some category shifts catch on while others remain controversial? Do different types of shifts function differently? Are there red lines that cannot be crossed when pursuing this sort of legal analysis? As we explore additional examples, we will aim to develop some criteria for thinking about this mode of halakhic development.

III. Ranges and Ovens: Shifting Temperatures and Laws

In the third chapter of Mishnah Shabbat, we hear about permissible and impermissible ways of cooking and heating up food as one enters into Shabbat on a Friday afternoon. The Mishnah offers the following rule:

משנה שבת ג:א–ב
כירה שהסיקוה **בקש ובגבבא** נותנים עליה תבשיל בגפת **ובעצים** לא יתן עד שיגרוף או עד שיתן את האפר...**תנור** שהסיקוהו **בקש ובגבבא** לא יתן בין מתוכו בין מעל גביו.

Mishnah Shabbat 3:1–2
One may put food to cook on a **range** that is fired by **straw** [right before Shabbat], but if it was fired with **wood**, one may not put food to cook on it until the coals have either been raked away or smothered with ash…One many not put food either in or on top of an **oven** [right before Shabbat] even if it was only fired with **straw**.

These passages are the subject of intense talmudic analysis, but the principle in the Mishnah is fairly straightforward: It is permissible to place food on an insignificant heat source going into Shabbat, whereas it is impermissible to place food on a significant heat source going into Shabbat. A כירה, or a range, is an open-air device that does not concentrate heat well on the food placed on it. Therefore, as long as a relatively minor and ephemeral heat source is used—such as straw—it is not hot enough to present a problem. Wood, however, provides too much heat. If wood is used to fire a range, no food may be placed on it heading into Shabbat until the embers have been removed or stamped out. By contrast, a תנור, an enclosed oven into which food is placed, is highly insulating and retains significant heat, even when fired with a relatively insignificant heat source. As a result, one may never place food into a תנור on Friday afternoon, even if it was only fired with straw.

Just as laundry practices changed, so too did the nature of ovens. The Talmud already notes in other contexts[2] that some ovens are larger and hotter than others, and the same goes for ranges. A professional's range

2 See Bavli Bava Batra 20b.

might in fact generate heat equivalent to the common oven, such that various laws relating to ovens and ranges might not apply equally to all makes and models. Seizing on this point, Rabbeinu Ḥananel rules, in his commentary on Talmud Bavli Shabbat 38b, that the Mishnah's proscriptions here speaks only to the equipment of professional bakers: "וקי"ל מתני' בתנור של נחתומין — It is established for us that our *mishnah* is about a professional baker's oven." It was indeed forbidden to place anything in a baker's oven on Friday afternoon, but the common oven was, according to R. Ḥananel, subject to the Mishnah's discussion of a professional's range: As long as no live embers remained inside, one could use it.

This is another classic category shift. The word תנור is constant over time and place and signifies an oven used for cooking. However, the objects referred to in common language as תנורים have undergone a shift. Whereas the Mishnah applies to them the **legal** rule of a תנור, they have, according to R. Ḥananel, shifted to the **legal** category of כירה, a range. The ramifications are significant. We now permit putting food into an oven on Friday afternoon, an act that a surface reading of the Mishnah expressly forbids.[3] But once again, the category shift preserves the meaning and the intention of the law as focused on intensity of heat. In contemporary terms, R. Ḥananel is essentially asserting that the Mishnah meant to say something like: "One may put food on a heat source on Friday afternoon that is below 200 degrees Fahrenheit." In the time of the Mishnah, ovens and ranges were a decent proxy for this distinction. In R. Ḥananel's time, the category of "oven" itself must be subdivided to get at this distinction.

As in our example of laundering, this proposed shift was not uniformly accepted either. The Maharshal rejected this category shift:

> **דברי ר' שלמה לוריא המובאים בספר תפארת שמואל על רא"ש שבת ג:א**
>
> ואם קבלה היא נקבל. ואם לדין אומר אני דאדרבה דמתניתין איירי בסתם תנור של בעל הבית ולא איירי דוקא בנחתום. והרי"ף שרגיל לחלק ולהביא דברי הגאונים בכל דוכתא ולא חילק כלל הכא בין תנור שלנו ושלהם או של נתתום וכ"כ הרב רמב"ן וכן משמע בכל

3 Other Shabbat laws play out differently between ranges and ovens, including permissions on returning food to them on Shabbat. See Shulḥan Arukh OḤ 253.

דברי האחרונים דאף בסתם תנור שלהם נפיש הבלא כדין תנור הנאמר בתלמוד עכ"ל רש"ל ז"ל.

Maharshal as quoted in Tiferet Shmuel on Rosh Shabbat 3:1
If [this distinction between our ovens and the ovens of the Mishnah] is by a received tradition, I will accept it. But if this distinction is offered based on logical deduction alone, then I say that the Mishnah is in fact talking about the common oven found in people's homes and is not speaking about a professional baker's oven. The Rif, who commonly introduces such distinctions based on geonic traditions, did not distinguish here at all between our ovens and theirs or those of professional bakers...and this is implied by all the later authorities [who were silent about this distinction], for even their common ovens got very hot, [and they follow] the rule of the oven laid out in the Talmud.

The Maharshal argues that if an object is called a תנור and is shaped like a תנור, then it has the halakhic status of the Mishnah's תנור. He argues this point in part based on substance—perhaps the insulated heat of even a small oven is still a problem—but also on the notion that without explicit textual support, it is dangerous to say that words do not mean what they seem to mean. When earlier generations failed to distinguish between various objects or scenarios, one will have to make a clearer case for how contemporary reality is obviously different in order to convince skeptical voices such as the Maharshal.

IV. "Everyone Is Sick"— Asking Gentiles to Heat Jewish Homes on Shabbat

Such an obviously different reality is in play when Jews relocated to Northern Europe from the Middle East. Another useful and dramatic example of a category shift relates to using Gentiles to light fires for Jews on Shabbat. The following two basic principles are established without dispute in the Talmud. First, Gentiles may not do forbidden labor on Shabbat for Jews, and if they do so, Jews may not benefit from those labors. Second, on Bavli Beitzah 22b, Ulla b. R. Ilai rules that one may instruct a Gentile to do anything on Shabbat—including biblically forbidden labors—for the benefit of a sick Jew. This does not refer to someone in mortal danger—even a Jew can violate Shabbat for such a person—but someone whose entire body is in pain and discomfort.

Lighting a fire is a core biblical violation of Shabbat and it is thus forbidden for a Jew to benefit from a fire lit by a Gentile. Mishnah Shabbat 16:8 in fact already makes this explicit, saying that a Jew may not use a lamp lit by a Gentile for the Jew's own use. It is therefore initially quite surprising to find medieval authorities, like the Maharam of Rothenberg, who permitted Jews to tell Gentiles to light fires for them on Shabbat:

שו"ת מהר"ם מרוטנברג ד:צב
וששאלת על הגויות המחממות בית החורף בשבת בצרפת היו נוהגי' היתר בבית מורי ואמר שרבי' יעקב דאורליינ"ש התיר אפי' **לומר** לגוי לתקן האש משום חולה שאין בו סכנה [דאומר] לגוי [ועושה] והכל חולי' אצל האש לישב בקרירות. אמנם במלכותינו נ"ל לאסור משום דברים המותרים ואחרי' נוהגי' בהן איסור.

Responsa Maharam of Rothenberg IV:92
You asked about the Gentile women who heat up the furnace on Shabbat. In France, in the home of my teacher, they were lenient [to allow Jews to benefit from the heat], and my teacher said that R. Ya'akov of Orleans even gave permission to **instruct** a Gentile to light the fire under the permission to tell a Gentile to perform *melakhah* for a sick person, since we are all sick with respect to fire were we to sit in the freezing cold. However, in our land, I think we should forbid under the rubric of forbidding permitted things when others have already treated them stringently.

The category of חולה, a sick person, can be thought of in two different ways. On a surface level, it would seem to refer to a small subset of the population that is in a hopefully temporary state of illness. It is an abnormal state, recognized by the physically healthy majority as aberrant. This understanding of חולה would makes it virtually unfathomable to use this legal category as a basis for allowing the entire Jewish population to adopt a general practice of instructing Gentiles to light fires on Shabbat on account of the cold. On the other hand, one might think of חולה as a legal category that is simply a proxy for a standard of discomfort, the point at which one's entire body is in distress and one can no longer enjoy Shabbat. R. Ya'akov of Orleans read the category this way; the Talmud simply did not require Jews to be that uncomfortable on Shabbat when Gentiles could be of assistance. In fact, being "strict" and applying the Talmud's leniencies only to more generally sick people would distort the underlying value of that leniency, which involves ensuring, where possible, a certain level of comfort on Shabbat. Here we find an even more dramatic category shift: "Everyone is sick" with respect to the act of lighting a fire when it is cold.[4] The category of "well" still exists, but only with respect to other sorts of needs and their remedial violations.

The Maharam here adds an interesting German postscript to the French interpretive innovation. He "buys" the argument, describing the act of instructing a Gentile to light a fire on Shabbat in the cold as permitted. But he recommends against following through on this suggestion in Germany, where a surface reading of talmudic texts on this matter remains dominant.[5] Would it not be excessively destabilizing to march into a community that has routinely sat in the cold on Shabbat for generations and suddenly to pronounce that what was forbidden is now permitted? We get here another glimpse of the destabilizing nature of category shifts: If a word or legal category has already made the transition to another reality—in this case, continuing to apply the category of חולה only to those who are ill—it becomes a tricky proposition to institute a shift at a later point without unsettling religious norms more generally.

The Shulḥan Arukh codifies R. Ya'akov of Orleans, but with a caveat of his own:

שולחן ערוך או"ח רעו:ה

בארצות קרות, מותר לא"י לעשות מדורה בשביל הקטנים ומותרין הגדולים להתחמם בו, ואפי' בשביל הגדולים מותר אם הקור גדול,

4 The phrase הכל חולים אצל הצינה creatively evokes Rava's statement on Bavli Pesaḥim 69a that "הכל חולין הן אצל המילה — All [infants] have the status of a sick person with respect to circumcision," even if they are otherwise healthy. Rava's statement itself is a kind of category shift, putting children in the context of circumcision in the category of the ill, despite their general "health."

5 For a clear articulation of the earlier German position, in the name of R. Simḥah of Speyer, see Hagahot Mordekhai on Bavli Shabbat 19a.

שהכל חולים אצל הקור. ולא כאותם שנוהגים היתר אע"פ שאין הקור גדול ביום ההוא.

Shulḥan Arukh OḤ 276:5

In cold lands, it is permitted for a Gentile to make a large fire for children[6] and then adults may warm themselves by it as well. And it is even permitted for them to do it for adults if the cold is severe, since all are sick when it comes to cold. But one should not act like those who permit this even when the cold is not severe on that day.

We see here that the Shulḥan Arukh fundamentally endorses this sort of category shift as legitimate, without much concern for the destabilization of prior practice. In cold lands, it may indeed be the case that the category of "sick" is the best way to think about "healthy" people who are very cold, since חולה is intended to capture a level of discomfort in the context of this *halakhah*, not a standard of general bodily health. But he also notes, like the Ran before him on laundry, that one must be vigilant to make sure that the category shift does not become a tendentious formal leniency. The logic of R. Ya'akov of Orleans's position only makes sense in times and places when it is very cold, such that keeping a person without heat is truly a kind of suffering. There is no basis for relying on Gentiles to light fires when it will raise the temperature from 60 to 68 degrees. And yet, he is aware of many who do this nonetheless and he scolds them for doing so. Here we see another dynamic of category shifts: They are open to abuse. It is often simpler for people to function with a menu of cut-and-dried categories. Is it forbidden to tell a Gentile to light a fire on Shabbat or isn't it? When people are asked to engage with substantive categories—how cold is it? how uncomfortable am I?—the results can be subjective and inconsistent. And as in this case, the fact that a certain action is legitimate in some instances—as when it is very cold—can provide cover for those who want to manipulate the law for their convenience.

---

6 The assumption here is that children are routinely considered to be vulnerable and thus to have the status of sick people (albeit not in mortal danger). See Hagahot Mordekhai cited above and Rema OḤ 328:17. This is another model for thinking about otherwise healthy people as being in the category of "sick."

V. Reclining at the Seder Table— Two Shifts Are Better than One

Sometimes, multiple factors are involved in a category shift. This is on display when we look at halakhic material surrounding the practice of reclining at the Seder. Mishnah Pesaḥim 10:1 articulates what seems to be a universal obligation to recline: "ואפילו עני שבישראל לא יאכל עד שיסב — Even a poor Jew should not eat until they recline." The practice of reclining was firmly rooted in Greco-Roman mores and reflective of the posture adopted in a symposium-style meal. Diners ate on couches with small tables of food placed in front of them; the instruction to recline is asserting that this meal must be fancy and one of leisure, as opposed to a more rushed meal that might have been eaten sitting upright or even standing.[7]

Those mores changed over time. In northern Europe, kings would eat royal banquets at tables in upright chairs. How was the observant Jew to translate the practice of "reclining" to this new setting? Some continued a simulated practice of reclining by leaning to the left side while sitting in a chair. But others objected, claiming this distorted the original meaning and purpose of the practice. In Germany, a strong line of thinking developed arguing for discarding the practice, based on this shift in material culture, as can be seen in the Ra'avan:

ראב"ן פסחים דף קסד עמוד ד

והם היו נוהגין לישב על המיטות ולהסב בהסיבת שמאל. אבל אנו שאין אנו רגילין בכך יוצאין אנו כדרך הסיבתינו ואין לנטות ימין ושמאל.

---

7 As a historical matter, it is less than clear if this *mishnah* is **prescribing** reclining as opposed to **assuming** it for a fancy meal such as the Seder. If the latter, then the text is making a comment about the timing of eating: Even though poor people normally ate earlier than others—in part to save the cost of fuel required to light a lamp to eat by (see Talmud Bavli Berakhot 2b and Rashi there)—on this night they must not eat before the prescribed time for dining, which is after dark, in keeping with the biblical injunction, ואכלו את הבשר בלילה הזה (Shemot 12:8). In an Eretz Yisraeli-Roman context, reclining is simply the way a fancy meal like the Seder would have been eaten. In any event, later generations understood the Mishnah to be prescribing a particular **posture** while eating, and this is the basis for our discussion here.

Ra'avan Pesaḥim 164d
Their practice was to sit on couches and recline on the left side, but since that is not our normal practice, we fulfill our obligation the way we sit normally. One should not lean either to the right or to the left.

His grandson the Ra'aviah concurred,[8] and a later text cites another German authority as making this point with even greater force:

ספר מהרי"ל (מנהגים) סדר ההגדה
דדוקא בימיהם שהיו רגילין בהסיבה בשאר ימות השנה, אז מחוייבין בה בפסח, אבל לדידן שבשאר ימות השנה לא נהגינן בהסיבה, אין לנו לעשותה בלילי פסח, דמה חירות שייך בזה אדרבה דומה לחולה, וכ"כ אבי העזרי.

Sefer Maharil, Minhagim, Seder ha-Hagaddah
[The obligation to recline applied] specifically in their days, when they were accustomed to recline throughout the year. In that context it was obligatory to do so on Pesaḥ. But in our context, where we never recline the rest of the year, we should not do it on Pesaḥ. What does this have to do with freedom? On the contrary, it makes a person appear sick!

Here we see a passionate case for a category shift as preserving the true underlying value of the law. Whereas eating in a regular chair had once been the symbol of a rushed, common meal, by the Middle Ages in Europe, dining rooms were employing upright seating for all occasions. Sticking to the old form of reclining in this new context would not only have no meaning, but it would deprive the Seder of the very feeling of freedom it is intended to inspire. In the new style of dining room, "reclining" would be a ridiculous act that is counterproductive to the goal of the ritual! The claim is not that we need to phase out obsolete rituals, but rather that we must translate the underlying values of those rituals to different contexts. "Reclining" never really meant **reclining**, according to these German authorities; it meant adopting a posture that signifies elegance and freedom while eating.

---

8 See Ra'aviah II:525.

Despite the convincing nature of this analysis, legal authorities were reluctant to accept it. Hagahot Maimoniyot to Hilkhot Ḥameitz u-Matzah 7:2 reports this basis for eliminating reclining at the Seder, but declares it "a lone view" and therefore inappropriate to rely on. So follow almost all subsequent authorities. The Shulḥan Arukh exhorts the Seder participant to set up one's chair in order to recline on it, and the Rema glosses that while ideally one should cushion one's chair with pillows to fulfill this obligation, a poor person who owns no pillows should recline on a bench.

Why is this eminently reasonable category shift—sitting upright is the legal equivalent of the reclining of yore—so unsuccessful? This is no mere leniency, but a claim that the best way to demonstrate freedom is to eat in the formal posture of formal meals. Why did this shift not take?

It seems to us that this shift is different from the others we have seen so far, in that it **eliminates** the earlier legal category altogether. When laundering became ironing, ironing remained forbidden. When stoves became ranges, stoves fired with wood remained a problem. When cold people became sick with respect to fire, they were still forbidden to ask Gentiles to do other tasks for them. In other words, there was a true category **shift**, with a certain activity or person switching between two legal categories, each of which retained its integrity. In this case, German scholars were in fact arguing for category **elimination**. True, these German authorities held that one fails to fulfill the obligation to recline at the Seder by slumping over in one's upright chair, and in this sense, the legal category of reclining has not truly been eliminated but rather transposed to the category of normal sitting. But the average person would experience this category shift as dispensing with something that had once been unusual and obligatory in favor of something unremarkable and pedestrian. Indeed, the Ra'aviah formulates his instruction as "יושב כדרכו — One fulfills the obligation of reclining today by sitting normally." To the extent that category shifts work with old forms but fill them with new content, this one asks us to break the mold, and so we should not be surprised that it was not terribly successful.[9] In other words,

9 Though we should note that there are many Jews who have a Seder who do not hang off their chairs, or who make sure there is a pillow under them, which is in fact in keeping with the Ra'aviah.

category shifts may be less successful when they make practice thinner, eliminating rituals without replacing them with alternatives.[10]

Interestingly enough, the Ra'aviah got a second bite at the apple. To see how, we need to return to another set of texts and another category shift, ones that deal with women and their obligation to recline at the Seder. As we noted above, the Mishnah specifies that even the very poor must recline at the Seder, as a sign of the universal freedom granted to all Jews as a result of the Exodus. But displaying this kind of freedom may not be appropriate for all, especially for those who occupy subordinate social positions. On Pesaḥim 108a, the Talmud Bavli rules that a woman does not recline in the presence of her husband unless she is an אשה חשובה, "an important woman"—a woman of significant social status (and presumably wealth).[11] This distinction was codified and preserved by most authorities.[12] But a tradition ascribed to the Tosafot preserves a different perspective:

תולדות אדם וחוה נתיב ה חלק ד דף מב טור ד
וכתבו התו' כל הנשים שלנו חשובות הן וצריכות הסבה. והרמ"בם
כתב בסתם אשה אינה צריכה הסבה.

Toledot Adam ve-Ḥavah, Netiv 5, Part 4, 42d
The Tosafot wrote that all of our women are considered important and thus are obligated to recline. But the Rambam simply wrote that the average woman need not recline.

---

10 It is also worth noting that at a certain point, the "strange" ritual of reclining entered the liturgy of the Haggadah, in the form of the fourth question asked at the beginning of the Maggid section. Combine this with the fact that many "strange" things happen at the Seder, and you have a welcoming environment for stubbornly retaining an odd ritual form of the reclining posture out of context.

11 There is disagreement among interpreters as to whether the Talmud Bavli means merely to **exempt** women from reclining or to **forbid** them from doing so, on account of it being an inappropriate usurpation of a higher social status. We have deliberately elided that in translating the talmudic phrase לא בעיא as "does not." Other elements we are not engaging here include the question of whether married women and single women are different and whether the husband's physical presence is key for triggering a wife's removal from the obligation to recline.

12 See Rambam, Hilkhot Ḥameitz u-Matzah 7:8.

Here we have yet another category shift. The world once divided into men and important women, who were both required to recline, as opposed to ordinary women, who do not recline. Ordinary women shift categories, according to this view, and are now reckoned as important—and are therefore the equivalents of men with respect to this law. Others, such as students in the presence of their teachers, remain unencumbered by the obligation to recline.[13]

The gendered nature of reclining proved resilient, however, and the Rema reports that in 16th-century Poland most women had not adopted the practice of reclining at the Seder. Once again a category shift failed to take hold, perhaps because the claim of all women being considered "important" was insufficiently plausible,[14] or perhaps because the ramification of essentially eliminating the legal category of the common woman was too great a shift to bear. Interestingly, though, the Rema does not reject the Tosafistic claim of universal importance for women as a way of explaining this. Rather, somewhat surprisingly, he maintains that this category shift is indeed in place, but that women refrain from reclining because they rely on the German position that no one needs to recline in a cultural context where formal meals are eaten while sitting upright!

Aside from the Rema's support for the category shift that rendered all women as חשובות, we learn something else interesting about category shifts from this example: They are often much more successful as *post facto* explanations of behavior that no longer fits earlier sources than they are as guideposts for how to change practice to fit the times. When early medieval German authorities tried to argue proactively for abandoning the practice of reclining without replacing it with something else based on a category shift, they were largely unsuccessful, no matter how persuasive their arguments. On the other hand, when those who ostensibly should recline were not—in this case women—the category shift became an attractive

---

13 The exclusion of students from reclining in the presence of their teachers is grounded in the subsequent discussion on Bavli Pesaḥim 108a.

14 Historical and social context is important here as well, but beyond the scope of our discussion. Suffice it to say that the role of women in the surrounding non-Jewish society would have had significant effects on perceptions of female "importance." The medieval French context was one where women had a particularly influential role and greater freedoms. See discussion of R. Yoel Bin-Nun in Part Two, n. 76 and onward.

way to make sense of this behavior. This was further made easier by the fact that men continued to recline, thus removing the biggest obstacle to this approach: the elimination of any even pseudo-act of reclining from Jewish practice.

VI. Identities and Defining Categories of People

So far, most of the examples we have looked at concern actions and ritual obligations and prohibitions. Throughout, we have seen earlier authorities assessing the underlying meaning of various terms. Does "laundry" refer to a specific physical action, or to a standard of cleanliness? Do "ranges" and "ovens" speak of specific structures, or are they proxies for levels of heat? Does "reclining" refer to a specific posture, or is it a term that captures a socially dependent level of elegance and freedom?

A few examples we have seen begin to deal with classes of people, such as who counts as "sick" and "important." But these are still malleable states of being, which can change with climate and social standing. How would these sorts of category shifts play out with respect to what seem to be more fundamental groupings of human beings, based on physical attributes or national and ethnic origin? As we shall see, category shifts have been suggested in these areas as well, where they can often be even more vital to the ongoing coherence of Jewish law and practice, even if they are no less controversial.

A. חרשים, DEAF-MUTES

Those who can neither speak nor hear are routinely exempted by rabbinic sources from various obligations and banned from certain rituals. Mishnah Ḥagigah 1:1 states that a חרש, a "deaf-mute," is exempt from making a pilgrimage to Jerusalem on the three festivals. Mishnah Megillah 2:4 declares the deaf-mute invalid to read the *megillah*. Mishnah Bava Kama 4:4 explains that if the ox of a deaf-mute gores the ox of a פקח, "one who can hear and speak," the deaf-mute is exempt from payment. Mishnah Terumot 1:1 rules that a deaf-mute cannot separate out *terumah* (the portion of produce reserved for priests), and if they do so, the *terumah* has no status. Mishnah Terumot 1:2, however, considers a boundary case: What if a deaf person who can **speak** takes *terumah*? While the Mishnah maintains that they should not do so, it concedes that such *terumah* is indeed valid and sacred. Why? Because the term חרש, says the Mishnah, only refers to a deaf-**mute**, and the person in question here can speak.

It is fairly obvious from the context here that the legal category of חרש signifies—at least in most contexts—someone who is of impaired intelligence on account of their disability. Therefore, a deaf person who can speak, and who can thereby demonstrate intelligence, is not treated the same way as a deaf-mute. In other words, even though the word חרש really only means someone who cannot hear, it is understood to **signify** those who lack mental intelligence on account of their lack of hearing, and in most cases this is manifested by an inability to speak as well. Someone who can speak, even if they are deaf, is no longer in the legal category of חרש, even if they might commonly be described as a חרש in society.

In case this analysis was not clear, the Talmud Bavli hammers it home. The Talmud wants to understand the significance of the Mishnah's grouping of a חרש together with a שוטה, one of diminished mental capacity who could be clinically classified as insane, and a קטן, a minor. Why would these three categories of people, so utterly different from one another, be listed as a triplet when describing those who are exempt from making a pilgrimage on the three festivals? The Talmud Bavli's answer:

תלמוד בבלי חגיגה ב:

קתני חרש דומיא דשוטה וקטן. מה שוטה וקטן דלאו בני דעה, אף חרש דלאו בר דעה הוא. וקא משמע לן כדתנן: חרש שדיברו חכמים בכל מקום, שאינו שומע ואינו מדבר. הא מדבר ואינו שומע, שומע ואינו מדבר – חייב.

Talmud Bavli Ḥagigah 2b

The Mishnah teaches [about a חרש in juxtaposition to a שוטה and a קטן in order to indicate that we are speaking] about a deaf person who is similar to a mentally incompetent person and a minor. Just as those two do not have the requisite intelligence, so too we are dealing with a deaf person who does not have the requisite intelligence. This teaches us the rule laid out in the Mishnah [in Terumot]: "The deaf person about whom the Sages spoke everywhere is one who can neither hear nor speak." By implication, a deaf person who can speak or a mute who can hear is obligated.

The Talmud here sees the **context** in which the category of חרש is used to be determinative of the scope of its **definition**. Since חרש is discussed in the context of other mentally incompetent people, it must not be a category primarily about hearing, but rather about mental competence. Therefore, whenever there is someone who cannot hear but who is fully mentally competent, this person does not belong in the legal category of חרש.

This basic mode of thinking lays the groundwork for a potential category shift for deaf-mutes who learn sign language and receive a full education in schools designed to work around their disabilities. A category shift approach essentially says that such people, despite having a **physical condition** of being חרשים, inhabit the **legal reality** of the פקח and follow the legal rules that are applied to the mentally competent. And so have held many later halakhic authorities with respect to contemporary deaf-mutes who can communicate through lip reading, sign language, and writing. R. Markus Horovitz took this approach and thought that education in a school for deaf-mutes shifted the students' legal category from חרש to פקח.[15]

Nonetheless, others, beginning with Tzemaḥ Tzedek and continuing through the present day, resist any category shift of this sort. If someone can neither hear nor speak, they remain a חרש—and other indicators of mental competence cannot and should not shift this person's status. The reality that counts is not the intelligence that stands behind the physical disability, but rather the physical disability itself. The dynamics here are similar to what we saw in the case of reclining, though with some subtle differences. Those resisting the category shift are clearly nervous about abstracting from a physical category endorsed as significant by classical sources to a concept of intelligence that may be more subjective. On the other hand, in this case, the abstract category—intelligence—is already described by the Talmud as central to our understanding of the legal meaning of חרש. This gives those advocating the shift firmer textual ground on which to stand.

We find a poignant mixture of deep commitment to the category shift along with concern for stability and continuity in the writings of R. Asher Weiss. In a *teshuvah* published online,[16] he writes the following:

---

15 His view is quoted in Responsa Shevet Sofer Even ha-Ezer #21.

16 Weiss, "Status of a Deaf Person."

ואי בדידי תליא היה נראה דכל הפוסקים הנ״ל דיברו בזמנם שרוב החרשים אכן כשוטים היו ורק מעטים אחד בעיר ושנים במשפחה הצליחו להתגבר על מגבלתם ולהגיע לדעת שלימה. אבל בזמנינו שרובם המכריע מגיע לדעת שלימה והם מתפקדים כאחד האדם אם על ידי שפת הסימנים ואם על ידי קריאת שפתיים, דינם כפקחים גמורים.

ובירושלים עיר הקודש זכינו שיש כולל אברכים שכולם חרשים אילמים והם לומדים סוגיות הש״ס בעיון ובהבנה, וכמה רחוק לומר שדינם כשוטים.

ונראה עיקר להלכה דיש להחמיר בזה לכל צד, מחד גיסא לנהוג בהם דין פקח לכל דבר ולחייבם במצוות התורה, ומאידך להחמיר בהם כמסורת ההלכה דור דור כיון שהלכה זו עמומה ורפויה היא בידינו.

If it were up to me, it would seem that all the earlier authorities spoke about their own time, when most of the deaf-mutes were indeed like the mentally incompetent. Only a few here and there succeeded in overcoming their handicap and to develop a full mental faculty. But in our own time, when a clear majority of deaf-mutes attain full mental ability and they function like anyone else with sign language and lip reading, their status should be that of fully mentally competent people.

In the holy city of Jerusalem, we are privileged to have a *kollel* made entirely of deaf-mutes and they learn talmudic *sugyot* in depth and with understanding. How far from reality to say that they have the status of mental incompetents!

But it seems that the essence of the *halakhah* here is that we should be strict in all directions. On the one hand, we should treat deaf-mutes as fully mentally capable and to obligate them in *mitzvot*. On the other hand, we should be strict in keeping with the halakhic tradition of past generations, given that this *halakhah* remains unclear and unresolved.

Here we see in live and raw form many of the dynamics we have explored throughout this essay.[17]

B. GENTILES

Another famous example of a category shift in matters of identity relates to the status of Gentiles. Classical Jewish law is replete with distinctions between Jews and Gentiles. Jews are exempt from paying damages to Gentiles whose property they have destroyed (at least when such matters are adjudicated by Jewish courts), Jews may (at least on a biblical level) lend money on interest to Gentiles, and Jews may not eat many foods prepared by Gentiles.[18] Perhaps the peak moment of distinction between Jews and Gentiles is when Mishnah Yoma 8:7 takes for granted that Jews are forbidden from violating Shabbat in order to save the life of a Gentile.

At various points in Jewish history, some of these distinctions came into question. The most famous reassessment in this regard was argued for by R. Menaḥem ha-Meiri. The Meiri argued for a sophisticated sort of category shift: Whenever Gentiles seem to have a different status on account of their idolatrous practices (such as in bans on engaging in commerce with them on their festivals), then contemporary non-idolatrous, monotheistic Christians are no different from Jews.[19] Whenever Gentiles seem to have a different status on account of their moral or ontological inferiority (such as in the context of civil law or saving their lives on Shabbat), contemporary, non-barbarian, legally responsible Gentiles are to be treated like Jews.[20] When Gentiles seem to have a different status because of concerns about Jewish national distinctiveness (as in the case of forbidden Gentile foods and penumbral prohibitions around intermarriage), their status is unchanged.[21] In other words, the term נכרי means different things in different contexts:

---

17 For more on this topic, see Ancelovits, "Ma'amad ha-Ḥeresh."

18 See Mishnah Bava Kama 4:3 for one example of this sort of distinction.

19 See Beit ha-Beḥirah Avodah Zarah 2a.

20 See Beit ha-Beḥirah Yoma 84b, Gittin 62a, and Bava Kama 37b.

21 See Beit ha-Beḥirah Avodah Zarah 38a–b.

בית הבחירה להמאירי עבודה זרה כו.
הרבה ראינו שמתפלאים על שבזמנים אלו אין אדם נזהר מדברים אלו כלל, ואנו כבר ביארנו: עיקר כונת הספר על איזו אומה היא סובבת כמו שיעידו ימי אידיהן שהזכרנו שהם כלם לאמות הקדומות שלא היו גדורות בדרכי הדתות והן אדוקות ומתמידות בעבודת האלילים...ומ"מ לענין חשש איסור שבת וחשש איסור מאכלות ומשתאות כיין נסך וסתם יינם ושאר איסורין הדומים לאלו, הן שנאסרו בהנאה הן שנאסרו באכילה הן מאותם שגזרו עליהם מחשש חתנות, כל האומות שוות בו...ומעתה יהו דברים אלו מיושרים על לבך ולא נצטרך להשיבם בכל דבר ודבר, אלא שתהא אתה בוחן באיזו אתה מפרשם על האמות הקדומות ובאיזו אתה מפרש על כלל הכל ובין ותדע.

Beit ha-Beḥirah Avodah Zarah 26a
We have seen many people who are surprised than in our time, no one is careful about any of these things [the Mishnah's prohibitions on helping Gentiles give birth or on receiving medical treatment from them]. But we have already explained: The essence of [the Mishnah's] intention here is directed toward the nations of old that were not bounded in the ways of religion and they were entrenched in constant idolatry…Nonetheless, with respect to concerns about Shabbat prohibitions[22] and concerns about forbidden food and drink such as [Gentile] wine and other prohibitions like these, whether they are prohibitions around benefit or consumption or whether they were decrees to prevent intermarriage, all the nations are the same…So now, let this be clear to you so we need not explain it in each and every instance. You discern for yourself in which areas the laws are meant to apply [only] to the peoples of old

22 As we noted above, the Meiri explicitly distinguishes elsewhere between the Gentiles of the Talmud and his Provencal Christian neighbors when it comes to the question of saving a Gentile's life by violating Shabbat. This category, therefore, must refer to other areas of Shabbat law relevant to Gentiles, such as when one is able to ask a Gentile to do a *melakhah* on Shabbat for a Jew. For a broader analysis of the Meiri's approach to Gentiles in *halakhah*, see M. Halbertal, *ha-Meiri*, 80–108.

> and which are meant to apply generally. Know and understand this.

As was the case with the Talmud's analysis of deaf-mutes, the Meiri argues that we always look to see the legal context of the term נכרי. Sometimes it indeed refers to any sort of Gentile, but sometimes it means "idolater," "barbarian," "immoral citizen of a corrupt government that does not recognize my rights," "someone whose culture is hostile to mine," or "someone whose full humanity we do not and cannot respect"—think of a Nazi war criminal in our own time. The Meiri reveals that he considers these distinctions to be readily discerned, even intuitive, once we focus on the essence of what a legal category is about and what its context is.

This category shift is powerful in that it essentially denies that the term נכרי has any universal meaning at all, instead seeing this as code for a distinct underlying value that guides each area of law. Its vulnerability lies precisely in this unevenness of interpretation: Sometimes a Gentile is a Gentile and sometimes they are a Jew! It should not be surprising that the Meiri's category shift failed to persuade many Jews, and even those uncomfortable with letting a Gentile die on Shabbat found other ways of justifying their practice.[23] They might have said to the Meiri: Until we permit intermarriage and dissolve the Jewish people, we cannot claim that contemporary Gentiles have shifted categories with respect to civil law and Shabbat. The term נכרי cannot mean two things at once.

Nonetheless, there is no denying that the Meiri's category shift seems to be the reasoning for how many Jews reconcile their own relationships with contemporary Gentiles in light of classical rabbinic sources. However

---

23 The most common is to invoke the Talmud's category of איבה, "enmity," between Jews and Gentiles. The idea is that if Jews do not save a Gentile's life on Shabbat, Gentiles will not save Jews, or worse: Gentiles will use this legal discrimination against them to attack and kill Jews. Saving a Gentile life thus becomes justified even on Shabbat as an act of Jewish self-preservation. The outcome is the same, but the philosophical and textual basis is dramatically different. It is always hard to know in such contexts whether the *poskim* in question truly resist the notion that Gentile life is of equal value to Jewish life, or whether they are simply afraid of subjectivity run amok were they to follow the Meiri's lead. For a ruling that exudes the first attitude, see Responsa Tzitz Eliezer VIII:15:6. For a ruling that (perhaps) has echoes of the second attitude, see Responsa Yabia Omer VIII OḤ #38. Interestingly, neither of them cites the Meiri on this topic.

much his analysis has caught on in the world of the *poskim*, it shows that this sort of thinking about categories of identity and ontology is not a modern innovation but a natural continuation of the other sorts of shifts we have looked at.

C. WOMEN

Finally, we turn to and conclude with the most relevant category shift for the topic of this book, one that is very much still in process and in the infancy of being considered: gender. As is the case with respect to Gentiles, women are given a different status from men in many halakhic contexts. As contemporary Jews confront great equality between men and women in both social and economic spheres, some of these distinctions have come under strain and interrogation. Does Jewish law view men and women as ontologically different in all of these areas? Are these prescriptions meant to be in force even when they are countercultural? Are they sociologically based and malleable over time and place?

Deploying a category shift with respect to gender would seem to involve following the Talmud's lead on deaf-mutes and the Meiri's subtlety with respect to subdividing categories. When we look at the female exemption from various *mitzvot*, we find that women appear in a triplet of their own: "נשים עבדים וקטנים — women, slaves, and minors."[24] This is a jarring juxtaposition to the contemporary ear, but it seems fairly clear that it reflects a sociological grouping that would have been quite familiar to an ancient audience: These are social adjuncts and dependents, those who are subservient to the dominant group of free adult men. And, viewed in this context, many of the exemptions for women make perfect sense. Take, for instance, women's exemption from the twice-daily recitation of the Shema in Mishnah Berakhot 3:3. On its own terms, this is somewhat puzzling. Why would women be exempt from this most basic declaration of theological commitment? Aren't women also obligated to believe in one God and to affirm this on a daily basis, just like men? But when one considers that rabbinic sources understand the Shema at its core to be קבלת עול מלכות שמים, accepting God's ultimate authority over one's life

---

24 For just a few examples of this very common triplet, see Mishnah Berakhot 3:3, 7:2, Pesaḥim 8:7, Shekalim 1:3, 5–6, Sukkah 2:8, 3:10.

and one's choices, the exemption and those whom it affects make perfect sense. Who must affirm daily, upon waking up and before going to sleep, that God has unrivaled authority? The person who might be deluded by their own social status into thinking otherwise: the free adult male. Women, slaves, and minors live every moment of the day with a clear understanding that they do not sit at the top of the social pyramid. They are not poisoned with the potential arrogance to which the Shema is an antidote. A proponent of a category shift around gender would look at contemporary women who wield power and live lives independent of men and would suggest that these women in fact have the status of men with respect to this and other *mitzvot*. Put another way: Is it in keeping with the purpose of the *mitzvah* to recite the Shema twice daily to exempt a neurosurgeon, a CEO, or a secretary of state just because they happen to be biologically female?

We saw above, in the context of our discussion of reclining at the Seder, that medieval rabbis already entertained the notion that women's status had changed in a way that eliminated the gendered nature of reclining, a practice intimately bound up with social standing and hierarchy. But even those "important women" of the world of the Tosafot remained exempt from a slew of *mitzvot*, in keeping with a social status that was still that of an adjunct.[25] A category shift based on the triad נשים עבדים וקטנים would go one step further. Reading for context, as the Gemara directs us to do in the case of deaf-mutes, advocates of this category shift would argue that the **intended and original meaning** of the phrase נשים עבדים וקטנים is "social adjuncts." The category of נשים would thus only be understood as historically associated with biology, but, in its essence, the category would be just one example of **social standing**. In the time of the Mishnah, there were then two categories with respect to many *mitzvot*: principals and adjuncts. Free adult men fell into the first category, whereas women, slaves, and minors fell into the second. A category shift around gender would claim that women have shifted categories from adjunct to principal.

---

25 It is often hard to remember how recent many of the victories of feminism and egalitarianism are, even in the West.

Indeed, we have begun to see some contemporary rabbis articulate thoughts in this direction. R. Yoel Bin-Nun penned the following thoughts a few years ago:[26]

> רוב הנשים של ימינו בנות חורין הן...ואינן דומות לעבדים בשום פנים, שהרי אין רשות אחרים עליהן. לפיכך, כל מי שמצטט פסקי חכמים, שהתבססו על כך ש"אישה דומה לעבד" בכל מקום, איננו מבין שהוא מעביר הלכה ממציאות אחת למציאות אחרת, בלי יסוד. "נשים שלנו", לא רק שכולן חשובות, כדברי הרמ"א, אלא שהן "בנות חורין"...פשוט לא מדובר באותו סוג של נשים.

> Most women in our day are independent/liberated (*benot ḥorin*)...and they bear no resemblance to slaves, because there is no power of others over them. Therefore, anyone who cites the ruling of the Sages, which are based on the notion that "a woman is similar to a slave" in all arenas, fails to understand that they are transferring a *halakhah* from one reality to another without any basis whatsoever. "Our women" are not only all important—as the Rema already said—but they are independent/liberated...It is obvious that we are not speaking about the same category of *nashim*.

To be clear, advocating for this category shift entails claiming that this is the **correct** understanding of the underlying value of the texts in question. A proponent of a category shift on gender is afraid that **exempting** contemporary women from various *mitzvot* would be a **distortion** of the Mishnah's intention, arguing that the Mishnah never dreamed of exempting someone who could not plausibly be compared to a slave based on their biology alone. This is an excellent example of how debates over category shifts cannot be simply reduced to arguments over leniency and stringency. They are instead arguments of **right** and **wrong.** What is the correct way to understand what an earlier text is getting at and how do we then faithfully apply it to our context? Where the Meiri would see complicity in bloodshed when a Jew allows a Gentile to die on Shabbat, his opponents would see Jewish fundamentals being destroyed by Shabbat desecration if one takes action. Similarly, the question of a

---

26 This was quoted in Part Two, at n. 76.

category shift around gender is not about how lenient one can be in the name of egalitarianism; it is rather at its root a complex question of just how biologically based various *halakhot* are meant to be.

As even the Meiri points out, identities can be complex and have multiple components. This is surely true as well in the context of gender. There are many *halakhot* that clearly are grounded in biology and that do apply to **women**, and not to (male) slaves and minors. These would be unaffected by this category shift analysis, since those *halakhot* are not grounded in a sociological reality.[27] We would be forced to take up exactly the sort of work the Meiri proposes to his audience: Learn the laws and practices in their larger context and pay attention to the other groups they apply to. This can guide us to think about their proper application in our own day and age.

Even if one adopts R. Bin-Nun's approach—it seems obvious to us that more and more people will do so in the years ahead—many questions remain. If sociology is the true force here, then is it really the case that all women should shift to the category of men? What of all the women in the world who still experience subordination on a daily basis? And aren't there men—like the slaves of old—who inhabit an inferior social position and should therefore perhaps be exempt from certain *mitzvot*? Are we confident we can sort out the laws that relate to biology and sexuality from the ones that relate to socioeconomic status? We can expect that as this category shift continues to play out, the same dynamic that manifested in earlier conversations will emerge here as well. But we do think that any long-term horizon for a gender-equal Jewish practice that is grounded in Ḥazal will ultimately employ this category shift and integrate it into halakhic discourse, just as happened with many of the earlier examples we saw.

27 Of course, other factors and analyses might lead to those *halakhot* being applied differently as well, but it would not be on account of the juxtaposition of the term נשים with עבדים וקטנים. A useful parallel to think about might be someone who would contend that contemporary deaf-mutes who can speak sign language fluently are now obligated in all *mitzvot* except *shofar*, since it is a *mitzvah* specifically grounded in **hearing**, not just intellectual ability.

VII. Conclusion: Patterns and Red Lines

We would like to end with some summary thoughts on the dynamics we have seen and with an attempt to isolate the factors that may lead some category shifts to be more accepted than others.

A. PATTERNS

When we consider *halakhah*'s evolving relationship with reality through the dynamics we have described here, a number of patterns emerge:

1. *Correspondence to Reality*

A successful category shift is not an excuse for leniency or stringency, but one that speaks compellingly and directly to some sort of change in facts that warrants reading inherited language more creatively than a surface reading might suggest. Laundering simply produced different results in Babylonia and this made plausible the translation of כיבוס into גיהוץ. As soon as those facts no longer held up—as in the context of the much more effective laundering that went on in Europe—the category shift failed to hold, and appropriately so. And the converse is true as well: If a category shift is desperately needed for *halakhah* to make sense of reality, other risks inherent in its adoption may be overlooked. We have presented a number of examples of this dynamic and we would argue that this is the single most important factor in a category shift's success.

2. *Degree of Disruption to Common Practice*

The more a category shift threatens to undo a standing practice—whether the ban on laundering before Tisha B'Av or the refusal to tell Gentiles to light fires on Shabbat or the practice to sit in an unusual fashion at the Seder—the more it will be viewed with suspicion by the traditional population. The more the category shift strives to give legal language to facts already on the ground—as when women sit normally at the Seder table—the less controversial it will be.

3. *Local Versus Global Nature of the Shift*

The more tailored the category shift is to the *halakhah* in question, the less it threatens the global language of *halakhah*. It is simpler to digest a shift with respect to ovens and stoves than it is to redefine the category of "Gentile," with all of its massive implications for texts dealing with a host of issues.

4. *Economy of the Distribution of Legal Data*

If a category shift essentially renames or switches categories while leaving the ratio of forbidden to permitted untouched, it is more likely to be adopted with ease. In some cases, the data shifts mildly, as when one type of cleaning clothing is exchanged for another, or even when the specific activity of lighting a fire on a very cold day moves into the permitted column. In all of these cases, the category shift stands a good chance. Things get dicier when the balance is shifted more dramatically, as when Gentiles become Jews or when all women are supposed to behave like men, since society now thinks of being a principal independent of gender. Here we might expect greater resistance to full acceptance of the shift, as an entire category simply threatens to disappear as most of the data it contained migrates elsewhere and nothing else rushes in to replace it.

5. *Red Lines*

Part of what is so fascinating about category shifts is how bold and direct they are. Instead of chipping away at a received halakhic reality, they simply reassess it in its entirety and propose a new way of looking at things. This can be invigorating and inspiring. It can also be terrifying and destabilizing.

Consider the following example of taking a category shift too far in an antinomian direction. Paul, a first-century Jew, offered the following analysis and reached the following conclusion:

> **Romans 2:28–29 (KJV)**
> For he is not a Jew who is one outwardly; neither is that circumcision which is outward in the flesh: But he is a Jew who

> is one inwardly; and circumcision is that of the heart, in the spirit not in the letter; whose praise is not of men, but of God.

This passage from the Christian Bible features Paul suggesting a classic category shift, does it not? Our categories are מולים, those who are circumcised, and ערלים, those who are uncircumcised. Jews, following the *mitzvah* given to Avraham, who mark their (males') flesh, fall into the first category, whereas the unaltered bodies of Gentiles place them in the second category. After all, although Bereishit 17 introduces God's command to Avraham to circumcise himself, the same language (ומלתם) is used in Devarim 10:16 and Yirmiyahu 9:25 to talk about "circumcision of the heart." In light of this biblical background, Paul argues that in his own time the physical circumcision should be seen as a marker of something more spiritual. He claims that many people circumcised in the flesh do not manifest the circumcision of the heart that is the true sign of being God's servant, whereas many whose flesh has not been cut are truly open to the word of God. The underlying **value** of circumcision has nothing to do with the physical marker itself, argues Paul. That value is inward and of the spirit. To mistake the letter for the spirit is to distort the core intention of the Torah on this point. The major consequence for Paul and Christianity more generally: Gentiles can be a part of the covenant with the God of Israel without circumcision, and Jews, despite their circumcision of the flesh, may in fact be rejected by God and not truly Israel at all.

Whatever one thinks of the biblical interpretation here, there is no question that this analysis is completely incompatible with rabbinic interpretation of the Torah and what we recognize as non-negotiable Jewish practice throughout the ages. But why? How is Paul's analysis here so different from the category shifts we have seen? Why can't this move be assimilated, in the sense of "our hearts are like their foreskins"? Or, framed from the other direction: Why won't the dynamic of category shifts lead us down a Pauline slippery slope toward antinomianism, the evisceration of *halakhah*, and even the dissolution of Jewish identity?

I want to suggest the red line that Paul crosses here and that must serve as a boundary to any halakhic engagement with category shifts. Most of the category shifts we saw propose that a person fulfill an obligation by **acting** differently. Instead of refraining from laundering, one refrains from ironing. Instead of claiming an exemption from a ritual, one must now perform it. The German approach to reclining at the Seder was a bit different, arguing that the act of reclining no longer fulfilled the obligation of feeling free and that this state of mind could now be accomplished by sitting upright. It should not surprise us that this was rejected by many later authorities. This begins to verge into a different sort of shift, one where one's understanding of the deeper purpose of a law allows one to **eliminate** it.[28] Paul's pronouncement in Romans that the true benefits of circumcision can be realized without taking an actual knife to the flesh is precisely the sort of category shift *halakhah* has generally been unwilling to bear. The more durable shifts have tended to be those that replace one physical act with another, such that the Jew fulfilling the *mitzvah* still does so in the flesh, in keeping with *halakhah*'s distinctive emphasis on concrete action above intention and state of mind alone. *Halakhah* is a pathway of the letter and the flesh; rendering concrete actions into abstract states of mind is incompatible with rabbinic law and practice.

Another red line is how we speak and what our canon is. Often the boundary between acceptable and unacceptable ideas is as much how they are articulated as the substance they convey. The language of category shift can be used in flippant ways to depart from the tradition, or it can be used to tether us more tightly to its underlying values. Here, the words of R. Yitzḥak Hutner should ever ring in our ears. In describing the vast capacity of the discourse of Torah to contain multiple opinions and approaches, R. Hutner lays out one important criterion for an opinion to be in the canon: "אם רק נאמרה לפי גדרי המשא ומתן של תורה שבעל פה — provided it was articulated according to the boundaries of discussion of the Oral Torah."[29] R. Hutner here is trying to emphasize the centrality of engaging the traditional canon of halakhic sources and feeling duty-bound to interpret them, as opposed to simply replacing them with one's own opinions. Perhaps even more so than other halakhic ideas, category shifts can risk being broad pronouncements about how "today, everything is different" in a way that can threaten the continuity of discourse that represents a commitment to the eternity of God's will. The "boundaries of discussion" point us back to the canon of rabbinic sources through the

28 We emphasize "verge," since the Ra'aviah still required a very specific physical action of sitting at the table—walking around would not have been permitted in his regime. Nonetheless, because it is not apparent to the observer or the participant that any distinctive action is being taken at that moment, it almost feels as if the ritual of reclining is being eliminated entirely.

29 Paḥad Yitzḥak, Hanukkah, Ma'amar 3.

ages and force category shifts to be a best effort to understand and apply that which we have received from the past. Category shifts with integrity and staying power will be those that aim to capture a deep truth embedded in earlier texts rather than aiming to replace the insights of the past with our own.

Our hope is that this exploration of this critical dynamic in *halakhah* can help deepen that search for God's will as refracted throughout our people's history of learning and practice.

APPENDIX B:
Talmud Bavli Berakhot 20b

MISHNAH BERAKHOT 3:3 discusses women's obligation in *tefillah,* and there are many variants in the Talmud Bavli's analysis of this *mishnah* on Berakhot 20b. Here is a synopsis of various textual witnesses:[1]

1 Transcriptions taken from The Saul and Evelyn Henkind Talmud Text Databank of The Saul Lieberman Institute of Talmud Research of the Jewish Theological Seminary of America

Soncino (1484)

מאי שנא ק״ש ותפילין דמצות עשה שהזמן גרמ׳ וכל מצות עשה שהזמן גרמ׳ נשים פטורות תפלה ומזוזה וברכת המזון דמצות עשה שלא הזמן גרמ׳ נשים חייבות ק״ש פשיטא מצות עשה שהזמן גרמ׳ הוא וכל מצות עשה שהזמן גרמא נשים פטורות מהו דתימ׳ הואיל ואית בה מלכות שמים קמ״ל ומן התפילין פשיטא מהו דתימ׳ הואיל ואתקוש למזוזה קמ״ל וחייבין בתפלה דרחמי נינהו מהו דתימ׳ הואיל וכתי׳ בה ערב ובקר וצהרים כמצות עשה שהזמן גרמ׳ דמי קמ״ל ובמזוזה פשיטא מהו דתימ׳ הואיל ואתקש לתלמוד תורה קמ״ל ובברכת המזון פשיטא מהו דתימ׳ הואיל וכתי׳ בתת ה׳ לכם בערב בשר לאכל ולחם בבקר לשבע כמצו׳ עשה שהזמן גרמא דמי קמ״ל

Oxford Opp. Add. fol. 23

פשיטא מהו דתימא הואיל ואית בה מלכות שמים אימא לא ק׳מ׳ל׳ ומן התפילין פשיטא מהו דתימא הואיל ואיתקש למזוז׳ אימא לא ק׳מ׳ל׳ וחייבין בתפלה פשיטא מהו דתימא הואיל וכתיב ערב ובקר וצהרים אשיחה ואהמה הויא לה מצות עשה שהזמן גרמה וכל מצות עשה שהזמן גרמה נשים פטורות ק׳מ׳ל׳ ובמזוזה פשיטא מהו דתימא הואיל ומזוזה איתקש לתלמוד תורה ליפטרינהו ק׳מ׳ל׳ וברכת המזון פשיט׳ דמצות עשה שאין הזמן גרמה היא ס׳ד׳א׳ הואיל וכתי׳ ויאמר משה בתת ייי לכם בערב בשר לאכול ולחם בבקר לשבע תהוי כמצות עשה שהזמן גרמה ק׳מ׳ל׳ **מאי שנא ק״ש ותפילין דהויא להו מצות עשה שהזמן גרמה וכל מצות עשה שהזמן גרמה נשים פטורו׳ אבל תפלה ומזוזה וברכת המזון מצות עשה שלא הזמן גרמה היא ומשום הכי נשים חייבות**

Paris 671

מאי שנא קרית שמע וכל מצות עשה שהזמן (ש) גרמה נשים פטורות משום דכתי׳ ביה בשכבך ובקומך הוייא ליה מצות עשה שהזמן גרמה **תפלין** נמי לילה לאו זמן תפילין הוא **הוו להו מצות עשה שהזמן גרמה נשים פטורות אבל תפלה ומזוזה וברכת המזון כיון דהוייא להו מצות עשה שלא הזמן גרמה חייבות מאי טעמ׳ כל מצות עשה שלא הזמן גרמה נשים חייבות** פטורין מקרית שמע פשיטא דהא מצות עשה שהזמן גרמה הוא מהו דתימ׳ כיון דמלכות שמים (הוא) היא הכל חייבין ק׳מ׳ל׳ ומן התפילין פשיטא מהו דתימ׳ הקיש תפילין למזוזה מה מזוזה מיחייבי תפילין נמי מיחייבי ק׳מ׳ל׳ וחייבים בתפלה פשיטא מהו דתימ׳ הואיל וכתי׳ ערב ובקר וצהרים כי מצות עשה שהזמן גרמה היא ק׳מ׳ל׳ כיון דרחמוי נחילא ובמזוזה פשיטא מהו דתימ׳ אקיש מזוזה לתלמוד תורה מה תלמוד תורה פטירי אף מזוזה נמי פטירי ק׳מ׳ל׳ דמחייבי וברכת המזון פשיטא מצות עשה שלא הזמן גרמה היא ס״ד אמינ׳ הואיל וכתי׳ בתת יי לכם בערב בשר לאכול ובבקר תשבעו לחם כי מ(..)[צ]וות עשה שהזמן גרמה היא ק׳מ׳ל׳

Florence II-I-7

[נ'א' קרית שמע ותפילין דהויא לה מצות עשה שהזמן גרמה וכל ( ) מצות (לא) תעשה שהזמן גרמה נשים פטורות תפילה ומזוזה וברכת המזון דהויא להי מצות עשה שלא הזמן גרמה וכל מצות עשה שלא הזמן גרמה נשים חייבות] פשיטא מצות עשה שהזמן גרמא הוא ונשים פטורו' מהו דתימא הואיל ואי(ן)[ת] בה מלכות [שמים] (לא) [חייבות] ק'מ'ל' מן התפילין פשיטא [+נ'א' ל'ג'+] מצות עשה שהזמן גרמא הוא ונשים פטור' מהו דתימא נקיש תפילין למזוזה [מה מזוזה מיחיבי] [אף תפילין נמי ליחייבי ק'מ'ל'] ק'מ'ל' מן התפילה פש' מהו דתי' הואיל וכתי' בה ערב ובק' וצהר' כמצות עשה שהזמן גרמא הוא [דדמיא] ק'מ'ל' [תפילה רחמי היא] מתני' (?וחייבי?.. ....
..........) ומזוזה [פשיטא מהו דתימא ניקוש מזוזה (לתפילה)לתלמ' תורה מה תלמ' תורה פטירי אף מזוזה נמי פטירי ק'מ'ל' ?פשי?ט?א?? מצות עשה שלא הזמן גרמה היא איצטריך ס'ד'א' הואיל וכת' בתת ה' לכם וכו' תהוי כמצות עשה שהזמן גרמה ק'מ'ל' אמ' רב אדא בר] (פשיטא מצות עשה שלא הזמן גרמא וכל מצות עשה שלא הזמן גרמא נשים חייבות מהו דתי' נקיש מזוזה לתלמוד תורה ק'מ'ל')

Munich 95

(מאי טעמ' דק"ש ותפילין הוי להו מצות עשה שהזמן גרמא וכל מצות עשה שהזמן גרמא נשים פטורות תפלה ומזווה וברכת המזון דהוו מצות עשה לא הזמן גרמא נשים חייבו') [אינו מלשון התלמוד דאין צריך לפרש אלא גרסינן פשיטא כו'] ופטורין מק"ש פשיטא מצות עשה שהזמן גרמא הוא מהו דתימ' הואיל ואית ביה מלכות שמים ליחייבינהו ק'מ'ל' ומן התפילין פשיטא מהו דתימ' הואיל ואיתקש תפילין למזווה מה מזווה מיחייבי אף תפילין מחייבי ק'מ'ל' וחייבין בתפילה [גירס ר'ש'י' תפלה דרחמי ננהו וא"ד פשיטא מ"ד הואיל דכתיב ערב ובקר וצהרים אשיחה כמצות עשה שהזמן גרמ' דמי ק'מ'ל' ובמזווה פשיטא מהו דתימא הואיל ואיתקש מזווה לתלמוד תורה מה תלמוד תורה פטירי אף מזווה פטירי ק'מ'ל' מתניתין ובברכת המזון פשיט' מ"ד הואיל וכתיב ויאמ' משה כו'] פשיטא דמצות עשה שלא הזמן גרמא הוא (........ ..)[מהו דתי'] הואיל וכתי' ויאמר משה בתת יי לכם בערב בשר לאכול כמצות עשה שהזמן גרמא הוא ק'מ'ל **(מאי שנא ק"ש ותפילין דלא דמצות עשה שהזמן גרמא הוא וכל מצות עשה שהזמן גרמא נשים פטורות תפלה ומזוזות וברכת המזון מצות עשה שלא הזמן גרמא הוא ומשום הכי חייבות) [אינו תלמוד]**

A quick look at these parallels reveals two basic versions of the Gemara here:

1. A statement explaining why the different *mitzvot* are treated differently: Those that are caused by time are obligatory for women and those that are not caused by time are not obligatory for women. This version appears in bolded text above.
2. A series of short פשיטא exchanges on all five *mitzvot* in the Mishnah, with an expression of shock that one might ever have thought otherwise. In the case of the obligatory *mitzvot,* we imagine how they might have been considered caused by time (*tefillah* and Birkat ha-Mazon), or how they might have been closely linked to another *mitzvah* from which women are exempt (*mezuzah*). In the case of the exemptions, either the value at stake is high enough (*keri'at Shema*) or the *mitzvah* is similar enough to an obligatory *mitzvah* (*tefillin*) that we might have thought women were obligated. This version appears in highlighting above. There are also a few sections of plain text, which reflect later additions from other sources and processes.

Though there is much to say about these manuscripts, the following picture emerges. The Florence manuscript lacked the bolded version in the body of the text and bears witness to a version of the Gemara with five פשיטא passages and no general explanation. A later hand then added the other version of the Gemara into the margins. The double appearance of the bolded text in the body of the Munich manuscript suggests that it was a marginal gloss to a textual ancestor of this text that crept into the body in two separate places. A later hand, however, clearly possessed something like the body of ms. Florence and was careful to note that the bolded version ought not to be considered an original part of the Gemara (in his opinion, at least). The parallel nature of these two versions of the Gemara is confirmed by Rishonim, with both the Rashba and Tosafot R. Yehudah he-Ḥasid stating that they knew of texts that lacked the פשיטא passages entirely and only featured the general statement in the bolded text. The other textual witnesses thus represent a hybrid picture, reporting both versions of the Gemara together. Mss. Oxford and Paris nonetheless switch the order of the two versions, a classic sign that one of them is a later addition that crept in from the margins (a process we described above for ms. Munich). The first printing solidifies this process, with both versions of the text achieving canonical status until today, even though they were originally dueling versions.

It is thus clear that when the Rif offers his summary statement of the reasoning behind the Mishnah's ruling, he is citing his version of the Talmud Bavli, which itself offers this sort of blanket statement and does not engage the פשיטא structure at all (the bolded text above). The same is true of many other Rishonim, including the Talmidei R. Yonah, who offer their own explanations of their version of the Talmud, which asserts without explanation that *tefillah* is not a time-caused commandment.[2]

The next significant change to the text comes about as a result of Rashi:

> רש"י ברכות כ:
> הכי גרסינן תפלה דרחמי נינהו ולא גרס פשיטא דהא לאו דאורייתא היא.

Rashi clearly had the version of the Gemara that featured multiple פשיטא passages, like the bolded section of ms. Oxford. Rashi assumed two points that created a problem for him:

1. that the term מצות עשה refers to something biblical, and
2. that *tefillah* had no biblical component and was entirely rabbinic in provenance.[3]

He therefore considered this passage as the work of an unlearned copyist and argued for its erasure. In place of the פשיטא passage on *tefillah,* he suggested the phrase דרחמי נינהו in an assertion of the basis for obligating women in *tefillah* independent of the question of its status as a time-caused commandment.[4] In other words, the word "פשיטא" in Rashi's comment

---

2 This confirms the instinct of Ma'adanei Yom Tov letter *tzadi* on Rosh Berakhot 3:13, who said that the Talmidei R. Yonah seem not to have had anything in their Gemara. To put it more precisely: They did not have a version with any פשיטא statements, just a blanket statement about the nature of these different obligations.

3 The first assumption seems to be a linguistic point, though it is disputed by Tosafot Berakhot 20b s.v. *peshita*; the second point is supported by Bavli Berakhot 21a: אלא: קריאת שמע וברכת המזון — דאורייתא, ותפלה — דרבנן.

4 The phrase is borrowed from Bavli Sotah 33a, where it is used to explain why *tefillah* can be said in any language. The phrase also appears on Bavli Pesaḥim 117b, where it helps explain why blessings in the Amidah are formulated with present-tense verbs. Other passages describe tefillah as רחמי with different

above meant "פשיטא..." covering that word and the entire conceptually linked section that followed it, through the קמ"ל.[5] We can see this process at work in ms. Munich. The base text there begins with a text that reads identically to the bolded section of ms. Oxford, but which gets cut off in the middle due to a copyist's error caused by the next section of text.[6] A later hand adds a note that Rashi replaced this section with the words דרחמי נינהו and that the alternative he was arguing against read as does the italicized section of ms. Oxford. In ms. Florence, we see how Rashi's version is suggested as an alternative in the margins to a passage virtually identical to the italicized section of ms. Oxford. In ms. Paris, this alternative has already crept into the base text.[7]

Our printed version represents the final stage of this process. Either the manuscript used by the printer or the printer himself wanted to update the text of the Gemara to reflect Rashi's emendation. But this editor did not properly understand Rashi's comment. He thought that when Rashi wrote ולא גרס פשיטא, he was merely referring to the **word**, פשיטא, as opposed to the **entire phrase that begins with that word**. As a result, the first printing features a text that replaces the word פשיטא with the words דרחמי נינהו, and then continues on with the rest of the פשיטא text. This hybrid does not really make any sense—having a מהו דתימא without a prior expression of surprise is syntactically awkward—but we can now understand how it came about.

---

phrasing; see Bavli Berakhot 26a for one example. The concept that *tefillah*'s essence as a personal request for mercy is at the core of women's obligation in it is already found in the Talmud Yerushalmi parallel to our *sugya*: כדי שיהא כל אחד ואחד מבקש רחמים על עצמו.

5 That this is Rashi's intent is clear from Tosafot Berakhot 20b *s.v. peshita*.

6 The copyist seems to have jumped from the words מהו דתימא הואיל וכתיב in the section on תפילה to the same words in the later section on ברכת המזון, a common type of scribal error.

7 See also Meiri s.v. *maḥloket*. Note that some versions of Halakhot Gedolot report the phrase דרחמי היא in their summary of this *sugya*. But see Halakhot Gedolot, ed. Hildesheimer, vol. I, 17, n. 82, which demonstrates that this is not the original text of Halakhot Gedolot, but rather a later addition based on Rashi's highly influential correction.

APPENDIX C:
The "*Mitzvah*" of Public Prayer

A NUMBER OF TALMUDIC sources engage with the question of public prayer ("praying with a *minyan*"). The Talmud Bavli discusses R. Eliezer's decision to free his slave so that the ex-slave could be the tenth in a *minyan*:

תלמוד בבלי ברכות מז:

מעשה ברבי אליעזר שנכנס לבית הכנסת ולא מצא עשרה, ושחרר עבדו והשלימו לעשרה...

והיכי עביד הכי? והאמר רב יהודה: כל המשחרר עבדו עובר בעשה, שנאמר: "לעלם בהם תעבדו" (ויקרא כה:מו)!

לדבר מצוה שאני.

מצוה הבאה בעבירה היא!

מצוה דרבים שאני.

ואמר רבי יהושע בן לוי: לעולם ישכים אדם לבית הכנסת כדי שיזכה וימנה עם עשרה הראשונים.

Talmud Bavli Berakhot 47b

It happened that R. Eliezer entered the synagogue and did not find ten, so he freed his slave and rendered him the completion of the ten....

How could he act thus? Did not Rav Yehudah say, "Anyone who frees his slave transgresses a positive commandment, as it said, 'Forever treat them as slaves' (Vayikra 25:46)"?!

For a *mitzvah* it is different.

[But] it is a *mitzvah* that is performed through a transgression!

A communal *mitzvah* is different.

And R. Yehoshua b. Levi said, "A person should always get up and go early to the synagogue in order to merit and be counted with the first ten."

The critical phrase in this passage is מצוה דרבים, literally "a *mitzvah* of the many" (and translated above as "a communal *mitzvah*"). This quality of praying with a *minyan* is what justified R. Eliezer's violation of the Gemara's assumed ban on freeing slaves. There are multiple ways to interpret this phrase, each interpretation having different consequences for how we understand the practice of public prayer and its relationship to the individual:

1. מצוה דרבים means an individual obligation possessed by many people. R. Eliezer's action was warranted because he enabled multiple people to fulfill their individual obligations in public prayer. This reading supports the notion of an individual obligation to pray with a *minyan*.
2. מצוה דרבים means a communal obligation to have a *minyan* and, as such, devolves on all individuals, though not as a specifically individual obligation. Once the community has assured the presence of a *minyan*, no individual obligation to be present remains. According to this reading, all individuals who count in a *minyan* are responsible to do what they can to make sure the community has a *minyan*, but there is no individual obligation beyond that communal imperative.

3. מצוה דרבים simply means a praiseworthy act that involves many people, but does not signify a neatly quantifiable personal obligation. The term מצוה is used here to mean something like "a good deed" or "the ideal way to do things."[1] This reading maintains that while it is certainly praiseworthy, beneficial, and possibly even of deep importance to pray in a *minyan*, it is not a formal obligation like other *mitzvot*.

Various sources within the Talmud Bavli can be marshaled to support these various readings. R. Abahu cryptically says in the name of Reish Lakish: "לגבל ולתפלה ולנטילת ידים: ארבעה מילין — For a kneader, for prayer, and for the washing of the hands: four *mil*." Rashi explains "prayer" here to refer to the degree one must inconvenience oneself to pray in a synagogue:

רש"י פסחים מו.
וכן לתפלה, אם מהלך אדם בדרך ובא עת ללון ולהתפלל, אם יש בית הכנסת לפניו ברחוק ארבע מילין – הולך ומתפלל שם ולן שם.

Rashi Pesaḥim 46a
And so, too, for prayer: If a person is traveling along the way and the time comes to sleep and to pray, if there is a synagogue ahead within a distance of four *mil*, then one should go on and pray there and sleep there.[2]

This may argue for an individual obligation to pray in a *minyan*, even when one is on the road, outside of one's local community, though it may be speaking more about importance of setting—when one can pray in a sacred location, one should do so.[3] It might also be **specific** to a case of one who is traveling who can easily reconfigure their itinerary to end up at a synagogue. In any event, Rashi's interpretation is disputed by Rabbeinu Ḥananel, who explains "prayer" here to refer to the distance that one needs

1 For a similar usage of מצוה, see Bavli Makkot 10b.

2 There is a parallel passage containing both R. Abahu's statement and a similar comment by Rashi on Bavli Ḥullin 122b.

3 A series of statements at the beginning of Talmud Yerushalmi Berakhot 5 (8d) seem to evince this perspective.

to travel to find **water** so that one can wash one's hands before praying.[4] If one adopts this reading, there is certainly no clear source formally mandating the individual to pray in a *minyan*.

Other sources seem to militate against the notion of an individual obligation, even as they may leave room for the notion of a communal imperative. When Reish Lakish says, on Talmud Bavli Berakhot 8a, "כל מי שיש לו בית הכנסת בעירו ואינו נכנס שם להתפלל נקרא שכן רע — Anyone who has a synagogue in their city and does not enter there to pray is called a bad neighbor," the emphasis is not on fulfilling an individual obligation, but rather on the need to make sure that the community can live out its collective obligations.

Yet other passages suggest that the act of public prayer should not be engaged on the axis of obligation at all. These sources suggest that public prayer is to be judged by its metaphysical value, not by its ability to fulfill personal obligations.[5] It is a spiritual means rather than a personal or communal end. Theological expression for this value can be found in the following passage:

> **תלמוד בבלי ברכות ז:–ח.**
>
> אמר רבי יוחנן משום רבי שמעון בן יוחי, מאי דכתיב, "ואני תפלתי לך ה׳ עת רצון" (תהלים סט:יד), אימתי עת רצון – בשעה שהצבור מתפללין.
>
> רבי יוסי ברבי חנינא אמר מהכא: "כה אמר ה׳ בעת רצון עניתיך" (ישעיהו מט:ח).
>
> רבי אחא ברבי חנינא אמר מהכא: "הן אל כביר ולא ימאס" (איוב לו:ה), וכתיב: "פדה בשלום נפשי מקרב לי כי ברבים היו עמדי" (תהלים נה:יט).

---

4 The interpretational advantage of this reading is obvious: All three portions of the statement then deal with water, with "washing of the hands" referring to the water required before eating bread. Of course, R. Ḥananel may also be pushed to this perhaps less intuitive reading of the the word *li-tfillah* by the total foreignness of the idea that one would be obligated to pray with a *minyan*.

5 The exhortatory tone of R. Yehoshua b. Levi's statement in the passage we opened with fits with this framing as well.

תניא נמי הכי, רבי נתן אומר: מנין שאין הקדוש ברוך הוא מואס בתפלתן של רבים, שנאמר "הן אל כביר ולא ימאס" (איוב לו:ה), וכתיב "פדה בשלום נפשי מקרב לי" וגו' (תהלים נה:יט). אמר הקדוש ברוך הוא: כל העוסק בתורה ובגמילות חסדים ומתפלל עם הצבור – מעלה אני עליו כאילו פדאני, לי ולבני, מבין אומות העולם.

Talmud Bavli Berakhot 7b–8a

R. Yoḥanan said in the name of R. Shimon b. Yoḥai: What is the meaning of the verse "I am my prayer to You, God, at a time of goodwill" (Tehillim 69:14)? When is a time of goodwill? When the community is praying.

R. Yose b. R. Ḥanina derives it from here: "So says God: At the hour of favor I answer you" (Yeshayahu 49:8).

R. Aḥa b. R. Ḥanina derives it from here: "See, God is great[6] and is not contemptuous" (Iyov 36:5), and it is written: "[God] redeems my life in peace from the battle against me, as though there were many with me" (Tehillim 55:19).

So was it also taught [in a *baraita*]: R. Natan said, From where do we learn that the Holy One never despises the prayers of the many? As it is said, "See, God is great and is not contemptuous" (Iyov 36:5), and it is written: "[God] redeems my life in peace from the battle against me" (Tehillim 55:19). Said the Holy One: Anyone who engages in Torah and acts of lovingkindness and who prays with the community, I relate to that person as though they had redeemed Me—Me and My children—from the nations.

Prayers are more likely to be accepted in an עת רצון, a time of favor—interpreted here by these Sages as synchronizing one's prayers with those of the community. Similarly, R. Natan argues that though individuals risk God not hearing their prayers because of the offending consequence of

6 This translation reflects the contextual meaning of the verse. The proof is based on reading the word for "great" as referring to the greatness—in quantitative terms—of the community.

their sins, a community's prayers will always be heard; the corporate voice drowns out individual shortcomings. These paeans to communal prayer are focused on its metaphysical efficacy, not on any notion of personal obligation.

Indeed, classical sources never clearly articulate a full-fledged personal obligation for an individual to pray in a *minyan*. This is likely explainable, in part, because of a person's inability to fulfill such a "*mitzvah*" on their own. Moreover, we find views that some commitments trump praying with a *minyan* if there is a conflict. For example, in the material surrounding the above talmudic passage, we find Rav Naḥman justifying not bothering to go to the synagogue because he was "unable" and not convening a *minyan* where he was, because that would be "difficult." A few lines later, we find several sages concluding that those deeply engaged in Torah study should pray where they are, in the *beit midrash*, rather than interrupting their study to join the community:

תלמוד בבלי ברכות ח.

אמר ליה רבי יצחק לרב נחמן: מאי טעמא לא אתי מר לבי כנישתא לצלויי?

אמר ליה: לא יכילנא.

אמר ליה: לכנפי למר עשרה וליצלי.

אמר ליה: טריחא לי מלתא.

ולימא ליה מר לשלוחא דצבורא, בעידנא דמצלי צבורא ליתי ולודעיה למר.

אמר ליה: מאי כולי האי?

אמר ליה: דאמר רבי יוחנן משום רבי שמעון בן יוחי...

ואמר אביי: מריש הוה גריסנא בגו ביתא ומצלינא בבי כנישתא, כיון דשמענא להא דאמר רבי חייא בר אמי משמיה דעולא: מיום שחרב בית המקדש אין לו להקדוש ברוך הוא בעולמו אלא ארבע אמות של הלכה בלבד, לא הוה מצלינא אלא היכא דגריסנא.

רבי אמי ורבי אסי אף על גב דהוו להו תליסר בי כנישתא בטבריא לא מצלו אלא ביני עמודי, היכא דהוו גרסי.

> **Talmud Bavli Berakhot 8a**
> R. Yitzḥak asked Rav Naḥman: Why do you not come to synagogue to pray?
>
> He said to him: I cannot.
>
> He said to him: Then gather ten and pray.
>
> He said to him: That would be difficult for me.
>
> Then why not tell the *ḥazzan*[7] to inform you of when they are praying?
>
> He said to him: Why should I go to such lengths?
>
> He said to him: Because R. Yoḥanan said in the name of R. Shimon b. Yoḥai...[8]
>
> And Abaye said: Originally, I would study in the house and pray in the synagogue. When I heard that which R. Ḥiyya b. Ami said in the name of Ulla, "From the time the Temple was destroyed, the Holy Blessed One has only the four cubits of *halakhah*"—I would pray only where I studied.
>
> R. Ami and R. Asi—even though there were thirteen synagogues in Tiberias—would pray only between the columns where they studied.

Various Rishonim cite these voices and weigh them differently. As noted above, Rashi may well argue for some sort of personal obligation in public prayer.[9] The Rambam, by contrast, quite clearly emphasizes the

---

7 In this context, the *ḥazzan* is more like what we would call "*gabbai*" than "cantor."

8 Here, the Gemara continues with the passage we cited above about the positive values associated with praying with the community.

9 R. Ya'akov b. Asher in Tur OḤ 90 favors Rashi's reading of the Gemara over that of R. Ḥananel. Nonetheless, he seems not to embrace the obligation in nearly as full terms, in principle accepting the notion that other values—such as praying where one learns—can trump the value of praying in a *minyan*. The Tur, following the Rosh, doubts whether contemporary scholars are truly so engaged in Torah study as to justify such an exemption from supporting the community, and out of

metaphysical benefits highlighted on Bavli Berakhot 8a while pointedly avoiding any language suggesting a personal obligation. It is fairly clear that for him there is no concrete individual obligation in play at all here:

רמב״ם הלכות תפילה ח:א, ג
תפלת הציבור נשמעת תמיד ואפילו היו בהן חוטאים אין הקדוש ברוך הוא מואס בתפלתן של רבים, לפיכך צריך אדם לשתף עצמו עם הציבור, ולא יתפלל ביחיד כל זמן שיכול להתפלל עם הציבור, ולעולם ישכים אדם ויעריב לבית הכנסת...וכל מי שיש לו בית הכנסת בעירו ואינו מתפלל בו עם הציבור נקרא שכן רע...בית המדרש גדול מבית הכנסת, וחכמים גדולים אף על פי שהיו להם בעירם בתי כנסיות הרבה לא היו מתפללין אלא במקום שהיו עוסקין שם בתורה והוא שיתפלל שם תפלת הציבור.

Rambam, Hilkhot Tefillah 8:1, 3
The prayer of the community is always heard, and even if there are sinners in it, the Blessed Holy One does not reject the prayer of the many. Therefore, a person needs to participate with the community, and not to pray alone when one could pray with the community, and a person should always arrive early and leave late from the synagogue…and anyone who has a synagogue in one's city and does not pray with the community is called a bad neighbor…A *beit midrash* is greater than a synagogue, and great sages, even though they have many synagogues in their city, would pray only in the place where they would engage with Torah—and this is provided that there is communal prayer there.

---

concern that the masses would misunderstand the nature of the exemption. He therefore rules that this exemption no longer applies. (The Rambam, whom we will cite shortly, limits the exemption for scholars by saying that sages may pray in their places of study only when there is a *minyan* there.) But the idea that praying with a *minyan* is ultimately a highly valued, strongly preferred act rather than a hard and fast obligation seems to prevail for the Tur. This explains the Tur's language of "צריך להשתדל בכל כחו — One should try with all one's might" to pray with the community, plaintive language not normally used with straightforward, individual obligations. The Shulḥan Arukh borrows this language.

Others make clear that while the community may have an obligation to constitute a *minyan*, this is not an individual obligation *per se*. For example, the Maharil addressed the legitimate parameters for establishing an *eruv teḥumin*, the placing of a food source far out in one direction of one's home in order to enable one to directionally extend the distance permissible to walk on Shabbat:

ספר מהרי"ל, הלכות עירובי חצירות
תנן אין מניחין עירוב תחומין רק לסמוך עליו לילך לדבר מצוה כגון לבית האבל או לבית המשתה. אמר מהר"י סג"ל דלא ראה בשום פוסק שמותר לערב תחומין לילך לבה"כ כדי להתפלל בעשרה רק בסמ"ק ובספר אגודה. א"ל הר"ר איקא ולא יהא פחות מבית המשתה, א"ל הרב להתפלל בעשרה אינה כ"כ מצוה דיכול לכוון תפלתו בביתו, **דלא אשכחן אשר הצריכו חכמים להתפלל בי'.**

Sefer Maharil, Hilkhot Eruvei Ḥatzeirot
It is taught: We set an *eruv teḥumin* only to rely on it for a *mitzvah*, such as to go to a house of mourning or to a wedding celebration. [The Maharil] said that he did not see in any authority that it is permitted to make an *eruv teḥumin* to go to synagogue in order to pray with ten, except for the Semak[10] and the Agudah.[11] R. Ika said to [the Maharil], "And should it be of less status than a wedding?" [The Maharil] said to him: "To pray with ten is not truly a *mitzvah*, because one can direct one's prayer in one's house, **for we do not find that the Sages required one to pray with ten**."

---

10 *Siman* 282.

11 We have not found a passage in the Agudah that states this explicitly. However, Agudah Berakhot 2:41 and Pesaḥim 3:44 both reveal an understanding of R. Abahu's statement on Bavli Pesaḥim 46a as requiring praying with a *minyan*. The Maharil may just be noting that someone who reads the Talmud in this way would naturally extend that interpretation to considering praying with a *minyan* to be sufficiently required to validate the use of an *eruv teḥumin*. As the end of this passage in the Maharil indicates, the latter rejects any notion that there is a talmudic passage outlining such an individual obligation.

The Maharil's North African contemporary, R. Shimon Tzemaḥ Duran, concisely summed up this conception of praying with a *minyan*:

שו"ת תשב"ץ א:צ
שחובת צבור היא להתפלל בעשר' אבל אם יש שם יותר מעשרה כל אחד יכול לומר לו והלא יש עשרה חוץ ממני וא"כ הריני יכול להשמט מלבא אצלך באותה שעה.

Responsa Tashbetz I:90
It is an obligation on the community to pray with ten, but if there are there more than ten, each one can say, "But without me there are still ten, and if so, I can refrain from coming to join you at that time."

Four centuries later, R. Yair Ḥayyim Bacharach explicitly rejected the notion that there is a personal obligation to pray in a *minyan*. In that case, why did R. Eliezer free his slave to be a tenth in a *minyan* and why did the Gemara justify this on the grounds that this was a "*mitzvah*"?

שו"ת חוות יאיר סימן קטו
ונ"ל דאין הכוונה דהמצוה נהוגה בכל ישראל רק ר"ל שהוא קידוש השם ודווקא ברבים ואם לא שחררו היה בטל המצוה מכל הרבים ההם שהיו נאספין יחד.

Responsa Ḥavvot Yair #115
It seems to me that the intent is not that such a *mitzvah* [of praying in a *minyan*] is incumbent on every Jew; rather it means to suggest that it is the sanctification of God's name, and only among the many, and had he not freed him, this *mitzvah* would have been unfulfilled by all of the people gathered together.

This claim, that praying in a *minyan* is a public responsibility but not an individual *mitzvah*, seems to be the dominant perspective on this important activity. Not being a personal obligation does not mean it is valueless, of course. Far from it: If a community must convene public prayer, each citizen has a certain categorical imperative to contribute toward its successful formation, even if there might not be a full-fledged personal obligation. This explains the language of the codes, such as the Shulḥan Arukh: "**ישתדל** אדם להתפלל בבית הכנסת עם הציבור — A person **should make great effort** to pray in the synagogue with the community"

(OḤ 90:9). Nonetheless, many authorities also codify the expectation that individuals will normally go out of their way to attend public prayer, whether or not this can be formally classified as an individual obligation.[12]

In sum, there are Rishonim whose words suggest an idea that individuals are obligated to pray in a *minyan*.[13] Others expect individuals to attend as part of their civic duty to help the community fulfill its **communal** obligation, but balk at the notion that the individual is obligated *per se*, allowing individuals to absent themselves when a *minyan* is otherwise present. Finally, other voices suggest that a discourse of obligation misses the point and that the community gathers in prayer as an effective strategy for communicating with God.

No gender gap is ever articulated with regard to this responsibility—such as it is—before the late 17th century. Some recent authors have cited a few Aḥaronim to buttress the claim that there is such an obligation, that women are exempt from it, and that said exemption prevents them from leading the community in prayer. Of particular prominence in these claims is the statement of R. Ya'akov Reischer that "האשה אינה מצוה כלל להתפלל בעשרה — A woman is not commanded at all to pray with ten." Here is a fuller citation:

שו"ת שבות יעקב ג:נד

נשאלתי מישוב אחד שבעל הבית אחד יש לו חדר בתוך ביתו והניח ליכנס הצבור בתוך החדר אנשים לחוד ונשים לחוד להתפלל ועכשיו נולד קטטה גדולה בין בע"הב עם אחד מאנשים ואשתו שרגילין לבוא לבה"כ שלא יבואו עוד לבה"כ...עליהם להביא הראיה אך שהם טוענים כיון שחדר זו שהי' שייך לבעלים הראשונים נכנסו ג"כ בחדר זו להתפלל כמה וכמה שנים ע"כ הוא בחזקת הצבור ומסתמא השאילו להם ומידי ספיקא לא נפקא ופסקתי שלא יוכל לאסור מספיקא על אחד מן הקהל להסתפח מנחלת ה' אבל על אשתו המתחלת תמיד במריבה יוכל לאסור עליה שלא תבא לבה"כ כלל כי אע"פ שהאשה ג"כ מחויבת בתפלה כמבואר בא"ח סי' ק"ו מ"מ כיון

---

12 For instance, Shulḥan Arukh OḤ 90:16, after using the language of ישתדל, "make great effort" earlier in the *siman*, follows Rashi in articulating expectations on travelers going out of their way to pray in a *minyan*. Mishnah Berurah 90:52 codifies later views that explicitly apply this to someone who is at home as well.

13 For a more recent adherent of this approach, see Iggerot Moshe OḤ 11:27: הנה להתפלל בעשרה הוא חיוב מצוה על האדם ולא רק הדור ומעלה בעלמא.

שהאשה אינה מצוה כלל להתפלל בעשרה ואינה מצטרפת למנין ולא לקדושה כלל כדאמרינן "אשה בעזרה מנין?" [קדושין נ"ב:] ו"בתולה צייל‍נית מבלי עולם" ע"ש בסוטה דף כ"ב וכבר כתב המ"א בסי' ק"ו ס"ק ב' וז"ל ולכן נהגו רוב נשים שאינן מתפללים בתמידות משום דאומרים מיד סמוך לנטיל' איזה בקשה ומדאורייתא די בזה עכ"ל המ"א לכן נ"ל דיכול למחו' בידה עד שיפייסו וימחול זה לזה כי הנשי' עלולת להרבה בקטטות ומריבות וכן דנתי למעשה.

Responsa Shevut Ya'akov 3:54

I was asked by a certain community regarding a homeowner who had a room in his house, and he had given permission to the community to enter into that room, men and women separately, to pray. And now, a great dispute had come about between the homeowner and one of the men and his wife who were accustomed to go to this synagogue, such that [the owner determined that] they should no longer go to the synagogue... The community must bring proof [that they have rights to pray there] even though they claim that they used to pray in this room for many years in the time of the prior owners of the house, such that the room has the status of a public space [which would prevent the current owner from excluding specific people from coming there]. Nonetheless, the matter is still in doubt, and I ruled that he could not forbid one of the members of the community from joining on to God's portion [in this case, where there is doubt as to whether prior owners of the house might have explicitly and clearly licensed it for public prayer use], but regarding his wife, who was always starting arguments, he could forbid her from going to [that] synagogue at all, because even though the woman is obligated in prayer, as is clear in [Shulḥan Arukh] OḤ 106, nevertheless, since the woman is not commanded at all to pray with ten, and she does not count toward the *minyan,* nor for Kedushah at all, as we say, "What would a woman be doing in the Temple Court?"

[Kiddushin 52b][14] and "A young woman who prays excessively destroys the world"—see Sotah 22[15]—and the Magen Avraham has written [that perhaps women are not obligated in the daily Amidah, but only in one freeform prayer a day][16]...therefore it seems to me that he can prevent her [from going to the synagogue in his house] until they reconcile and forgive each other, for women are likely to bicker and fight a lot. So have I ruled.

---

14 Here, the Shevut Ya'akov quotes R. Yehudah's words in a *baraita* in which he accuses R. Meir's students of badgering him with irrelevant and picayune questions, such as regarding the status of a marriage transaction of a *kohen* with the parts of the sacrificial meat that are his portion. Rashi understands R. Yehudah's point to be that this is a foolish question because the meat is useless if it leaves the Temple court, and women are not allowed in the Temple court. The Shevut Ya'akov imports this sense of the words to bolster his rhetorical point about women's presence in the synagogue being unnecessary: If they weren't even allowed in the main Temple court, and the synagogue is in some way an imitation of the Temple, then their presence there is extraneous as well, giving license to the homeowner to exclude a difficult woman. However, note that Tosafot s.v. *ve-khi* attack this interpretation of Rashi, pointing out that, counter to Rashi's claim, no *mishnah* stipulates that women are excluded from the Temple court. Moreover, they argue, Mishnah Zevaḥim 3:1 assumes women's legitimate presence there, as it teaches that a sacrifice slaughtered by a woman is legitimate, and further, a *sotah* (woman accused of adultery) and a female Nazirite *must* bring offerings in the Temple court. The Tosafot, therefore, interpret the *baraita*'s words more modestly to mean, "What would a woman be doing getting betrothed in the Temple court?!" That is, "This whole case is so preposterous and remote that you shouldn't be wasting my time with it." Both the Tosafot's point and the observation that women were rarely found in the Temple court is summed up by Tosefta Arakhin 2:1: לעולם לא נראית אשה בעזרה אלא בשעת קרבנה בלבד. The Shevut Ya'akov is using the paradigm of the Temple here to emphasize that there is a long tradition of women being more marginal in public sacred spaces and thus they can be more easily excluded when a problem arises on their account.

15 This opaque statement displays an aversion to excessive piety in female figures, though it is immediately challenged by another source in the Gemara that features R. Yoḥanan praising a young woman whom he finds praying. Rashi understands the core problem here to be one of sorcery and witchcraft being dressed up as genuine religious expression. In any event, the passage is not referring to the Amidah and Shevut Ya'akov's use of the phrase here is clearly part of a larger rhetorical flourish he is building to make his case for excluding this woman from the prayer space.

16 See our lengthy discussion of the Magen Avraham above, Part One, nn. 28–33.

In order to understand the Shevut Ya'akov's logic here, we need a little background. One of the many ordinances promulgated by Rabbeinu Gershom pertained to an individual who allows the community to use their home as a synagogue space. R. Gershom legislated that when a person lends their house out to community for public prayer, they cannot then exclude a specific individual from praying there unless they forbid the entire community from using the space at all.[17] This ordinance seems to have been set up to make sure that those with resources and power not use their leverage to isolate people from the communal experience of public prayer. R. Meir Katzenellenbogen of Padua later ruled that this ordinance only applied when the homeowner's space had been explicitly lent to the community. In cases where a homeowner merely allowed people to gather in their house for prayer but never formally "leased" the space, they would retain total control over who could enter, as they would with respect to guests in his home more generally.[18]

With this background in mind, the Shevut Ya'akov confronts the case of a homeowner who wants to exclude a married couple from the *minyan* being held in his home. The facts of the case are under dispute: The owner of the house never formally leased the space to the community for public prayer, but the community claims that they had an arrangement in place prior to the current owner's purchase of the house. Because the matter is in doubt, the Shevut Ya'akov will not allow the community to potentially violate R. Gershom's ordinance by excluding an individual man from praying there while allowing the rest of the community to do so. Nonetheless, he argues that the homeowner may exclude the man's wife from coming. He perceives the woman in this case to be the troublemaker and sees women in general as more prone to bickering and fighting. He justifies this exclusion of the wife specifically by appealing to a number of points that indicate a more marginal application of communal prayer

---

17 For one citation of this ordinance, see Orḥot Ḥayyim, Dinei Beit Kenesset #25:

כתב הר׳ רבינו גרשום בתקנותיו שעשה איש שהשאיל ביתו לבית הכנסת ויש לו מריבה עם אחד מהקהל שאינו רשאי לאוסרה לו אלא אם כן יאסור אותה לכל הקהל כאחד.

18 Responsa Maharam of Padua #85:

כי לשון התקנה הוא וז״ל ואם אדם משאיל לרבים כו׳ ואלו היתה התקנה אפילו בסתם היה לו לומר ב״ה של יחיד שרבים נכנסים שם גו׳ אלא ודאי ר״ל משאיל בפירוש.

obligations to women, perhaps suggesting that they are not protected by R. Gershom's ordinance in the same way as are men:

1. Women, though they are obligated to pray, are not obligated to pray with a *minyan*, whereas men are.
2. Women do not count in a *minyan*.
3. According to the Magen Avraham, maybe they are not even obligated in the Amidah at all.

All of these factors, which place the woman on a different footing than her husband with respect to public prayer, lead the Shevut Ya'akov to justify removing the woman from this home-based synagogue.

The second point, that women do not count in a *minyan*, is straightforwardly based in Shulḥan Arukh OḤ 55's holding that women do not count in a *minyan*. We dealt with this issue at length above. Shevut Ya'akov here seems to appeal to the notion that one who cannot help form a *minyan* cannot possibly be essential to that space. The third point above is based on the reading of the Magen Avraham that we dealt with at length as well. As we noted, building any firm legal argument based on the Magen Avraham's analysis—particularly given that he seems to have abandoned it himself—is difficult. Any use of the Magen Avraham to bolster an argument for female exemption from the Amidah must be balanced against the overwhelming evidence to the contrary that we amassed in our discussion of his view.

The first point is our main concern here. The Shevut Ya'akov makes the unsourced claim that women, as opposed to men, are exempt from public prayer. As we saw above, this claim is grounded in a contentious assumption, given that men's obligation to pray in a *minyan* is by no means universally agreed upon. Moreover, the notion that the obligation of public prayer is gendered has no antecedent that we can find, whereas the values attached to praying with a *minyan* by the Talmud seem to apply to anyone who is required to pray.

Indeed, other Aḥaronim emphasize the gender-blind aspects of praying with a *minyan*. R. Eliyahu Ragoler writes as follows:

יד אליהו, פסקים א:ז
שאלה: אם יש באיזה בית הכנסת קטן או מנין של ששה או שבעה אנשים שלא התפללו ושלשה התפללו, ונמצא שא"א לקיים רק מצות קדיש וברכו וקדושה, אבל אין זה עולה לתפלה בציבור כי אם בעשרה ממש...אכן נסתפק לי לכאורה אם יש בבית הזה ג' נשים שמתפללים אם יש לצרף הנשים עמהם, אם נחשבת תפלת הנשים בכלל הציבור?

ונראה לי לפשוט מהא דאמר...תשעה ועבד מצטרפין, ומקשה מעובדא דר"א דשחרר עבדו, ומתרץ תרי הוי חסר, ושחרר אחד וצירף אחד עיין שם, והשתא אי אמרת דתפלת נשים אינם בכלל תפלת הצבור כמו דלא מצטרפין אותם לקדיש ולקדושה, אם כן הוה ליה לתלמודא לשנויי דלכן שחרר עבדו בכדי להתפלל בציבור – דהא אשה ועבד שקולין לענין צירוף וחיוב מצוות עשה...אלא **על כרחך דתפלת נשים** ועבדים **מצטרפים לתפלת הציבור**, ולא היה צריך ר"א לשחרר עבדו בשביל זה.

Yad Eliyahu, Pesakim I:7
Question: In a small community, when there are only six or seven men who have not prayed and three who have, one can only fulfill the *mitzvah* of Kaddish, Barekhu, and Kedushah, but praying in such a group does not count as public prayer unless there are actually ten [who have not prayed]...What I am unsure about is what if there are three women in this house who have not prayed, do the three women join with them such that the prayer of the women is considered part of the community?

It seems to me we can answer this from the fact that it says... nine and a slave join [to make a *minyan*] and then it challenges this point from the case of R. Eliezer, who freed his slave, and then resolves by saying that they needed two additional participants and so he freed one and counted the other slave as the tenth. If you claim that the prayer of women is not a part of the public prayer just as they are not joined to the *minyan* for Kaddish and Kedushah, then the Talmud should have resolved that R. Eliezer freed his slave in order to have public prayer—given that a woman and a slave have the same status with respect to joining a *minyan* and in their obligations in positive

> commandments…Rather it must be that **the prayer of women** and slaves **counts toward public prayer**, and R. Eliezer had no need to free his slave for this purpose.

Though Yad Eliyahu would have excluded women from the *minyan* required to recite *devarim shebikdushah,* he thought the *mitzvah* of public prayer—**which he understands to be the recitation of the private Amidah in a group of ten**[19]—was equally applicable to men and women (and slaves).

R. Ya'akov Ariel addresses the case of a woman who arrives late to synagogue on Shabbat morning, such that she can either pray in the usual order by beginning with Shaḥarit, or she can begin with Musaf in order to synchronize her prayer with that of the community. R. Ariel concludes that this comes down to the question of whether she is obligated to pray with the community:

> **שו"ת באהלה של תורה ב:כז**
> ואם כי אשה חייבת בתפילת המוסף, אך השאלה היא אם היא חייבת להתפלל **בציבור** דוקא...מיהו נראה שגם אשה חייבת להתפלל בציבור, שנאמר "הן קל כביר ולא ימאס"...ועדיין י"ל שהאשה יכולה להתפלל מוסף עם הציבור ושחרית אחרי מוסף.

> **Responsa be-Aholah shel Torah II:27**
> But even if a woman is obligated in the Musaf prayer, we must still address the question of whether she is obligated specifically to pray it **with the community**[20]…it seems that a woman is also obligated to pray communally, as it is said: "See God is mighty, but not contemptuous…"[21] [Therefore,] a woman who arrives late should pray Musaf with the community and then pray Shaḥarit after Musaf.

---

19 We will return to this point below.

20 R. Ariel's emphasis.

21 This verse, from Iyov 36:5, is cited in the passage on Bavli Berakhot 8a that we cited above.

R. Ariel notes that the core basis given for praying with a *minyan* in the Talmud—the greater effectiveness of prayers uttered as a community—is a gender-blind consideration. To the extent that communal prayer leads to better, more acceptable prayer, then this obligation in communal prayer will devolve on anyone obligated to **pray**. Thus, since women are obligated to pray, they must also be obligated to pray with a *minyan*.

Alternatively, perhaps the Shevut Ya'akov means to link the first and second point here, suggesting that one's exclusion from the quorum for *minyan* not only means that the public prayer space does not depend on them, but that they themselves have no real need of that space. In other words, he might be arguing that the whole notion of requiring people to pray in *minyan* devolves from the communal imperative to make sure that people show up to make a *minyan*. This would then be legal expression of that sense that many people in non-egalitarian communities have, in which many men feel driven to go to *shul* during the week "to help make the *minyan*," whereas women in the same communities are much less likely to make that effort, since they are not "needed." Here, the Shevut Ya'akov seems to be saying that in such a community, the homeowner may not restrict a troublemaking man from the synagogue in his home, since the man's presence fulfills more than his own personal desire to come to *shul*. His presence represents his portion of the communal duty to sustain the *minyan*; his absence weakens the community. A troublemaking woman, on the other hand, could be restricted. Since she shoulders no part of the communal duty, her presence reflects just her own personal desire to attend and participate in the life of the community, which can be forfeited because of antisocial behavior. Obviously, this claim would fall away in any context in which women were potential members of the required quorum, per our discussion above.[22]

---

22 This conversation continues among later authorities as well. R. Avraham Ḥayyim Rodrigues, in Responsa Oraḥ la-Tzaddik #3, also asserts, as we saw above, that women are exempt from praying with a *minyan*. He also does not source this claim, though he makes clear that it is **not** derivative of women's exclusion from *minyan*. His insistence on the gendered nature of public *tefillah* is thus all the more puzzling. See Part Two, nn. 73–74. R. Ovadiah Yosef, in Yalkut Yosef *siman* 106, offers the analysis we are suggesting for the Shevut Ya'akov here: Women are not obligated to pray with a *minyan*, because only those who count in a *minyan* are expected to be there. Nissel, *Rigshei Lev*, chapter 7, cites R. Yosef Shalom Elyashiv as ruling that women **are** obligated to pray with the community and R. Ḥayyim Pinḥas

All of this helps clarify why there might be a debate about the gendered nature of an obligation to pray with a *minyan*. But even if one posits such a gender gap in the "obligation in communal prayer," one point is particularly central: Whatever the obligation in communal prayer may be, it seems to be about **attending** communal prayer and is something that cannot and need not be fulfilled vicariously through the prayer leader. Note that the Shevut Ya'akov nowhere suggests that the leader somehow fulfills the obligations of **others** in communal prayer. An assumption that women need not go to *shul* in the same way as men do is irrelevant to the obligations of others in the Amidah; nothing in the Shevut Ya'akov argues this point. Indeed, the Yad Eliyahu's analysis makes clear that תפילה בציבור refers to the **private** Amidah, and this obligation, such as it is, is in no way fulfilled through the prayer leader. Questions of obligation in public prayer, while possibly relevant for our expectations of who should **attend** communal *tefillah*, are not relevant for the question of who may **lead** such *tefillot*.

Summary

Praying with the community is an important social responsibility in which members of the community should make every effort to engage. It is also a personal desideratum, insofar as it improves the acceptability of one's individual prayer. If one focuses on the latter of these two elements, then women, being obligated to pray, also share an obligation to pray communally (and thus, the view of R. Ariel). If we focus on the former element—the responsibility to help make a *minyan*—then the proper location for the full examination of this question is the exploration of the question of women's inclusion in the *minyan* in contemporary contexts. Even for those who argue, however, that women do not count and that they therefore lack the social responsibility or the personal obligation to pray in a *minyan*, there is no basis to claim that this in any way affects women's

---

Scheinberg and R. Eliyahu Greenblatt as opining that women should do so, while R. Shlomo Zalman Auerbach and R. Moshe Shternbuch rule that women usually have no special responsibility to pray with the community. See also the Frimers' citation of R. Ahron Soloveichik that whatever the status of the obligation to pray with a *minyan*, there is no gender component involved; see Part Two, n. 70.

fitness to serve as *sha"tz*. Such a claim requires making three points in concert, each of which is far from self-evident in the sources:

1. There is an individual obligation to pray with a *minyan*. This notion is challenged by many Rishonim.
2. Men and women are not equally obligated to pray with a *minyan*. This is counterintuitive given women's equal obligation in *tefillah* and is unsupported by any evidence in the Rishonim. It is most intelligible as a corollary of women's exclusion from *minyan*, which would then relegate this discussion to a subunit of the conversation around gender and the quorum required for public prayer. Even given this, many Aḥaronim explicitly describe the obligations around public prayer as being gender-blind.
3. The assumed gender gap plays a role in one's ability to serve as *sha"tz*—a point that makes little sense, given that an individual obligation in public prayer seems to be about **attending** public prayer, not leading it, and that seems to have no reflection in any source prior to the contemporary period.

APPENDIX D:
The Relationship of *Zimmun* to Other Quorums of Ten

OUR MAIN ANALYSIS of *minyan* above focused on the *minyan* required for aspects of public prayer. We only tangentially addressed sources regarding the required quorums for *zimmun*. In this appendix, we will aim to give a clearer picture of the history of the quorum of ten for *zimmun*, its gendered history, and the relationship of this quorum of ten to the quorums required for public prayer and Torah reading. In particular, do sources that ban the possibility of a *zimmun* of ten for women or groups of women and men necessarily clarify anything about other quorums of ten?

While classical rabbinic sources have nothing explicit and unambiguous to say about the role of gender in any quorum of ten, a number of sources do address the question about the role of gender in forming a *zimmun*.

Mishnah Berakhot 7:2 states concisely: נשים ועבדים וקטנים אין מזמנין עליהם; adult males (the presumed addressees of this *mishnah*) may not form a *zimmun* with women, slaves, and minors. A *baraita* on Bavli Berakhot 45b clarifies that women form their own *zimmun* and slaves form their own *zimmun*, but a group of women and slaves may not form a joint group. The Gemara on Bavli Arakhin 3a cites a text of unclear provenance but of undisputed authority stating that women are obligated to form a *zimmun*. This is all the direct evidence that classical sources present on the question of women and *zimmun*.[1]

Regarding women's obligation in Birkat ha-Mazon more generally, Mishnah Berakhot 3:3 clearly states that they are obligated. Tosefta Berakhot 5:17, as reflected in ms. Vienna and the first printing, however, exempts women (along with slaves and minors) from Birkat ha-Mazon and explains that they may not fulfill the obligations of others. It then adds that a woman may say Birkat ha-Mazon for her husband (and a slave may do so for his master and a son for his father):

> נשים ועבדים וקטנים פטורין ואין מוציאין את הרבים ידי חובתן
> באמת אמרו אשה מברכת לבעלה בן מברך לאביו עבד מברך לרבו.

This then leaves unclear exactly what the status of women's obligation is. Is there indeed a gender gap with respect to obligation in Birkat ha-Mazon, while there was nonetheless, at least at one point, some tolerance for a woman saying Birkat ha-Mazon for her husband, at deviance with the usual rule that one can only fulfill the obligations of others if one is equally obligated?[2] Alternatively, should we conclude that a woman's ability to say

---

1 Koren, "Kullam Baki'im ba-Hallel," has argued that the Gemara in Arakhin also assumes that women and men may join together to form a *zimmun* and that this ought to be our understanding of Mishnah Berakhot 7:2 as well. According to her reading, the Mishnah only forbids **entire groups** of women, slaves, **and** minors to form a *minyan*, but women's capacity to form a *zimmun* on their own or with adult men was never in question in the tannaitic period; it was only the conceptual and literary creativity of Ravina on Bavli Berakhot 20b and the anonymous editor of Bavli Berakhot 47b that introduced the notion that *zimmun* was not a gender-blind practice. See above, Part Two, n. 7 and n. 14, for more on this argument and some of our concerns regarding it.

2 There is an even more intriguing possibility that should be considered here: Perhaps the phrase מוציאין את הרבים **is not** synonymous with the notion of להוציא את האחר. In other words, lack of obligation may not preclude one's ability to fulfill the obligations of another individual. Rather, it may be that a lack of obligation disqualifies one from serving in a **public** capacity to discharge the obligations of those assembled as a **group**. That would make perfect sense of this version of the Tosefta: Women, slaves, and minors cannot lead a communal Birkat ha-Mazon for a group including men. However, on a one-to-one basis, the Tosefta may be telling us that there is no issue. This would also fit with the general pattern of the phrase באמת אמרו, which in no other place contradicts what comes before, but rather makes a qualifying statement consistent with the prior phrase, albeit counterintuitive or unexpected. While later sources clearly assume that sources like Mishnah Rosh Hashanah 3:8

Birkat ha-Mazon for her husband proves that women and men have an equal obligation in Birkat ha-Mazon, in which case we would have to say that the word פטורין is an error? Indeed, ms. Erfurt of the Tosefta here omits the word פטורין and simply states that women do not fulfill the obligations of others, which is possibly a statement that they are not **allowed** to do so, not that they are **unable** to do so.[3]

However we understand the Tosefta, the Mishnah's clear obligation of women in Birkat ha-Mazon seems to dominate subsequent discussion. On Bavli Berakhot 49a, Rav derives details about the essential core text of Birkat ha-Mazon from the assumption that anything that does not apply to women cannot possibly be a core part of Birkat ha-Mazon, which seems to reflect an assumption that Birkat ha-Mazon is not gendered in any way. Therefore, Rav concludes, given that women are not circumcised nor commanded to study Torah, nor does the Davidic line flow through them, mentioning these themes in Birkat ha-Mazon must not be essential.

Nonetheless, possible echoes of a version of the Tosefta that spoke about exemption, along with the Mishnah's treatment of women as a separate and seemingly inferior class with respect to *zimmun*,[4] may have sown doubt as to whether the Mishnah's claim that women are obligated in

---

(כל שאינו מחוייב בדבר אינו מוציא את הרבים ידי חובתן) apply to individual interactions as well—a reading perhaps influenced by Mishnah Sukkah 3:10—it might be that this Tosefta gives us a glimpse at a different approach to this question. Nonetheless, a later passage in Tosefta Berakhot 5:15 seems to apply concerns of obligation to even individual interactions: "אנדרוגינוס מוציא את מינו ואינו מוציא את שאינו מינו — A hermaphrodite can fulfill the obligations of another hermaphrodite, but not of a non-hermaphrodite."

3 Lieberman in Tosefta Kifshutah I:83 argues that ms. Erfurt preserves a more original and accurate reading here and points out that the Tosafot and Tosafot ha-Rosh on Sukkah 38a clearly had a text of the Tosefta that lacked the word פטורין. The Meiri, in Beit ha-Beḥirah Megillah 4a, emends a parallel text that reads חייבין ואין מוציאין to פטואין ואין מוציאין, and in Beit ha-Beḥirah Berakhot 20b he simply reports the text of our Tosefta as חייבין ואין מוציאין. Lieberman argues that that last report is a conscious correction and indicates that he had a text that read like ms. Vienna. It seems more likely to us that ms. Vienna is the original here and that all other versions are corrections in one way or another, but it is hard to make a solid case either way. See also Koren, "Tziruf Nashim le-Zimmun," 44–50.

4 The language of the Mishnah is **not** לא יזמן איש עם שתי נשים ולא תזמן אשה עם שני אנשים, following the structure of Mishnah Kiddushin 4:12.

Birkat ha-Mazon is unequivocal. Indeed, on Bavli Berakhot 20b, Ravina wonders if women's obligation in Birkat ha-Mazon might only be of rabbinic authority. Rava responds by quoting the end of the Tosefta cited above, which seems to indicate a full-blown obligation for women, given that a wife is said to be able, in principle, to fulfill her husband's obligation in this regard. (Notably, this parallel omits the first part of the Tosefta as we have it, which states that women are exempt. It further adds a coda condemning any husband who would rely on his wife to perform such a task for him.) A final passage questions this interpretation, given that it seems to suggest that a minor can fulfill his father's obligation in Birkat ha-Mazon, even though the former's obligation is rabbinic, while the latter's is biblical. Therefore, says the Gemara, Rava's prooftext can be deflected as assuming women's obligation is rabbinic and that they (like minors) can only fulfill the obligations of adult males who have eaten so little that their obligation in Birkat ha-Mazon after that meal is only rabbinic.

The impact of this final passage on the *sugya*'s conclusion is an area of dispute. Most Rishonim, like the Ra'avad, hold that this final section is a mere deflection devoid of halakhic weight and still assume that the *sugya*'s conclusion follows Rava that women are biblically obligated.[5] Some, like the Rambam, take the deflection seriously and as the final legal word here: Ravina's question is left unanswered and we do not know if women are biblically obligated in Birkat ha-Mazon, and therefore we cannot allow them to fulfill the obligations of men in this regard.[6]

Returning to the question of women and *zimmun*, the Gemara in Arakhin seems crystal clear that women are obligated to form their own

---

5 Hasagot ha-Ra'avad letter *alef* on Rif Berakhot 12a. These authorities address the problem of the child blessing for the father by saying that the father repeats the words of Birkat ha-Mazon after his son, following the resolution to this problem in Yerushalmi Berakhot 3:3 (6b). Alternatively, perhaps בן in the Bavli's version of the *baraita* means an adult son, who only presents a problem of social boundaries but not of an obligation gap. Regarding the last point, see Ramban, Milḥamot Hashem on Rif Berakhot 12a, where he claims that the words וליטעמיך קטן בר חיובא הוא are a later addition to the base text, such that the Gemara here never even took a stand on the notion of whether a minor is in play. We suggested above, n. 2, that the plain sense of the *baraita* may hark back to a time when obligation (and certainly equal obligation) was not a presumed prerequisite for discharging the obligations of others in more private settings.

6 Rambam, Hilkhot Berakhot 5:1.

zimmun. If one reads Mishnah Berakhot and the Gemara in Arakhin as a pair, without engaging Ravina's question in the Bavli, one could easily conclude that Birkat ha-Mazon and *zimmun* are "separate but equal" rituals. Men and women share an obligation, but they must execute this obligation in gender-distinct groups. This approach can be found in various Rishonim. We noted above the Rishonim who say that women are biblically obligated in Birkat ha-Mazon. R. Yonah[7] and the Rosh,[8] even though they do not endorse a biblical obligation in Birkat ha-Mazon for women, nonetheless obligate women in *zimmun* in the same way as men. Women and men, however, do not join together to form a *zimmun* but rather form groups on their own. This is a social concern; in the words of Rashi as cited by R. Yonah: אין חברתן נאה.[9] According to this view, there is something improper about a joint fellowship of men and women.[10] But as we noted above, the gender-blindness of Birkat ha-Mazon does not seem to have been universally agreed upon throughout the rabbinic period, and this trend seems to have spilled over into the question of obligation in *zimmun*. Rashi already suggests that the reason men and women may not form a *zimmun* together is because women and men say different texts of Birkat ha-Mazon, with only men mentioning the concept of ברית, i.e., circumcision.[11] The Tosafot also report that common practice—perhaps fueled by many women's ignorance of Hebrew—was for women **not** to ever lead a *zimmun* on their own. They therefore proposed a reading of the *baraita* on Bavli Berakhot 45b that only **allowed** three women to form a *zimmun*, but did not **require** them to do so.[12] In the face of the blatant evidence to the contrary in Arakhin, Rabbeinu Yitzḥak of Dampierre explains that women are obligated in *zimmun* when they have eaten in

---

7 R. Yonah on Rif Berakhot 33a s.v. *nashim* and s.v. *ve-nir'eh*.

8 Rosh Berakhot 7:4.

9 R. Yonah on Rif Berakhot 33a s.v. *nashim*.

10 Note that this concern would apply even if there were three men and three women. They would seemingly be required to split into two groups. It is not clear if R. Yonah is specifically concerned about a meal-based environment, or if the problem is broader and goes to the question of any sort of mixed-gender group.

11 Rashi Arakhin 3a s.v. *mezamnot*.

12 Tosafot Berakhot 45b s.v. *shanei*.

the presence of three or more men and that this is the meaning of Bavli Arakhin 3a.[13] Note that this potentially shifts the discussion of a ban on mixed-gender *zimmun* from the realm of social policy to a problem regarding equality of obligation. More generally, the notion that perhaps groups of women are **not** obligated to have a *zimmun* plays a key role in later discussions of women and quorums in general.

The classical sources leave us with a few key ambiguities. Even if men and women may not join together to form a *zimmun* of three,[14] may men and women join to mention God's name in a *zimmun* of ten? We know that three women make a *zimmun* on their own. Does a group of ten women make a *zimmun* with God's name? Does one's stance on these questions affect whether ten women or mixed groups of ten can form other quorums, a topic not taken up explicitly in classical sources?

---

13 Cited in Semag Positive Commandments #27 s.v. *tenan bi-vrakhot*. This is a forced interpretation aimed at shoring up a practice that deviates from a central text. Note that it eviscerates any notion of impropriety just by dint of sharing a meal and then joining for Birkat ha-Mazon, such that, for the Semag, it is obvious that three women can answer to the *zimmun* of three men and need not break off and make their own. This is not an obvious point and we will see sources below that fall on the other side of this question.

14 Since we are primarily interested here in quorums of ten, we will not address the unexpected position of R. Yehudah ha-Kohen, cited in Responsa Maharam of Rothenberg IV:2227, who ruled that יכולה אשה לצרף בשלשה בברכת המזון. Later commentators struggle with how he reconciled this view with what they assume to be the Mishnah's ban on including women in a *zimmun*. Ḥiddushei Hagahot suggests that he thought the Mishnah only banned one man joining with two women, whereas Derishah thought he read the Mishnah as only banning creating groups of men, women, slaves, and minors all together. According to Ḥiddushei Hagahot, it seems R. Yehudah ha-Kohen would only have allowed **one** woman to count toward the ten needed for *zimmun* with God's name, whereas Derishah would likely have him endorsing treating women as equals with respect to any *zimmun*, including *zimmun* with God's name together with men or on their own. See also Agur #289 and Baḥ OḤ 199. The Maharam of Rothenberg argues against this view, in part appealing to his assumption that ten women cannot perform *zimmun* with God's name on their own, a view we will return to below. D. Koren tries to argue even more forcefully than Derishah that Mishnah Berakhot 7:2 never intended to ban a mixed-gender *zimmun*. See above, Part Two, n. 7 and n. 14. If she is correct—we are less sure than she—then the questions we ask here are even more open.

Above, we tracked the post-talmudic history of the gendered nature of the quorum of ten required for *devarim shebikdushah*.[15] We saw how R. Sa'adiah Gaon seems to be the earliest source to make any explicit statement that a community of Jews for the purposes of public prayer consists of ten men. This statement is descriptive and almost instinctive, without any discussion of the basis for it or the reasons surrounding it. And most medieval sources maintain this sort of approach, either omitting any mention of gender when describing quorums of ten, or simply excluding women from them as a matter of fact without any need for comment. We analyzed above the few sources that do engage the question somewhat, either to uphold a strict male standard, or to open the possibility for female involvement.

Post-talmudic discussions around the quorums of ten required for mentioning God's name in *zimmun* and for the public reading of the *megillah* can help fill in the picture we described above. The question of women and these quorums of ten is first meaningfully engaged in the 12th century. The Rambam in Hilkhot Berakhot 5:7 states that ten women may not make a *zimmun* with God's name, without providing any reason.[16]

---

15 See Part Two, n. 19 and onward.

16 The Frankel edition of Hilkhot Berakhot 5:7 reads as follows:

> נשים ועבדים וקטנים אין מזמנין עליהם אבל מזמנין לעצמן, ולא תהא חבורה של נשים ועבדים וקטנים מפני הפריצות, אלא נשים לעצמן או עבדים לעצמן או קטנים לעצמן ובלבד שלא יזמנו בשם.
>
> One does not make a *zimmun* over women, slaves, and minors, but they may make a *zimmun* on their own. There should not be a group of women, slaves, and minors on account of [sexual] impropriety. Rather women on their own or slaves on their own or minors on their own, provided they do not make a *zimmun* with God's name.

The phrase או קטנים לעצמן is attested in a number of Rishonim, including Tur OḤ 199. But other Rishonim seem not to have had it and it was missing from the printed editions. See the notes in the Frankel edition. Note that while the Rambam has always been read as forbidding women from making a *zimmun* with God's name, it is technically possible to read the Rambam as only forbidding ten slaves (or ten minors) from engaging in this ritual. The Gemara on Bavli Berakhot 47b cites R. Yehoshua b. Levi's view that nine free people and one slave may join together. The immediate prior context is another ruling by R. Yehoshua b. Levi that an infant can be counted as an adjunct member of a *zimmun* of ten. This juxtaposition could easily lead one to assume that his ruling about a slave also applies to a case of a *zimmun* of ten. One might then infer that if the most lenient position only allowed

While he does not comment on the possibility of a mixed quorum of ten men and ten women for *zimmun*, it would seem that his citation of the Mishnah's language, נשים ועבדים וקטנים אין מזמנין עליהן, without exception is meant to endorse a ban on a mixed-gender *zimmun* encompassing the *zimmun* of ten as well.[17] The Ittur argues that *ab initio*, women should not count toward the ten of *megillah*, just as they don't count toward the ten or the three of *zimmun*.[18] For him, the exclusion of women from *zimmun* is paradigmatic for excluding women from all mixed groups with men, albeit ideally, suggesting that after the fact and/or in certain kinds of situations, such a mixed quorum does not compromise the integrity of the ritual. He says nothing about ten women reading the *megillah* on their own (or performing *zimmun* with God's name).

The next figure to contribute to this debate is R. Meir b. Shimon ha-Me'ili, who resists the Rambam's ruling that ten women may not perform *zimmun* with God's name, suggesting that the statement that women form their own *zimmun* in the Gemara is comprehensive and applies both to quorums of three and ten.[19] He offers two suggestions for the basis for the Rambam's ruling:

---

counting a slave as a tenth (or a minor as an adjunct), then certainly a group of ten slaves (or ten minors) cannot form their own group of ten, despite their ability to form an independent group of three. This would then provide some more basis for the Rambam's ruling here, which puzzled various authorities as devoid of any talmudic source, and he would not be making a comment on women at all. In fact, the Kesef Mishneh on Hilkhot Berakhot 5:7 only seems to explain the exclusion of slaves and minors from a *zimmun* with God's name and cross-references to chapter 8 of Hilkhot Tefillah, which does not engage the question of gender at all. But Beit Yosef OḤ 199 seems to throw gender into the mix as well when using the phrase אנשים גדולים ובני חורין. We have not, however, found any reader of the Rambam who is explicit that his phrase, ובלבד שלא יזמנו בשם, does not apply to a group of ten women.

17 This is indeed how almost all later authorities understood the Rambam. Note that Koren, "Kullam Beki'im ba-Hallel," who thinks that the language of the Mishnah itself does not preclude a mixed-gender *zimmun*, would make the same claim about the Rambam's phrasing here. We do not find this to be a plausible reading of the Rambam. If the first phrase, נשים ועבדים וקטנים אין מזמנין עליהם, means nothing more than a ban on groups of women, slaves, and minors joining together to make a *zimmun*, the next phrase in the Rambam becomes redundant.

18 Ittur Aseret ha-Diberot, Hilkhot Megillah 110a.

19 Sefer ha-Me'orot 45b.

1. He holds that women are permitted but not obligated to form a *zimmun* and, therefore, consistent with his view that women do not say *berakhot* over *mitzvot* from which they are exempt, they may not mention God's name in an optional *zimmun*.[20]
2. A group of women lacks "קביעות — fixity," the kind of social cohesion necessary to create a *zimmun*.[21] The Rambam felt that women and slaves do not generate a social center of gravity the way free men do, and perhaps this is the reason that they may not do *zimmun* with God's name.[22]

Despite these justifications, he argues that one should not stop groups of ten women who do *zimmun* with God's name, since there is no source in the Gemara that opposes it.[23] He then goes further, however, actively permitting an adult male to lead a group of either ten minors or ten women in *zimmun* with God's name, revealing a rejection of the Rambam's

---

20 According to this logic, communities that followed R. Tam and did permit women to say such *berakhot* would indeed allow to women to perform *zimmun* with God's name. Note that Sefer ha-Me'orot's reading of the Rambam here does not seem to be the plain sense of Hilkhot Berakhot 5:1, 7 (see the Meiri's understanding of the Rambam on this question); it also contradicts some versions of Hilkhot Berakhot 5:6 that explicitly obligate women in *zimmun* (see the Frankel edition), and it is borrowed from the Tosafot's notion that women are exempt from *zimmun*. Likely for this reason, and out of a desire to understand how the Rambam's ruling might apply to all communities, he suggests a second basis for the ruling here.

21 The concept of קביעות appears in talmudic discussions as a necessary factor for establishing a *zimmun*. See Bavli Berakhot 47b for one example. Rashi applies this notion to considerations of gender in a comment on Berakhot 45b s.v. *im ratzu*. Ha-Me'ili here is mapping the Rambam's ruling onto this concept, suggesting it is one of the underpinning bases for stating that ten women, even if they form a *zimmun*, would not include God's name in the formula.

22 Sefer ha-Me'orot's approach here seems to draw on the approach of the Ra'avad in Temim De'im #1, where he lays out the idea that a lack of קביעות is the core of the problem with mixed-gender *zimmun*, arguing that a group of men and women never coheres into a single unit with its own single center of gravity. Sefer ha-Me'orot extends this notion to suggest that women on their own have the same problem.

23 As we noted above, this sort of measured perspective would be welcome throughout the larger topic under discussion here, with Sefer ha-Me'orot's principle applying to women's participation in the *minyan* for *devarim shebikdushah* as well.

principle that a group of ten women or ten minors cannot mention God's name in the *zimmun*.[24]

With respect to the Ittur's restrictive position on a mixed-gender group of ten for *megillah*, Sefer ha-Me'orot echoes this view on Bavli Megillah 5a, saying that whenever ten are needed, men are required. In fact, this seems to go further than the Ittur, in that it suggests that ten women on their own are also ineligible to compose the ten for *megillah*, the first view to do so explicitly. This statement seems to reflect the kind of reflexive

24 Sefer ha-Me'orot is thus likely the יש חולקין בכך cited in Meiri Berakhot 47b that supports ten women performing a *zimmun* with God's name. The scenario of one adult male leading the *zimmun* with God's name for ten women is not intended to convey the notion that ten women cannot do this on their own, given that he otherwise rejects the notion that women join together with men and the only reason to say God's name is thus the presence of ten women. Rather, he discusses the case of a man leading for ten women in order to argue the case—which he does in the next part of the passage—that there is never an issue of *peritzut* when free men lead rituals for women; that concern is limited to slaves and women joining together for ritual performance. Though he also cites those who think that *peritzut* is a wide-ranging problem in the context of meals, and that this would be a problem for allowing a man to lead a *zimmun* for women, he rejects this view. In the end, he therefore in principle endorses the notion that a woman would lead other women in a *zimmun* with God's name as well. Note also that R. Shmuel b. Meshullam Gerondi, in Ohel Mo'ed 107b, cites a view identical to that of Sefer ha-Me'orot on this point in the name of R. Avraham, which may refer to the Ra'avad. Given our citation of the Ra'avad in Temim De'im above, Ohel Mo'ed seems to argue that if the problem with mixed-gender *zimmun* is the inability of men and women to cohere as a group, then there ought to be no issues with treating a group of women on its own identically to a group of men on its own. See Repsonsa Benei Banim 3:1. This view of Sefer ha-Me'orot does not get much traction with later *poskim* and the Meiri explicitly rejects him in his commentary on Berakhot 47b by echoing R. Manoaḥ's claim—explored above, Part Two, n. 23 and onward—that *zimmun* with God's name requires a קהל, and ten women cannot form a קהל. (R. Ben-Tziyyon Lichtman, in Benei Tziyyon 199:6, struggles with this passage in the Meiri and suggests instead that perhaps the Meiri had a different text on Megillah 23b that explicitly tied the requirement of ten for *zimmun* with God's name to the notion of קהל.) Most later authorities display no awareness of Sefer ha-Me'orot's position. But note that Shiltei ha-Gibborim on Rif Berakhot 33a, letter *bet*, cites the Rosh as permitting women to count toward the *zimmun* of ten in language that sounds unrestricted.

assumption that women are generally excluded from *minyanim* of ten that we saw above, extending this notion into the realm of *megillah*.[25]

At around the same time, R. Simḥah of Speyer, whose rulings we examined above,[26] also took for granted that at least one woman could count toward the ten of *zimmun*. We suggested above that he might have had an even bolder position, permitting women to function as equals in this quorum of ten, whether with or without men.[27] What is striking about R. Simḥah is that he carries the participation into the realm of the *minyan* of *tefillah*, something that no one before him did explicitly, even though the logic for doing so is similar to that of those, like Sefer ha-Me'orot, who argued for the ability of ten women to form a *zimmun*. Nonetheless, as we saw above and will see again below, even those authorities entertaining including women in the ten of *zimmun* or *megillah* seem to have taken for granted their exclusion from the ten of *devarim shebikdushah* during communal prayer, for reasons we argued for elsewhere.[28]

The next voice to weigh in is that of R. Aharon ha-Levi of Barcelona, who is cited in Ritva Megillah 4a. He argues there that women ought to

---

25 Sefer ha-Me'orot then offers a reason why women should not join with men toward the ten of *megillah*, the Ittur's original point: Such a mixed-gender group is a problem of *peritzut*. But, in light of his analysis on Bavli Berakhot 45a, where he suggests that free adults are not subject to such concerns, he comments here that the concern of *peritzut* could be easily dismissed. He thus seems to fall back on his first general statement that groups of ten are not the domain of women. This itself is a problematic statement, in that he is on record, as we saw, as permitting ten women to perform a *zimmun* with God's name. One might question whether his endorsement of the latter position also began to put into play the possibility of ten women reading the *megillah* on their own, a possibility not yet proposed in his day. It seems most reasonable to see Sefer ha-Me'orot's inconsistency as emerging from the pioneering nature of much of his analysis.

26 See Part Two, n. 38 and onward.

27 Agur #289 reports that R. Simḥah agreed with R. Yehudah ha-Kohen that men and women could join toward the quorum of three. This strengthens the notion that R. Simḥah might simply have said that any combination of ten adults is valid for *zimmun* with God's name. If this report is incorrect and R. Simḥah only permitted women to count toward the quorum of ten, he maximally would have permitted combinations of up to seven of one gender with three of the other, so as not to violate the Mishnah's ban on combining men and women to form the core *zimmun* of three.

28 See Part Two, n. 33 and onward.

be able to join with men toward the quorum of ten for *megillah,* directly rejecting the Ittur, and his logic makes clear that he would permit ten women on their own to count as a quorum for this purpose. He then attempts to distinguish the mixed-gender group he permits here from the one explicitly banned by the Mishnah. A *zimmun* constituted by men and women is problematic because an entirely new ritual (*zimmun*) is being added due to the joint participation of men and women, and this presents a concern of *peritzut.* Since neither the men on their own nor the women on their own could do this ritual, their joint participation is blatantly obvious, and thus problematic. In the case of *megillah,* however, the ritual looks the same irrespective of the size of the group, and therefore there is no issue of *peritzut.*[29]

As a summary of this topic, it is worth looking at a passage from Sefer ha-Mikhtam, which tries to synthesize all of this various material regarding women and various quorums and to work through how controlling a paradigm the material on women and *zimmun* ought to be. He writes as follows:

ספר המכתם ברכות מה.
נשים ועבדים וקטנים אין מזמנין עליהן.

פי׳ דלאו בני חיובא נינהו כאנשים, ואע״פ שהנשים חייבות בבכרת המזון, ספק הוא אם חייבות מדאוריית׳ או מדרבנן, והאנשים חייבות מן התורה...

וכתב הרמ׳ דנשים אם מזמנות לעצמן לעולם אין מזמנות לעצמן בשם, אפי׳ ביותר מעשה.

ועוד מפרש בגמ׳ דשנים ועבדים אפי׳ אם רצו לזמן אין מזמנין משום פריצותא, כלומ׳ כדי להרחיק שלא לעשות מסיבה של נשים ועבדים.

ויש שאומ׳ דדוקא בעבדים שהם פרוצים, כדאמ׳ עבדא בהפקירא ניחא ליה, אבל בחבורה של נשים עם בני חורין הכשרין אין מפקירין.

אבל מכל מקום הנשים אינן מצטרפות עם האנשים, דסתמא דמתני׳ דנשי׳ ועבדים וקטנים אין מזמנין עליהן, ואפי׳ סניפין לעשרה אין עושין מהן.

---

29 We explored this view and some of its ramifications above, Part Two, nn. 82–87.

ולא עוד אלא במה שמצטרפין הקטן היודע למי מברכין אין מצרפין אותן לענין זמון, דקטן אתי לכלל חיובא בגדול, אבל נשים לא.

ואע"ג דלענין מקרא מגילה מצטרפות לעשרה לדעת קצת הפוסקים, ומוציאות את האנשים אם היו יודעות לקרות, שאני התם דחיובן שוה לאנשים.

ואע"ג דאמרי' נמי אשה לא [תקרא] בתורה בציבור מפני כבוד [הציבור], דמשמע טעמא משום כבוד צבור הוא דלא, הא לאו הכי שרי, התם נמי אפשר דקריאתה אינה עולה למנין השבעה, או אפילו תימא דעולה מ"מ איהי לא מצטרפא לעשרה דאין קורין בתורה בפחות מעשרה.

ויש שאומרי' דלהכי לא פסלינן נשים לספר תורה ולמקרא מגילה משום דלא נתמעטו נשים אלא מזימון, משום דבסעודה שכיחא שכרות ושחוק וקלות ראש וכל זה איננו שוה להכשירן לענין צירוף שלשה או עשרה אפי' בכשרים.

1. Sefer ha-Mikhtam begins here by explaining why it is, in his view, that women and men do not join together to make a *zimmun*: Women may lack equal obligation to men. Even though they are obligated, once the Gemara on Berakhot 20b raises a doubt as to whether their obligation is biblical, they are no longer necessarily on the same plane as men with regard to *zimmun* and may not join them.[30]
2. He notes that the Rambam says ten women may not perform *zimmun* with God's name.
3. The Gemara clarifies that women and slaves may not form a joint group for *zimmun,* because of concerns of sexual impropriety. There should never be a joint meal of women and slaves.[31]

---

30 Sefer ha-Mikhtam here follows the Rambam, Hilkhot Berakhot 5:1. As we noted above, this is a highly disputed point; most Rishonim thought that women were biblically obligated in Birkat ha-Mazon just like men.

31 Note that the logic here applies even if the women and slaves are not relying on one another for a quorum. In other words, when the *baraita* on Bavli Berakhot 45b forbids women and slaves from mixing together because of פריצותא, the plain sense is that even three women and three slaves cannot combine to the same *zimmun*. This coerced separation is intended to prevent their inappropriate cohesion as a group.

4. The above logic would seem to ban men and women from ever having a joint *zimmun* or meal, so Sefer ha-Mikhtam now cites the view of Sefer ha-Me'orot that there is no fear of [sexual] impropriety with regard to free men and women. Therefore, three men and three women may participate in the same *zimmun*.[32]
5. Nonetheless, even if free men and women present no problem of [sexual] impropriety, such that they can participate in the same *zimmun*, they still may not join together to form a quorum of three or ten; the Mishnah's ban must minimally prevent these sorts of joint quorums (even if it might still allow for joint participation in a *zimmun* formed by a single-gender quorum). Even nine men and one woman may not perform *zimmun* with God's name.[33]
6. You might object that the Mishnah also forbids including minors in a *zimmun* and, yet, voices in the Gemara legitimate counting at least one minor.[34] Why shouldn't at least one woman be allowed to count toward the ten required for *zimmun* with God's name? He deflects this problem by insisting that minors are different, since

---

See above, n. 13, our comment regarding the question of whether three men and three women may join together to form a *zimmun*; based on Sefer ha-Mikhtam's understanding here, we would not permit in such a case if we felt there was a problem of פריצותא in a mixed-gender group of free adults.

32 Note that one who did not accept Sefer ha-Me'orot's distinction, or who felt that other problematic social issues arose from a mixed-gender meal, might reject this permission. Indeed, this seems to be the view of Rashi cited by R. Yonah that we cited above, who says that women do not join with men because אין חברתם נאה, a concern that would apply to any kind of joint *zimmun*, whether or not the men need the women to attain the quorum. While Beit Yosef OḤ 199:8–9 rejects this view in favor of Semag cited above, he agrees that this is the proper reading of R. Yonah, and this section of Sefer ha-Mikhtam confirms the plausibility of such a position.

33 Obviously, R. Simḥah read the Mishnah differently. See also Part Two, n. 7 and n. 14, for Koren's even bolder alternate reading of the Mishnah.

34 This is a reference to the idea that a minor who is sufficiently intelligent to understand the notion of blessing God for the food one has eaten may indeed help form the *zimmun*. Rav Naḥman rules this way on Bavli Berakhot 48a and the Gemara on Arakhin 3a endorses this view as normative. This then leads to a geonic gloss that creeps into the text of Bavli Berakhot 48a affirming Rav Naḥman's statement as accepted law.

they will eventually be fully obligated in Birkat ha-Mazon as adults, whereas women's obligation will never be on par with men's.[35]

7. Given the blanket ban Sefer ha-Mikhtam argues for on men and women forming a joint quorum for *zimmun*, you might be surprised by those authorities (like the Ra'ah) who permit women and men to join for the ten of *megillah*. Shouldn't women and men be banned from ever forming a joint quorum, based on the model of *zimmun*? Sefer ha-Mikhtam argues that *megillah* is different from *zimmun*, because women's obligation in *megillah* is equal to that of men, whereas this is not (at least clearly) the case, in his view, with regard to Birkat ha-Mazon.
8. Given the blanket ban Sefer ha-Mikhtam argues for on men and women forming a joint quorum for *zimmun*, you might be surprised that the *baraita* on Bavli Megillah 23b makes it sound like a woman can be among the total of seven readers for the Torah (assuming

---

35 The logic of distinguishing minors from other categories of people via the claim אתי לכלל חיובא, their eventual status as free adult Jewish males renders them more similar to the latter group than others outside of that category, was an innovation of Tosafistic circles. In fact, the almost certain referent here is a passage that appears in two parallel Tosafot (on Eruvin 96b and Rosh Hashanah 33a) that discuss the question of whether women are allowed to say *berakhot* over the voluntary performance of *mitzvot* from which they are exempt. After citing R. Tam's support for this position, the Tosafot deflect several suggested proofs for this view (even though they do not challenge the validity of R. Tam's view itself). The end of the Tosafot reads as follows: ומקטן דמברך ברכת המזון אף על פי שהוא פטור אין ראיה לאשה דקטן בא לכלל חיוב וחייב לחנכו מוזהר על לא תשא. The potential argument here is that Mishnah Berakhot 3:3 (which we looked at above) rules (according to Rashi and the Tosafot's interpretation of that text) that minors say Birkat ha-Mazon. Given that minors are exempt and yet allowed to say these blessings, one might argue that women, even though exempt, can say blessings over *mitzvot* that they voluntarily perform. The Tosafot reject this potential argument by suggesting that we would more readily let a minor bless than an exempt adult: Minors will eventually become obligated and must be educated; moreover, they are not yet culpable for taking God's name in vain. The Tosafot's claim here seems to be that because minors will eventually be obligated in these *mitzvot*, there is a value in educating them to perform them. This is supported by the Tosafot on Nazir 57b, where they consider it a forced suggestion that one would be stricter in the case of minors simply because they will eventually become obligated in the absence of educational concerns. Sefer ha-Mikhtam borrows that concept here to claim that we are more invested in including minors in a *zimmun* as part of their training to become adults. Therefore, our leniencies with them have no implications for women.

we control for the concern of *kevod tzibbur*). Sefer ha-Mikhtam offers two ways of explaining how women are indeed not really joining together with men to form a Torah reading quorum. First of all, some say that her reading cannot count toward the total of seven.[36] And even if one follows the plain sense of the *baraita*, which poses no objections to women's *aliyot* other than *kevod ha-tzibbur*,[37] women are still excluded from the quorum of ten required to enable the reading to happen in the first place.[38] Therefore, even if men and women can join to form the total of seven, we still see a disability analogous to the ban on a joint *zimmun* in the context of the ritual of Torah reading as well. In short, Torah reading in fact conforms to the ban on a mixed-gender *zimmun* quorum in one way or another.

9. Alternatively, there is another way of explaining why men and women might not jointly create a quorum for *zimmun* even though they can join for the ten required for the *megillah* and the seven required for Torah reading:[39] *Zimmun* presents a serious problem

---

36 This very likely refers to the view that women were only ever allowed to read when they did not have to make a *berakhah* over the reading, since originally only the first and last reader did so. Once each person coming to the Torah was required to make a blessing, women, who were classically exempt from Torah study, were no longer eligible to participate in Torah reading at all. This view is first suggested as a deflection in Tosafot Rosh Hashanah 33a and is later picked up as an actual ruling by later authorities, such as R. David Kokhavi, in Sefer ha-Batim, Sha'arei Keri'at ha-Torah 2:6, and R. Menaḥem ha-Meiri, in Beit ha-Beḥirah Megillah 23a. See above (Part One, n. 118, toward the end).

37 This is likely not just a theoretical point raised here in Sefer ha-Mikhtam. The author was likely aware of rulings like the one cited in Sefer ha-Batim—which we discussed above, Part One, n. 107 and onward—permitting women to read Torah in a private home where *kevod ha-tzibbur* might be said not to apply.

38 This fact is asserted as obvious by simply appealing to the text of the Mishnah. Obviously, Sefer ha-Mikhtam here is subject to the same analysis we offered earlier in our discussion of all such statements in the Rishonim, and he is another good example of the phenomenon of asserting this assumption of religious practice.

39 In other words, this is another effort to justify the rulings permitting women and men to combine for the ten of *megillah* (the Ra'ah) and permitting women to read Torah (Sefer ha-Batim) without running afoul of the Mishnah's opposition to mixed-gender groups in the context of *zimmun*.

> for mixed-gender activity, because mealtimes are prone to alcoholic consumption and inappropriate levity and gaiety; *zimmun* is not paradigmatic for other rituals that lack this quality, such as Torah reading and *megillah*. Therefore, one might entertain including women with men in the latter rituals while maintaining an ironclad ban on allowing even free men and women to jointly form the quorums of three and ten for *zimmun*. (This is the view cited by Sefer ha-Me'orot on Bavli Berakhot 45a, though he rejects it).

Even though almost every one of his points is substantively disputed by some medieval authority, Sefer ha-Mikhtam is a good place to end our discussion because of his fairly comprehensive survey of the material we have covered.[40] He also demonstrates the deeply embedded assumption of so many Rishonim that women are excluded from the ten required for *devarim shebikdushah*. This exclusion, for many Rishonim, is a truth in need of no justification, even as some of those same Rishonim entertain including women in other quorums of ten. We examined this pattern and its significance above. Finally, this source, along with the others we have explored in this appendix, demonstrates how the thin record on women and quorums in classical sources can be taken in a variety of directions with respect to a variety of rituals. Whether one views *zimmun* as paradigmatic or exceptional ultimately reflects what each authority understood to be the principles underlying the gendering of that practice. This should help put in perspective our analysis of the underlying principles of the gendering of the ten required for *devarim shebikdushah* and how one might apply that information in different religious times and places.

---

40 The Meiri on Berakhot 47b essentially cites Sefer ha-Mikhtam here, almost verbatim. His main contribution is to add a brief discussion on the question of whether ten women can perform *zimmun* with God's name, citing Sefer ha-Me'orot's opposing view to that of the Rambam, though ultimately rejecting it.

BIBLIOGRAPHY

Hebrew Works

E. Ancelovits, "Ma'amad ha-Ḥeresh" =

א. אנצ׳ילוביץ, ״מעמד החרש במציאות זמננו״, *תחומין* כא (תשסא): 152–141.

D. Bigman, "Kol Ishah Ervah" =

ד. ביגמן, ״עיון ב׳קול באשה ערוה׳״, באתר קולך.

Y. Bin-Nun, "Birkat Ḥatanim" =

י. בן-נון, תגובה ל ״ברכת חתנים: האם מניין גברים הוא הכרחי?״, *גרנות* 3 (תשסג): 172–173.

E. Fleischer, "ha-Pores al Shema" =

ע. פליישר, ״לליבון ענין הפורס על שמע״, *תרביץ* מא (תשלב): 133–144.

A. Frimer, "Nashim u-Minyan" =

א׳ פרימר, ״מעמד האשה בהלכה: נשים ומנין״, *אור המזרח* לד (תשמו): 69–86.

Y. Gershon, "Tzirufan shel Nashim le-Zimmun" =

י. גרשון, ״שלש דעות מזמנות: לשאילת צירופן של נשים לזימון בחוג המשפחה״, *אקדמות* כו (תשעא): 7–23.

Y. D. Gilat, *Hishtalshelut ha-Halakhah* =

י.ד. גילת, פרקים *בהשתלשלות ההלכה* (בר-אילן, תשנב), 19–31.

D. Golinkin, "Nashim u-Kri'at ha-Torah" =
ד. גולינקין, "נשים וקריאת התורה בציבור", *תשובות ועד ההלכה* ג (תשמח): 77–54.

D. Golinkin, "Nashim be-Minyan" =
ד. גולינקין, "נשים במנין וכשליחות ציבור," *תשובות ועד ההלכה* ו (תשנז): 79–59.

M. Halbertal, *ha-Meiri* =
מ. הלברטל, *בין תורה לחכמה: ר' מנחם המאירי ובעלי ההלכה המיינונים בפרובנס* (ירושלים, תשסג), 108–80.

E. B. Halivni, *Bein ha-Ish la-Ishah* =
א. ב. הלבני, *בין האיש לאישה* (ירושלים, תשסז).

D. Koren, "Kullam Baki'im ba-Hallel" =
ד. קורן, "כולם בקיאים בהלל", *מלין חביבין* ב (תשסו): ג-י.

D. Koren, "Tziruf Nashim le-Zimmun" =
ד. קורן, "על שיטת ר' יהודה הכהן בעניין צירוף נשים לזימון עם גברים", *מילין חביבין* ה (תשעא): כו-נ.

V. Noam, "la-Meḥitzah ha-Penimit" =
ו. נעם, "מעבר למחיצה הפנימית", *מקור ראשון* 11.1.2013.

Ḥ. Safrai and S. Safrai, "Minyan Shiv'ah" =
ח. וש. ספראי, "הכל עולין למניין שבעה", *תרביץ* סו (תשנז): 401–395.

A. Shochetman, "Aliyat Nashim" =
א. שוחטמן, "עליית נשים לתורה", *סיני* קלה-קלו (תשסה): רעא-שמט.

D. Sperber, *Darkah shel Halakhah* =
ד. שפרבר, *דרכה של הלכה: קריאת נשים תצורה, פרקים במדיניות פסיקה* (ירושלים, תשסז).

S. Wald, "Ha-Ishah bi-Tfillat ha-Tzibbur" =
ש. וולד, "מאמר על מעמד האשה בתפלת הציבור" (תשנו), [שלא פורסם].

English Works

R. Berkovits, "Women's Obligation in *Kiddush* of Shabbat," from *Ta Shma: The Halakhic Source Guide Series* (JOFA, 2008) (= "Women's Obligation").

S. Berman, "Kol 'Isha," in *Rabbi Joseph H. Lookstein Memorial Volume* (Ktav, 1981), 45–66 (= "Kol Ishah").

G. Blidstein, "Sheliaḥ Zibbur: Historical and Phenomenological Considerations," *Tradition* 12 (1971): 69–77 (= "Sheliaḥ Tzibbur").

M. J. Broyde and J. B. Wolowelsky, "Further on Women as Prayer Leaders and Their Role in Communal Prayer," *Judaism* 42.4 (1993): 387–395 (= "Women as Prayer Leaders").

A. Frimer, "Women and Minyan," *Tradition* 23.4 (1988): 54–77 (= "Women and Minyan").

A. and D. Frimer, "Partnership *Minyanim*," in *Text and Texture*, available on text.rcarabbis.org (= "Partnership Minyanim").

A. and D. Frimer, "Women's Prayer Services—Theory and Practice," *Tradition* 32.2 (1998): 5–118 (= "Women's Prayer Services").

A. Grossman, *Pious and Rebellious: Jewish Women in Medieval Europe* (Brandeis University Press, 2004) (= *Pious and Rebellious*).

J. Hauptman, "Some Thoughts on the Nature of Halakhic Adjudication: Women and *Minyan*," *Judaism* 42.4 (1993): 396–413 (= "Women and Minyan").

J. Hauptman, "Women and Prayer: An Attempt to Dispel Some Fallacies," *Judaism* 42.1 (1993): 94–103 (= "Women and Prayer").

Y. H. Henkin, *Equality Lost* (Urim, 1999) (= *Equality Lost*).

Y. H. Henkin, *Understanding Tzniut: Modern Controversies in the Jewish Community* (Urim, 2008) (= *Understanding Tzniut*).

E. Kaunfer, "*Aval Chatanu* ("But / In Truth, We Have Sinned"): A Literary Investigation," in L. Hoffman, ed., *We Have Sinned: Sin and*

Confession in Judaism—Ashamnu *and* Al Chet (Jewish Lights, 2012), 181–185 (= "Aval Ḥatanu").

S. Metso, "Whom Does the Term Yaḥad Identify?" in *Defining Identities: We, You, and the Other in the Dead Sea Scrolls*, ed. F. Garcia Martinez and M. Popovic (Brill, 2007). (= "The Term Yaḥad").

M. Nissel, *Rigshei Lev, Women and Tefillah: Perspectives, Laws, and Customs* (Targum/Feldheim, 2001), 82–87 (= *Rigshei Lev*).

M. Rabinowitz, "An Advocate's Halakhic Responses on the Ordination of Women," in S. Greenberg, ed., *The Ordination of Women as Rabbis: Studies and Responsa* (JTS, 1988) (= "Advocate's Halakhic Responses").

D. Reed Blank, "The Medieval French Practice of Repeating *Qaddish* and *Barekhu* for Latecomers to the Synagogue," *Liturgy and the Life of the Synagogue* (2008): 84–88 (= "Medieval French Practice").

S. Riskin and M. Shapiro, "Torah *Aliyyot* for Women—A Continuing Discussion," *Me'orot* 7.1 (2008): 2–19 (= "Aliyot for Women").

J. Roth, "On the Ordination of Women as Rabbis," in S. Greenberg, ed., *The Ordination of Women as Rabbis: Studies and Responsa* (JTS, 1988) (= "Ordination of Women").

G. Rothstein, "Women's *Aliyyot* in Contemporary Synagogues," *Tradition* 39.2 (2005): 36–58 (= "Women's Aliyot").

M. Shapiro, "*Qeri'at ha-Torah* by Women: A Halakhic Analysis," *Edah* 1.2 (2001), and see also the follow-up comments by Y. H. Henkin and M. Shapiro in the same issue (= "Keri'at ha-Torah").

D. Sperber, "Congregational Dignity and Human Dignity: Women and Public Torah Reading," *Edah* 3.2 (2003) (= "Congregational Dignity").

E. Tucker, "Equality Without Adjuncts?: Confronting the Limits of Gender Egalitarianism," available on hadar.org. (= "Equality Without Adjuncts?").

E. Tucker, "Good Fences Make Good Neighbors?" available on hadar.org (= "Good Fences").

A. Weiss, "Ruling of Rav Asher Weiss Regarding the Status of a Deaf Person," available on yctorah.org (= "Status of a Deaf Person").

LIST OF AUTHORITIES CITED

INDEX OF CLASSICAL SOURCES

TORAH

NEVI'IM

KETUVIM

MISHNAH

TOSEFTA

MIDRASH

TALMUD YERUSHALMI

TALMUD BAVLI

MASSEKHTOT KETANOT

www.ingramcontent.com/pod-product-compliance
Ingram Content Group UK Ltd.
Pitfield, Milton Keynes, MK11 3LW, UK
UKHW041634190726
13854UKWH00006B/2491